Jacques Moeschler
Why Language?

Mouton Series in Pragmatics

Editor
Istvan Kecskes

Editorial Board
Reinhard Blutner (Universiteit van Amsterdam)
N.J. Enfield (Max-Planck-Institute for Psycholinguistics)
Raymond W. Gibbs (University of California, Santa Cruz)
Laurence R. Horn (Yale University)
Boaz Keysar (University of Chicago)
Ferenc Kiefer (Hungarian Academy of Sciences)
Lluís Payrató (University of Barcelona)
François Recanati (Institut Jean-Nicod)
John Searle (University of California, Berkeley)
Deirdre Wilson (University College London)

Volume 25

Jacques Moeschler
Why Language?

What Pragmatics Tells Us About Language
And Communication

ISBN 978-3-11-126676-3
e-ISBN (PDF) 978-3-11-072338-0
e-ISBN (EPUB) 978-3-11-072344-1
ISSN 1864-6409

Library of Congress Control Number: 2021938384

Bibliographic information published by the Deutsche Nationalbibliothek
The Deutsche Nationalbibliothek lists this publication in the Deutsche Nationalbibliografie;
detailed bibliographic data are available on the Internet at http://dnb.dnb.de.

© 2023 Walter de Gruyter GmbH, Berlin/Boston
This volume is text- and page-identical with the hardback published in 2021.
Typesetting: Integra Software Services Pvt. Ltd.
Printing and binding: CPI books GmbH, Leck

www.degruyter.com

To Anne

Foreword

When I sent the original version of my book (*Pourquoi le langage? Des Inuits à Google*, Paris, Armand Colin, La Lettre et l'Idée, 2020) to Istvan Kecskes, he said he was very interested in having MSP publish an English version. I initially felt sceptical about his suggestion, because the book had been written with a general French-speaking audience in mind, focused on the French language, and aimed at discussing general issues about language, cognition and communication without using any jargon.

My book originated through concerns about the new orientation of the professorship I held at the Department of Linguistics at the University of Geneva. The issue was the scope of French linguistics, which was defined by my literary colleagues as the history of ideas in linguistics – from Saussure to Benveniste – and not as an empirical field, which implied that domains and methods developed over the past century were not worthy of notice. The discovery of this cultural gap was unexpected, and confirmed that those working in the humanities are unaware of the most important discoveries in linguistics.

Since many clever and well-documented books are available in English on language and linguistics, I understand that the reader might have doubts about an English adaptation of a French book for an international readership. However, positive feedback from English and American linguists encouraged me to think about and write this English adaptation. Doing so created a new and different challenge: How could I make sense of a book on language, cognition, and communication for an English readership, which is neither textbook nor monograph? During recent years, I have co-authored a textbook on implicatures (Zufferey, Moeschler, and Reboul 2019) and published a research monograph in pragmatics for MPS (Moeschler 2019).

There are two types of researchers: those who contribute to scientific knowledge and research by satisfying peer-review constraints and engaging in competitive fundraising, and those who engage in outreach and the dissemination of scientific knowledge. The second category often specialises in writing textbooks and introductory tomes for BA and MA students.[1] But remarkable changes have

---

[1] The most successful example is Transformational syntax, by Andrew Radford (1981), which has been republished many times. There have of course been exceptions. For instance, certain textbooks have been written by reputed researchers, and this trend began many years ago: Akmajian, Demers, and Harnish (1980) and Smith and Wilson (1980) for general linguistics; Haegeman (1994) for theoretical syntax; Dowty, Wall, and Peters (1981), Bach (1989), Chierchia and McConnell-Ginet (1990), Larson and Segal (1995), Heim and Kratzer (1998), Cann, Kempson, and

recently taken place in the second category of researchers, mainly because outreach and dissemination have become more highly valued. Good examples of this type of outreach publication, some of which have become best-sellers, are Yuval Harari on cultural history (Harari 2014, 2016, 2018), Thomas Piketty (2014), Abhijit Banerjee and Esther Duflo (2019) on economics, Steven Pinker on cognitive science (Pinker 1995, 1997, 2002, 2018), Noam Chomsky on theoretical linguistics (Chomsky 2016), Jared Diamond on the history of ancient and modern societies (Diamond 1997, 2005, 2012, 2019), Julien Musolino and Hugo Mercier on experimental psychology (Musolino 2015, Mercier 2020), Florian Cova on experimental philosophy (Cova 2011), Gloria Origgi on social psychology (Origgi 2015), and Ian Roberts on linguistics (Robert 2017). All these examples show that documented research is now readily accessible to non-specialist readers.

However, my main goal is not as ambitious as those of the above-mentioned authors. My contribution instead aims at proposing a new division of labour between linguistics and pragmatics. In other words, my primary contribution is to show, in subjects ranging from language and communication, language structure and pragmatic rules, to language and society, language and discourse, and language and literature, how pragmatics, and particularly Relevance Theory, can suggest new solutions to the linguistics-pragmatics interface and, above all, afford new perspectives.

Gregoromichelaki (2009) for semantics. For pragmatics, Levinson (1983) is still the basic textbook for traditional topics (speech acts, presuppositions, implicatures).

Acknowledgments

I was encouraged to write an English version of *Pourquoi le langage?* (Moeschler 2020a) by many people, and would like to acknowledge them all. Firstly, Frederick Newmeyer and Ian Robert gave me positive feedback on the first French draft and persuaded me to submit a proposal for an English version of the book. My thanks also go to Istvan Kecskes, whose invitation to submit to MSP convinced me that it was the right publisher for this book.

I am grateful to the first readers of the French draft: Sandrine Zufferey, Cristina Grisot, Joanna Blochowiak, Éric Wehrli, Guillaume Mathelier, David Giauque, Radu Suciu, David Blunier, Tijana Asic, Olivier Lombard, and my daughter Abigaël Moeschler. I am also indebted to Anne Reboul, whose work in pragmatics, cognitive science, and language evolution were more than a roadmap. Her encyclopaedic knowledge was on many occasions a shortcut as well as a highway.

I would like to thank the people who have most influenced my ideas about language and communication: Luigi Rizzi, Frederick Newmeyer and Stephen Anderson for linguistics; Deirdre Wilson, and Dan Sperber and Larry Horn for pragmatics.

Finally, many thanks to Marcia Hadjimarkos, who supervised the final English version with patience and competence and made this book readable.

Caveats

I would like to set forth five caveats regarding certain formal and content choices I made in writing this book.

First, I decided to adhere to the convention used in pragmatics articles and books and to employ the third person feminine pronoun *she* to refer to the speaker and the third person masculine pronoun *he* to the addressee. I am aware of alternatives, such as using both pronouns (*he/she*) and of the neutral plural form (*they*). My choice follows a convention that is well established in certain approaches to pragmatics, including Relevance Theory. During the last years of my academic career, I systematically used the French feminine gender to refer to the speaker (*la locutrice* 'the-fem speaker-fem'). The feminine gender was also my default morphological clue in terms of institutional roles. And I addressed students in my classes as *chères étudiantes* 'dear-fem students-fem'.

Second, in chapter 1, whose topic is traditional commonplaces about language, I was advised to refer to language ideology rather than to "false ideas about language" as I had originally done. Though I agree that most educated and cultured people share a language ideology, my purpose was not to describe an entire system, but only to touch on some of the traditional claims whose origins are in Western cultures (and specifically the culture of the French language) and which are commonplace. This is why I refer to these instances as *commonplace assumptions* rather than *language ideologies*.

Third, the topic of the origin of language, which frequently recurs, though it is not the main topic of my book, is necessarily presented in a sketchy and incomplete way. I chose to emphasize a pragmatic approach to the evolution of language and communication issues, and have primarily focused on the cognitive function of language. Communication is in fact an adaptative use of language when defined as a system of communication in the weak sense (Reboul 2017a). This choice is consistent with the general aim of this book, which is to show that language and communication are two different things, and how pragmatic meaning is not a matter of convention but of inference. I am aware that there are alternative stories and theories represented in the work of Christiansen and Kirby (2003), Hurford (2007, 2012), Tomasello (2008), Dessalles (2009), Fitch (2010), Scott-Phillips (2015), to name but a few.[2] To sum up, I have chosen to present a coherent picture of language and communication with pragmatics serving as a common thread.

---

[2] A new journal was founded recently: see Bidese and Reboul (2019–2020).

Fourth, one of my main points about language and languages is the multilingual situation of most speakers around the world. Monolingualism, which is dominant in France, is an exception to this rule. The diversity of languages in most countries does not mean that prehistoric societies were multilingual or multicultural; multilingualism is instead the result of new geographic and political entities or nations that came into being, mainly in the 19th and 20th centuries. I quote Jared Diamond in chapter 1 (in the section *One nation, one language*) to describe the sudden change in the linguistic situation in Papua New Guinea thirty years ago.

And finally, since the book opens with a discussion of social issues such as culture and politeness, I would like to clearly acknowledge my universalist approach to social issues like politeness. I am aware that the references mentioned in chapter 3 on cooperation (Grice), and in chapter 4 on face (Goffman) and politeness (Brown and Levinson), have been criticized as being typical of Western American and European cultures. In chapter 4, I give an example of the clash involved when presumably polite behavior (offering a gift) is interpreted as negative or even insulting in a non-European cultural setting. However, although it has been demonstrated that rules of conversation are not universal – see for example the systematic infringement of the *quantity maxim* in Malagasy (Keenan 1976), and the non-universality of the concept of face for explaining politeness (Bargiela-Chiappini 2003) – the common thread in my argument is to discuss the interplay of two kind of logic at work in verbal communication: the logic of conversation and the logic of politeness. Perhaps some readers will find this issue irrelevant; however, in a rather uniform cultural context like that of our Western societies, it raises interesting questions in terms about comprehension and cognition.

In a nutshell, it is clear that looking for a general and consistent way to discuss language and communication is inevitably risky. I have taken this risk, and hope that the questions addressed in discussing complex issues will be, if not relevant, at least interesting.

Contents

Foreword —— VII

Acknowledgments —— IX

Caveats —— XI

Introduction —— 1
1 Why is language a difficult topic? —— 1
2 What is this book about? —— 6

Part I: Language and Communication

Chapter 1
Eight commonplace assumptions about language —— 13
1 Non-written languages are not "real" languages —— 13
2 Some languages are more important than others —— 16
3 Logic, clarity, and beauty in languages: The case for French —— 18
4 Languages change when influenced by other languages —— 22
5 One country, one language —— 27
6 Children learn their mother tongue by imitating their parents' speech —— 31
7 Only words in dictionaries belong to languages —— 34
8 Linguists are interested in word origins —— 38
9 Conclusion —— 43

Chapter 2
Why is language not communication, and why is communication not language? —— 45
1 What is communication? —— 45
2 Verbal and animal communication —— 49
3 Animal communication systems —— 51
4 Intentional systems and non-natural meaning —— 53
5 Two models for communication —— 56
6 Why communication is non-literal —— 59
7 What is language? —— 60
8 The two functions of language: Communication and cognition —— 63
9 Conclusion —— 64

Chapter 3
Language structure and usage — 66
1   Linguistic rules first — 66
2   Principle of linguistic organisation — 69
3   FLN and FLB — 72
4   Protolanguage and modern language — 75
5   Cooperative principle and maxims of conversation — 78
6   Principles of relevance — 85
7   Relevance and implicit communication — 89
8   Conclusion — 90

Part II: Language, society, and discourse

Chapter 4
The social dimension of language — 97
1   Language as a social phenomenon — 98
2   The Sapir-Whorf hypothesis and linguistic relativism — 101
3   The reasons for the success of the relativist thesis — 105
4   Linguistic variation: The example of French — 111
5   The example of AAEV as a linguistic variety — 114
6   A question of politeness — 116
7   Face and face-work — 120
8   Face and politeness — 122
9   Conclusion — 126

Chapter 5
Language and discourse — 127
1   Some conversational rules — 128
2   Is discourse a linguistic fact? — 132
3   Are there discourse rules? — 134
4   Cohesion and coherence — 136
5   Discourse relations as life buoys? — 142
6   Discourse pragmatics — 146
7   Non-propositional effects, emotion and adhesion — 149
8   Propositional effects, argumentation and persuasion — 153
9   Conclusion — 156

Chapter 6
Ordinary and non-ordinary usages of language —— 157
1   Ordinary and non-ordinary usages of language —— 158
2   Figure of speech: The classic version —— 161
3   Metaphorical thought —— 164
4   Weak implicatures and non-propositional effects —— 169
5   Narration and temporal order between events —— 175
6   The representation of speech and thought —— 181
7   Causality in narration —— 184
8   Conclusion —— 187

Chapter 7
Superpragmatics —— 189
1   Beyond meaning —— 190
2   The role of presupposition in communication —— 193
3   The role of implicature in communication —— 194
4   Anti-decipherment, for epistemic vigilance —— 199
5   To be or not to be Charlie —— 200
6   Conclusion —— 205

Conclusion: What we do and still do not know about language —— 206
1   What we know: From syntax to pragmatics, the interface issue —— 206
2   What we still do not know: Emotion, origin of language, machine translation, and man-machine communication —— 210
3   A conclusion for the book —— 214

Afterword —— 215

Glossary —— 217

References —— 227

Name Index —— 241

Subject Index —— 243

Introduction

The main goal of this book is to present and discuss certain aspects of recently acquired knowledge on language and its usage. I do not aim to be exhaustive, but to give a coherent picture of some aspects of language that have developed in linguistics and pragmatics over the past fifty years. My conviction is that this knowledge is crucial for thinking about language and the questions related to it: society, education, communication, and even business.

My targeted audience is not only an academic one – students and researchers – but also a larger, more general audience. Everyone is interested in language, everyone likes language, but language is often an overly simple or overly difficult topic. Overly simple because it is self-evident – we all speak at least one language; overly difficult because the tools taught in grammar courses, if they are taught at all, are too imprecise for comprehension to take place, and because linguists' jargon can make it difficult to understand their findings.

This book invites readers to delve into multiple aspects of language. However, it contains major gaps. For instance, research in computation linguistics and cognitive neuroscience is rarely mentioned. Experimental research will be referred to infrequently, simply because I am not an expert in this area. I refer to major philosophical traditions when necessary, particularly as concerns the issue of meaning. I will mainly focus on my own discipline – linguistics – as well as the area within linguistics that I investigated most: pragmatics, which studies meaning in context.

1 Why is language a difficult topic?

Why is it so difficult to speak about language? Three main reasons explain this difficulty. The first is that every speaker is an expert in her own language: she acquired it without effort; can speak it easily (barring physiological or neurological problems); and engages in linguistic behaviour in a socially suitable way, except in certain contexts and states. All in all her expertise as a speaker appears to be reliable. Moreover, one might ask why language specialists – linguists – earn a salary in universities, when every speaker is already an expert in her own language. But a little reflexion shows why language specialists are necessary: speech therapists solve problems in language development (spelling, dyslexia, more serious pathologies such as autism, speech and language impairment), and translators are very important, as are specialists of foreign language learning, mother tongue reading, spelling, and grammar. In fact, the argument that everyone is an expert in language and that language professionals are therefore useless is not a convincing one.

The second reason for the difficulty in speaking about language in certain academic fields is scepticism about a scientific approach to language. When this occurs the very possibility of a science of language is called into question. Scepticism mainly crops up when the nature of the object of study leans more towards the humanities and the human and social sciences than life sciences (medical studies, biology) and hard sciences such as mathematics, physics, and computational science. But linguists more and more frequently use methods borrowed from the hard sciences, such as mathematical or logical formal languages to formalise grammar and meaning, computational methods to develop grammatical parsers and in machine translation, as well as experimental methods in psycholinguistics and experimental pragmatics. All this research has an increasingly significant impact on daily life. Some examples are the alleviation of language pathology, computer tools for word processors, automatic translators, etc. Moreover, interdisciplinary research in the human and cognitive sciences is becoming more and more frequent; digital humanities is another field that uses linguistic and textual data. However, the divergence between commonplace ideas about language and the reality of research explains why so little expertise on societal issues is institutionally entrusted to linguists.

The third reason is the existence of commonplaces about language. These clichés or persistent ideas about language are pernicious because they are strongly anchored in academic communities. These readily accepted but problematic assumptions distort rational discussion about language, and are obstacles to the most interesting ideas about language. What are these persistent ideas? Here are two examples.

One persistent idea entertained by most academics (even those who have enrolled in at least one class in linguistics) is that languages determine our representation of the world and our way of thinking. According to the Sapir-Whorf hypothesis, language has a strong impact on our world perception and our cultural representations, and, more importantly, on the way our world representations are organised into concepts. Many examples can be given: the huge number of words used to describe snow in the Inuit language, the variety of colour terms in all languages of the world, and the nature of time representation – cyclic – in the Hopi*[3] language.[4] These theses have all been contested and refuted (Pinker

---

[3] Words with * are defined in the Glossary (p. 217–225)
[4] "Whorf wrote that the Hopi language contains 'no words, no grammatical forms, constructions, or expressions that refer directly to what we call 'time', or to past or future, or to enduring or lasting'" (Pinker 1995: 63).

1995, Pullum 1991), but they remain persistent and pervasive. The same is true of the debate on the Pirahã* language, launched by the ethnolinguist Dan Everett: despite refutations of his arguments (among others by Reboul 2017b), the idea that there is at least one language in the world with no recursion*,⁵ which is defined as the central property of the faculty of language in the narrow sense* (Hauser, Chomsky, and Fitch 2002), is still recognized as a fact.

The persistence of Everett's thesis must be explained. Briefly stated, the relativist assumption, which implies the absence of linguistic universals and therefore a typological specificity for almost every language, is more acceptable in the academic world than the alternative claim, according to which all world languages are variations of the same pattern, which is known as Universal Grammar*.⁶

The book's second topic is the assumption that communication is not language and language is not communication, as will be demonstrated in chapter 2. This difference can be illustrated through many examples. Many species in nature communicate without language. This point is important and needs to be explained. First, humans are the only species to communicate with what is called a language, or a complex system composed of a phonology* (a sounds system), a semantics* (a system connecting words and their meaning), and a syntax* (a system of sentence formation rules). Second, modalities of communication can vary, since we know now that sign language is a natural language, although it uses another modality – gestural signs in space and gazes – instead of sounds. We have known for several decades that the brain areas devoted to comprehension and production in sign language are the same as those associated with production and comprehension in spoken language (Emmory 2013).

On the other hand, if language is not communication, this is mainly because of its function. Language is certainly used in verbal communication, but assuming that language is communication is the same as defining language as a system of communication in the strong sense (Reboul 2017a), which evolved *for* communication. However, this conception of language should be able to explain, for example, how principles of grammar are motivated by communicative constraints. This is not always the case, however, as in interrogative sentences containing an interrogative pronoun like *who, what, when, where*. Some languages, like Romanian, require the mandatory anteposition of the interrogative marker *(who have you seen?)*; other languages, like Mandarin Chinese, leave the interrogative

---

5 Recursion is the property of clauses to contain or embed other clauses, such as in complex sentences: [*Mary said to me* [*that Paul confessed to her* [*that he was guilty*]]]. Noun Phrases are also a recursive category: [*the son of* [*the neighbour of* [*my daughter*]]].
6 For an anti-universalist approach to languages, see Evans and Levinson (2009). For a universalist approach, see Newmeyer (2005) and Shibatani and Bynon (1995).

pronouns in their origin position (in situ), as in *you have seen who?*, whereas French allows for both forms. If the forms of interrogative sentences depend on their function, they should be homogeneous: the only thing we can say about languages which put their interrogative markers at the beginning of the sentence is that they allow the hearer to anticipate the interrogative meaning; one cannot say, however, that a relationship between form and function exists.

What are the arguments showing that the main function of natural languages is not communication? Verbal communication is a mixed system based on a code – that is, a language – as well as on ostension and inference (Sperber and Wilson [1986] 1995). In other words, when we communicate, we show (ostension) with our speech acts that we are communicating, and we give our addressees clues for accessing our intentions, which can be accessed via inferences. The simplest example is non-literal communication: we say something to communicate something else, not because we cannot say what we mean, but because this way of communicating is more efficient, quicker, and more relevant. If this kind of communication works, it is because our cognition is able to compute, in a non-random manner, what the speaker means.

In other words, verbal communication – and this is the greatest contribution of pragmatics[7] – is intentional. Many examples of this will be cited. But I would like to anticipate a possible counterexample, illustrated by *slips of the tongue*, which are traditionally interpreted as communicating unintentional meanings. In a slip of tongue, there is an error in encoding the message, which triggers a different and unintentional meaning, often springing from the speaker's subconscience, as the following examples show:

(1) British Prime Minister Gordon Brown, in the presence of President Barack Obama at Omaha Beach, said:
Obama Beach as opposed to *Omaha* Beach

(2) Bernard Kouchner, the former French Minister of Foreign Affairs, talking about the Uighur movement, said:
la répression du mouvement des yogourts instead of *la répression du mouvement des ouïgours*
'the repression of the yogurts movement as opposed to the repression of the Uighurs movement'

---

[7] For an introduction to pragmatics, see Sandrine Zufferey, Moeschler, and Reboul (2019).

(3) François Fillon, the former French Prime Minister, talking about shale gas, said:
les gaz de <u>shit</u> instead of *les gaz de <u>schiste</u>*
'hashish gas as opposed to shale gas'

What happens in these examples, which are often funny and sometimes politically incorrect? My interpretation, far removed from psychoanalysis, which is based on the unconscious, is that the correct form primes a proximal expression, which for a variety of reasons is more easily accessible: *Omaha* is phonetically close to *Obama*, and since Gordon Brown was with the American President Obama, the two words came together and the most accessible form in the context took precedence. On the other hand, we can only wonder at what happens in the minds of speakers who confuse *ouïgours* 'Uighurs' and *yogourts* 'yogurts', or *shit* 'hashish' and *schiste* 'shale': a vowel substitution occurred in one case, a consonant was left out in the other. While the linguistic forms of these word pairs are close, their meanings are not connected, and that is why slips of the tongue can lead to damaging and often irrevocable errors for the speaker.

If language is not communication, then the traditional evolutionary explanation – that language evolved *for* communication – must be rejected. If it is rejected, then the emergence of language and its evolution must have had another cause. Convergent findings in theoretical linguistics and cognitive science hypothesise that language emerged along with the function of externalising the language of thought (Chomsky 2016, Berwick and Chomsky 2016), and that language is a system of communication in the weak sense (Reboul 2017a): language has exapted for communication; that is, it used its first function, cognition, for a new one (communication). This hypothesis will be discussed in chapter 2.

In other words, as Chomsky stated, recursion* is the central property of natural language. It defines the grammar of natural language as a combinatory and computational system, but not as a by-product of communication. Communication, in the sense of an information exchange, is based on other cognitive principles that ensure its efficiency, its rapidity, and especially its economy.

In the same vein, one might ask what characterises natural language in terms of its usage. Dan Sperber and Gloria Origgi, in an article on the evolution of language and communication (Sperber and Origgi 2000), argue that the imperfection of natural languages is caused by the way in which it is learned.[8] We know

---

8 The hypothesis of natural language imperfection is a traditional hypothesis in the philosophy of ordinary language set forth by the German logician Gottlob Frege in the late 19th century (Frege [1892] 1948).

that one part of language learning is innate (syntax), and that another part must be learned (lexicon). The individual part of learning is responsible, according to Sperber and Origgi, for polysemy* – which means that a word can have several meanings – and ambiguity*.

The following conclusions can now be drawn: the main function of language is not communication but the externalization of the language of thought; the faculty of language is innate, but the learning of the lexicon results in the imperfection of languages; and finally, language is a system of communication in the weak sense.

2 What is this book about?

The main aim of this book is to shed a new and explicit light on questions that deal with language issues as seen from a pragmatic perspective. The traditional way of addressing language issues in linguistics states that what has been defined as *performance* (today known as pragmatics) cannot be addressed until more central issues of competence are correctly addressed and answered. In the generative grammar language schema (see chapter 3), the T-model of grammar, connecting narrow syntax to its interfaces (phonology and semantics), does not include pragmatics. In Jackendoff's approach to language, pragmatic or contextualised meaning includes linguistic semantics (Jackendoff 2002: 283; Zufferey, Moeschler, and Reboul 2019: 40). And last but not least, in Levinson's theory of generalised conversational implicatures (Levinson 2000), clear cases of pragmatic intrusion, going beyond classic cases of indexicals, show that some pragmatic meanings are included in semantic meaning.[9] In other words, either pragmatics is outside the scope and agenda of linguistics, or it is closely intertwined with semantics.

In this book, another perspective is addressed and argued for. It is based on the central distinction between language and communication. Defined as a code, a language is a system that pairs sounds and meanings, and that is disconnected from communication. From the pragmatic perspective advocated by Relevance Theory (Sperber and Wilson [1986] 1995), communication is mainly an inferential process, and there is no need for a complete and perfect semantic decoding in order for communication to be successful. Even though the semantics-pragmatics interface will be superficially addressed in chapter 7 (see Moeschler 2019 for a

---

9 This is not the case of particularised conversational implicatures, which are not only conversational in Grice's sense, but primarily contextual.

development), the disconnection between structural rules and communication principles (chapters 2 and 3) has a great impact on the organisation of natural languages and their relation to communication. This difference impacts the social dimension of languages, which includes issues such as the relationship between language and culture, linguistic variation, and politeness. However, suggestions have been made to make politeness principles compatible with the conversational principles responsible for the comprehension of utterances (Brown and Levinson 1987, see chapter 4).

Another crucial issue is the relationship between a linguistic system and its usage in discourse in terms of a possible analogy between grammaticality (a property of sentences) and coherence (a property of discourse). In chapter 5, I suggest an alternative analysis of discourse comprehension based on pragmatic principles, which defines coherence as an effect of comprehension rather than a property of discourse. In other words, discourse is not a property of language structure, but merely a result of language usage.

Finally, a pragmatic approach to meaning must also address non-ordinary usages in fiction and literature. Within the academy literature is limited to literary studies, which are historically and theoretically unconnected to linguistics and even pragmatics. However, a new trend in cognitive pragmatics is bringing utterance comprehension closer to the interpretation of literary texts (Cave and Wilson 2018). The traditional approach to literature is based on rhetoric and stylistics, and is mainly concerned with the inventory of linguistic and discursive strategies specific to literature. One main goal of chapter 6 is to show to what extent figures of speech are cases of ordinary language use. Certain literary properties, such as narration and free indirect discourse, will be approached from a cognitive pragmatic perspective to show the difference between ordinary and non-ordinary language usage.

The last chapter is a natural extension of the domain of pragmatics, and addresses non-propositional effects caused by the emotions and emotive states of the audience. This new approach, called superpragmatics, is an extension of the traditional domain of cognitive pragmatics. It is not limited to understanding speaker meaning: it is about societal issues like political manipulation and the media, as well as messages on the Internet. Special attention will be paid in this chapter to the utterances *Je suis Charlie/Je ne suis pas Charlie* 'I am Charlie/I am not Charlie', which were widespread on the Internet after the terrorist attack in Paris against the satirical magazine *Charlie Hebdo* in January 2015.

In a nutshell, this book advocates a new and original approach to language and language usage, and goes beyond the traditional perimeters of linguistics and pragmatics. The first chapter discusses commonplace assumptions about language. The following chapters each present a fundamental aspect of language: communication (chapter 2), the difference between structure and usage of language (chapter 3), the social dimension of language (chapter 4), the relationship between language and discourse (chapter 5), language usage in literature (chapter 6), and finally two forward-looking chapters, one about superpragmatics (chapter 7) and the last one on the new horizon of a language science (chapter 8).

Part I: **Language and communication**

The main goal of the first part of this book is to disentangle language from communication. In order to accomplish this, I will suggest a definition of what language and communication are by showing that linguistic rules, such as those to do with syntax, belong to the domain of the linguistic system rather than to the domain of communication. On the contrary, communication rules have no linguistic justification, but are activated by principles of cognition and human communication.

However, in order to strengthen my approach to language and communication, I will start by showing what language is not. The commonplace assumptions about language that I address below have no scientific justification, but are consistent with a general view of language. These preconceptions take for granted a hierarchy between languages, an identification between languages and nations, a dominance of written languages over spoken languages, a simple imitation process responsible for language acquisition, and similarities between human languages and other animal communication systems. I will argue that all these propositions are false, and should be replaced by more scientifically consistent propositions.

Chapter 1
Eight commonplace assumptions about language

I would like to start this book not with what linguists know about language and its usage, but with certain ordinary assumptions, which certainly have a logic, but which are highly questionable. The interesting point is that they form a whole: they are all connected. Here are some assumptions about language and its usage that ought to be abolished.

1 Non-written languages are not "real" languages

The first assumption about language taps into the supposed qualitative difference between written and spoken languages. This idea is absurd to linguists, but is believed by many people. I suddenly realised this during a professors' council, in which I was advocating for the application of a Kenyan PhD student working on Swahili*, the official language of Kenya. A professor of Latin asked how it would be possible to write a PhD thesis on a "language which is not a language". I confess I was surprised by the question, and spluttered out an answer: more than fifty million people speak this language in Kenya, therefore, Swahili is certainly a language. It has variants such as Sheng, a variety of Swahili spoken by young people in the suburbs of Nairobi. When the Latin professor objected, "But it's not a written language!", I didn't have the presence of mind to mention Nairobi newspapers in Swahili or literature written in Swahili. But I did grasp the assumption behind the initial question: only written languages are real languages. Going beyond this anecdote, it is important to put forth arguments that demonstrate the importance of spoken languages.

Today there are more than 6,900 languages spoken around the world.[10] The vast majority of them are spoken; only two hundred are written. Certain initiatives of language description, particularly in Africa, are run by missionary linguists of the Summer Institute of Linguistics. Their goal is to translate parts of the Bible, generally one of the gospels, into spoken and non-described languages, thereby turning them into written languages.

A great number of languages will disappear before the end of the 21st century: fifty to seventy percent of them will die out. They are known as *potentially endan-*

---

[10] See Crystal (2010), Anderson (2012); the best website is ethnologue.com, written by SIL International. Crystal (2010) refers to 6,912 languages.

gered languages (Austin and Sallabank 2012). The process through which this happens is quite simple: a language dies with the death of its last speaker. The various causes of language extinction are easy to understand: globalisation, systematic usage of standard languages of communication, and bilingualism. Indeed, as soon as a population begins to use another language of communication, it takes only three generations for a borrowed language to become a mother tongue. This is what happened and is still happening in certain areas of the Swiss Valais region, where the Franco-Provençal patois of the Hérens and Bagnes Valleys is doomed to disappear.[11]

Many linguists study endangered languages, including the Aboriginal languages of Australia, those of the mountains of Borneo and Papua New Guinea, and those of the Andean highlands. Collected data is processed in large databases by linguistic typologists in a race against time. Interesting findings have been made about how time and space are expressed by speakers of these languages. Spatial orientation is governed in many languages by the cardinal points or the direction of streams, which contrasts with the way in which Indo-European languages are oriented by the subject – think of *before, behind, to the right, to the left*, for which the spatial points of reference are the human body and its vertical orientation. In French, temporal reference points are indicated by verb tenses (*imparfait* 'imperfect', *passé simple* 'simple past', *plus-que parfait* 'pluperfect', *passé composé* 'present perfect', *présent* 'present', *futur* 'future')[12] and are almost completely unconnected to the system of spatial reference. Exceptions include *la semaine prochaine* 'next week' (the future lies ahead) or *la semaine d'avant* 'the week before' (the past lies behind). In Yupno*, a language of Papua New Guinea, on the other hand, the expression *towards the sea* indicates the past, while *towards the mountain* indicates the future: water which flows towards the sea thus denotes the past, and water which has not yet flowed represents the future. The gestures that accompany speech are also significant: a hand pointing behind the shoulder indicates the future, while a hand pointing ahead indicates the past (Núñez *et al.* 2012).

Another factor which shows that languages are fundamentally spoken is acquisition: we naturally and easily acquire our mother tongue, whereas learning reading and writing during our school years is much more difficult. For some children this is extremely hard and for others it is easier, but years of learning and

---

[11] See Knecht (1995). Diglossia*, or the existence of a standard language* (for instance German) alongside the vernacular language* (Swiss German) (see chapter 4) explains the preservation of these varieties of the German language.

[12] Germanic languages do not have morphological future tenses, unlike Romance languages such as French and Italian.

practice are needed to master the spelling of written languages such as written French and English.

What can be said about the first languages of humanity? It is obvious that the first languages of Homo sapiens* could only have been spoken. There are good reasons to think that language is a phenomenon which emerged only with our species, certainly a long time after the emergence of Sapiens 300,000 years ago. The reasons for the gap between the appearance of Sapiens and the emergence of language are based on human migration, which took place 60,000 years ago, beginning in African and spreading over the globe to Oceania, Eurasia, and Europe, and passing through the Bering Strait to North America and finally South America. The dominant thesis for the emergence of human language today is monogenesis, with a single linguistic centre. Research in genetics confirms this hypothesis, which correlates with linguistic research on typology and language classification, or the history of linguistic families (Ruhlen 1994, Cavalli-Sforza 2000).

But the most interesting phenomenon that illustrates the difference between spoken and written languages is the emergence of writing 5,000 years ago. According to the evolutionary biologist, geographer, and historian Jared Diamond, sedentary and agricultural societies, which were politically organized and had begun dividing labour, were well enough off to pay scribes who specialized in writing. The scribes essentially took inventory: since it was necessary to archive and relay information about production, exchanges and goods, writing began as accounting. Here is how Jared Diamond describes the first Sumerian texts (Diamond 1997: 234):

> The uses of these telegraphic, clumsy, ambiguous early scripts were as restricted as the number of their users. Anyone hoping to discover how Sumerians of 3000 B.C. thought and felt is in for a disappointment. Instead, the first Sumerian texts are emotionless accounts of palace and temple bureaucrats. About 90 percent of the tablets in the earliest known Sumerian archives, from the city of Uruk, are clerical records of goods paid in, workers given rations, and agricultural products distributed. Only later, as Sumerians progressed beyond logograms to phonetic writing, did they begin to write prose narratives, such as propaganda and myths.

Like the Sumerians, I use abbreviated writing when I jot down a shopping list. However, I use a more complex style to answer emails, and express myself in an even more sophisticated manner for articles, books, and comments on my PhD students' research. At the beginning, writing had a completely different function. According to Jared Diamond (1997: 236–237),

> Writing arose independently only in the Fertile Crescent, Mexico, and probably China precisely because those were the first areas where food production emerged in their respective hemispheres. Once writing had been invented by those few societies, it then spread, by

> trade and conquest and religion, to other societies with similar economies and political organizations.
>
> While food production was thus a necessary condition for the evolution or early adoption of writing, it was not a sufficient condition.

This perspective helps us to understand why languages were not originally written, and why writing appeared much later than spoken language, as well as why it had a much less significant function than it does today.[13]

2 Some languages are more important than others

I encountered the second assumption in a lecture given by a famous French linguist, who tried to convince his audience that some languages, including French, have a "global purpose", whereas others, like Chinese, don't. He also tried to show that the place of English as the most common language of communication was not legitimate, because English can be ambiguous. To illustrate this, he gave the dramatic example of an airline disaster caused by the mistaken interpretation of the air traffic controller's *Right now!*, which was understood by the pilot as "turn right, now", even though the controller had just given the order *Turn left!*, and the meaning of *Right now!* was "immediately!".

The idea of a hierarchy between languages is often quantitatively correlated with the number of its speakers. The spoken language with the highest number of speakers, Mandarin Chinese, has little chance of becoming the most widespread language in the world, despite the impressive development of the Confucius Institutes, because political, economic and cultural hegemonies determine the spread of a language more than other factors. English, on the other hand, has succeeded in conquering fundamental areas of social, political, cultural, and scientific life. The worlds of banking, finance, and politics (consider the EU) are more and more dominated by English. All major international scientific conferences are held in English, and the vast majority of scientific publications, articles, books, conference proceedings, etc. are now almost mandatorily in English.[14]

---

[13] For the dissemination of agricultural societies from the Fertile Crescent, see Renfrew (1987), who explains the relationship between the dissemination of germs and Indo-European languages.
[14] This does not mean that publications in other languages than English are not valuable: they simply target a more limited scientific community. For instance, the original version of this book was written and published in French (*Pourquoi le langage? Des Inuits à Google*, Paris, Armand Colin, 2020), because I was targeting a French readership and also because I wanted to write about the situation of French in France and other French-speaking countries.

Does it make sense to quantify the importance of a language? The reasons for which some languages emerge as international languages are multiple. During the entire Middle Ages, Latin was the *lingua franca* for literate people and the clergy, and during the modern period, through the first half of the 20th century, French was the language of diplomacy. In documents produced by the European Union, the distribution of the main European languages (French, English, and German) was more or less equal until 1997. 45% of its documents were in English and 41% were in French. But from 2012 on, these numbers changed: 75% of documents produced are now in English, while only 21% of them are in French.[15]

But does it make sense to wonder whether a language does or doesn't have an international purpose? Languages with a strong cultural tradition – literary, artistic, scientific – are all international languages. However, what really counts is not the number of native speakers of a language, but the number of non-native speakers who use it to read, write, and communicate. Another way of assessing this phenomenon is to compare the most frequently spoken languages of the *Cambridge Encyclopedia of Language* (Crystal 2010) in terms of the ratio between native and non-native speakers.

The ratio between the mother tongue and the usual language of communication (Crystal 2010: 36) is 20% for Chinese Mandarin, 37% for Hindi-Urdu, 85% for English, and almost 90% for French. Other languages have weak ratios. Spanish is often referred to as a world language because it is the fourth most frequently spoken language in the world, but its ratio is less than 10%. In comparison, Portuguese has a ratio of about 20%, Arabic almost 30%, and Russian about 60%.[16] Some languages have a very low ration: 0% for Japanese and Bengali, and only 12% for German. The language with the highest ratio is Malay, with 160%. This means that there are many more non-native speakers of Malay than native ones, because of the very large number of languages – more than 600 – in use in Malaysia.[17]

This parameter – the ratio of native to non-native speakers – is certainly important, but it is not the only one. Languages, indeed, are the result of historical events, and are often unpredictable. French language historian Henriette Walter has made a very interesting conjecture about the One Hundred Years' War (1337–1453) between the Kingdom of Normandy and the Kingdom of France.

---

15 https://www.lemonde.fr/les-decodeurs/article/2016/05/06/l-usage-de-la-langue-francaise-recule-au-sein-des-institutions-europeennes_4914763_4355770.html, accessed on 5 November 2018.
16 This figure, which dates from the beginning of the 21st century, shows that at the beginning of the new century, Russian still had an influence in the former communist bloc countries, as well as in the former Socialist Soviet Republics.
17 See the excellent documentation in *Pour la Sciences, Les langues du monde*, October 1997.

It is not generally known that, had England won the war, the Kingdom of Normandy would certainly not have disappeared, mainly because it would have been strengthened and consolidated by this victory. The Normans, established in England since William the Conqueror's conquest in 1066, spoke French: they were the grandchildren of a small Viking population in Normandy which had sailed from the Scandinavian coast to Normandy between the 9th and 10th centuries, and they spoke French, or rather old French, because their mothers were Normans. It's amusing to imagine that if the Kingdom of Normandy had conquered the Kingdom of France, the British conquerors of North America would have spoken French. The conclusion of this counterfactual story is quite funny: had things really happened this way, French would hold the role currently held by English in the world!

Accidents of history are therefore the second factor in determining the importance of a language. An interesting anecdote explains why William the Conqueror managed to conquer England. Here is how Jared Diamond describes this event (Diamond 2005: 185):

> The year 1066, famous for the Battle of Hastings at which William the Conqueror (William of Normandy) led French-speaking descendants of former Viking raiders to conquer England, can also be taken to mark the end of the Viking raids. The reason why William was able to defeat the English king Harold at Hastings on England's southeast coast on October 14 was that Harold and his soldiers were exhausted. They had marched 220 miles south in less than three weeks after defeating the last Viking invading army and killing their king at Stamford Bridge in central England on September 25.

This explanation of the Norman victory in England is quite surprising: the main reason for the English defeat is that they arrived at the battle exhausted by a forced walk of 220 miles. On what does the importance of a language depend? It depends on several things, as these two examples, one counterfactual, and the other factual, have shown.

3 Logic, clarity, and beauty in languages: The case for French

Why do people say that some languages are more beautiful than others? Almost all Swiss-French speaking people, for example, feel that Swiss-German dialects are among the ugliest languages in the world. Such purely subjective judgements should logically include all Northern Germanic languages: the many varieties of Dutch, the Scandinavian languages, the varieties of German spoken in southern Germany and Austria, as well as Alsatian dialects and Luxemburgish.

This inacceptable position definitely has cultural, psychological, and sociological reasons. My own French-speaking family, for example, some of whom earned university degrees, lived in a city with a majority of Swiss German Speakers. However, the Swiss German language was considered by my family to be a dialect, a sublanguage when compared to the German spoken in Germany. This judgement was accompanied by strong contempt for Germanic culture, and especially German literature, which was contrasted with the link between Swiss French literature and French literature. The best explanation for this feeling of superiority is the fact we belonged to a linguistic minority in a largely German-speaking region whose economic centre was in German-speaking Switzerland (Zurich); these facts reinforced our need to inverse the hierarchy of cultural, literary, and linguistic values.

However, we know from a linguistic point of view that Swiss German varieties are in fact real languages. They are now used in the media (radio, television), have been standardised in their written form (which is more a social fact than a linguistic necessity), and above all are very interesting in terms of their grammars.[18] To sum up, beauty is neither a criterion for evaluation nor a guarantee for a language to belong to the category known as natural languages.

What about the second claim, that some languages are more *logical* than others. Logic[19] is even less acceptable as a criterion than is beauty.[20] For instance, why would a language like English or French, whose *word order* is SVO (subject-verb-object), be more logical than SOV languages like Japanese? And what about Latin, a final verb language, considered by most teachers in European secondary schools as a language that develops students' logical reasoning? From a typological point of view, languages are distributed between six possible combinations of word order, but with different statistical distributions: SVO, SOV, OSV, OVS, VSO and VOS (Greenberg 1963, 2005). English is clearly a VO language, whereas Japanese is OV. In his 1963 article, Greenberg proposed 45 language universals, the most important being about word order. Here are three of them:

(4) Three language universals (Greenberg 1963: 88)
  1. In declarative sentences with nominal subject and object, the dominant order is almost always one in which the subject precedes the object. [. . .]

---

18 See Scherrer (2012) for a description of some grammatical properties of Swiss German dialects compared to those in standard German.
19 The term *logic* is used in a non-technical way. However, most ordinary explanations given to grammatical facts refer to the "logical" criterion. I confess that I have never understood the meaning of the term in this context.
20 One criterion applied by American university students in choosing to study French as a foreign language is its supposed beauty, coupled with the fact that it is such a "romantic language" and the prospect of studying in Paris.

3. Languages with dominant VSO order are always prepositional.
4. With overwhelmingly greater than chance frequency, languages with normal SOV order are postpositional.

It is possible to show the correlation between word order and the presence of pre- or post-positions (*adpositions*). The languages investigated show that for the order VSO, all languages have prepositions; with the SOV order, all have postpositions; and in the SVO order (like in French), 10 out of 30 of the investigated languages by Greenberg have prepositions. Briefly stated, the rules that govern word order have nothing to do with logic: the differences in word order are not evenly distributed.[21]

We now come to the third assumption, which states that some languages are clearer than others, which in turn implies that some languages are more ambiguous than others. Now, *ambiguity** is a universal phenomenon in natural languages. Ambiguity can take different forms: (i) *lexical*, when the word is ambiguous because it is polysemous (5), such as the word *bank*, which denotes different types of entities; (ii) *syntactic* (6), when the Noun Phrase (NP) *an umbrella* is either a complement of the NP *the man*, or an adjunct to the Verb Phrase (VP) *hit the man*; (iii) *semantic* (7), when the word *Norwegian* designates either a specific person or someone that is from Norway; and (iv) *pragmatic*, when an unambiguous utterance has different meanings in different contexts, such as in (8):

(5) *A bank*
   a. a financial institution
   b. a place for storing things
   c. a hillside
   d. a mass of earth, cloud, or fog

(6) *Mary hit the man with an umbrella.*
   a. *Mary hit the man with [an umbrella].*
   b. *Mary hit [the man with an umbrella].*

(7) *John wants to marry a Norwegian woman.*
   a. John wants to marry a particular Norwegian woman, Ilse.
   b. John wants to marry whoever is a Norwegian woman.

---

21 For a discussion of Greenberg's theses, see Newmeyer (2005).

(8) *The postman has just come.*
   a. It is 11 o'clock.
   b. Go get the post.
   c. You can let the dog out now.

What conclusion can be drawn here? Simply that ambiguity* is a property of natural language, and French, as well as English – despite the French linguist's argument about the ambiguous *Right now!* – is a language like any other. This does not mean that the French writer Boileau (1636–1711) was incorrect in his *Art poétique* (Chant I, verses 150–154):

> Avant donc que d'écrire apprenez à penser.
> Selon que notre idée est plus ou moins obscure,
> L'expression la suit, ou moins nette, ou plus pure.
> Ce que l'on conçoit bien s'énonce clairement,
> Et les mots pour le dire arrivent aisément.
>
> [Thus, before writing, learn to think.
> Depending on whether our idea is more or less obscure,
> The expression follows, either less clear or purer.
> What has been well conceived is clearly uttered,
> And the words for saying it come easily.]

But Boileau's advice is about written language, since thought precedes its linguistic expression. When we speak, we produce utterances in about 6 seconds, and it is not surprising that clarity is not our primary concern; that said, the idea of clarity has been explored by the philosopher Paul Grice, the idea being that cooperative speakers respect a conversational maxim of clarity (maxim of manner) to avoid ambiguities and obscurities, and to be brief and ordered (Grice 1975: 46). It is interesting that this maxim explains the reasons why we are able to say less, which contrasts with situations in which another maxim, the maxim of quantity ("Make your contribution as informative as required", Grice 1975: 45), takes precedence. In some cases, both maxims can contradict each other. If Peter asks Mary where Anne lives and she answers (9), either Mary means that she doesn't know where Anne lives (Mary has given the strongest information), or that she is respecting the maxim of manner "be brief", which could lead to the understanding that she does not wish to give more information:

(9) *Somewhere in the south of Burgundy.*

Clarity, unlike beauty and logic, makes sense, but in a very different way: it is not language which is clear, but its usage.

4 Languages change when influenced by other languages

The fourth commonplace assumption about language is the influence of *language contact* on *language change*: when a language changes, this occurs through contact with another language. The issue is not so much knowing whether this idea is true or false – some questions linked to linguistic changes, like lexical borrowing, are currently explained by linguistic contact. The main issue is that language contact is often seen as having a harmful effect. For instance, in Switzerland there is a false assumption that the German language leads to grammatical mistakes in Swiss French, especially in bilingual regions. For instance, when compared to correct French syntax (10), the Swiss French sentence (11) is a copy of German (12): in German, the verb *helfen* 'to help' governs the dative case, whereas in French, *aider* 'to help' is transitive, governing the accusative case (*le* 'him') and not the dative case (*lui* 'him'):

(10) Il   l'   aide.
      3sgProSub   3sgProAcc   help
      'He helps him.'

(11) *Il   lui   aide.
      3sgProSub   3sgProDat   help
      'He helps him.'

(12) Er   hilft   ihm.
      3sgProSub   help   3sgProDat
      'He helps him.'

However, in (11) the pronoun *lui* is an old French pronoun, and the form *lui aider* 'to help him' is an archaism, an old-fashioned manner of speaking French. This phenomenon is general and easy to explain: regions on the periphery of French-speaking regions are more conservative. An a contrario argument is the type of French spoken in the canton of Valais in French-speaking Switzerland, which is a more recent version of French than the French spoken in Geneva, which is more conservative because it is an older version. The canton of Valais joined the Swiss Confederation relatively recently and, since it is a Catholic canton, only used French in the 19th century. Protestant cantons, like the one including Geneva, adopted French earlier, because people in this canton read the Bible in French.

Now, what can we say about contact between languages? Is it disadvantageous or advantageous? For instance, is English a threat to French because of the many terms the latter has borrowed from the former, including frequently used technical terms like *start-up, blog, podcast, PC, peer-review, upgrade, download*, etc.? In fact, contact between languages is not harmful. On the contrary, it is a common situation in the world. How can we explain this fact?

Let us begin with a banal and ordinary fact: languages change over time. We will use French as an example. The ancestor of French is a variety of Latin, Vulgar Latin, which gave rise to varieties of Gallo-Roman dialects during the Middle Ages. One of these varieties of old French yielded modern French. A moderately well-informed reader knows that texts from the Middle Ages texts are fairly difficult to read, whereas works by Rabelais, a Renaissance French physician and writer (1483 or 1494–1553), are much easier: although French from the 17th century has some syntactic differences with contemporary French, as (13) and (14) show, it is not a foreign language:

(13) 17th century French
 Il   le   peut faire.
 3sgProSub 3sgProAcc can   do
 'He can do it.'

(14) 21st century French
 Il   peut le   faire.
 3sgProSub can   3sgProAcc do
 'He can do it.'

Syntactically speaking, the French language has changed only a little since the 17th century. It has certainly evolved much more in terms of prosody, phonetics, and lexicon. This can be readily observed when the lexicon and prosody of current Parisian French is compared to Quebec French.[22]

One of the central questions for historical linguistics is to identify factors of linguistic change. A classic theory evokes language contact as an important factor. In other words, languages change under the influence of other languages with which they come in contact. According to this theory, change is an external (or exogenous) factor, essentially bound to linguistic contacts between speakers.

We must then ask how language contacts influence or modify a language. Stated in this way, the phenomenon sounds rather mysterious and gives a negative impression. Statements of the following sort often crop up: German has a harmful influence on Swiss French, and English, whose lexicon is more and more

---

[22] For instance, *a car* is in Quebec French *un char*, and in standard French *une voiture*.

common in French, negatively impacts the structure of French. Fortunately, both statements are false.

First, the influence of German has no impact on French syntax or phonology. Some German and French bilinguals' "slice" (*trancher* in French), or maintain some prosodic features of their most commonly used language. One example is my cousin from Bern, Switzerland, whose mother tongue is French. Her French is perfect, but she speaks with a German accent. Her older sister, on the other hand, raised in the same bilingual milieu (a native French-speaking mother and a native German-speaking father), has no German accent. What conclusions can be drawn here? It is clear that the German-speaking environment had a greater influence on my younger cousin, but that it did not impose German syntax or the German lexicon on her French syntax.

It is certain that German has an influence, albeit a limited one, on the lexicon of the bilingual regions of Switzerland. As children growing up in a bilingual region of French-speaking Switzerland, we delighted in lexical intrusions, making up sentences like (15), that mixed French syntax with the German lexicon, as the reference clause in German shows (16):

(15) *Le fatre a schlagué le katz avec un stock parce qu'il avait stohlé le speck.*
the father beat the cat with a stick because it had stolen the bacon
'Dad beat the cat with a stick because it stole the bacon'.

(16) *Der Vater hat die Katze mit einem Stock geschlagen, weil sie den Speck gestohlen hatte.*
the father has the cat with a stick beaten because she the bacon stolen had
'Dad beat the cat with a stick because she stole the bacon.'

These examples show that only the lexicon is affected – *fatre* for *père* 'father', *schlaguer* for *battre* 'to beat', *katz* for *chat* 'cat', *stohler* for *voler* 'to steal', etc. –, and not syntax.[23] No French-speaking child would have used German syntax – the German grammatical structure in which the verb falls at the end of the subordinate clause and the past participle falls at the end of the matrix clause, as in (17):

---

[23] It is not surprising that French morphology is applied to these lexical borrowings. For instance, the verb *schlaguer* behaves like a first group verb with an -*er* inflection. Nouns like *katz* or *stock* take the same morphological gender as their French counterparts (*le chat* 'the cat', *le baton* 'the stick').

(17) *Le fatre a le katz avec un stock schlagué parce qu'il le speck stohlé avait.*
 the father has the cat with a stick beaten because he the bacon stole had
 'Dad beat the cat with a stick because she stole the bacon.'

When we consider the 'bad' influence of English on French, the crucial point is also the lexicon. Some French speakers condemn inappropriate usage of what they call *franglais*, or 'Frenglish', a mix of French and English. A typical example, from the article on franglais in Wikipedia,[24] is shown in (18), with the standard French version in (19):

(18) *Je reboote pour que les drivers que je viens d'updater soient loadés sans que le système ne bugue.*
 'I'm rebooting so the drivers I have just updated can be loaded without the system bugging.'

(19) *Je redémarre pour que les pilotes que je viens de mettre à jour soient chargés sans que le système ne plante.*
 'I'm rebooting so the drivers I have just updated can be loaded without the system bugging.'

Note that today, lexical units like *redémarrer* 'to reboot', *pilote* 'driver', *mettre à jour* 'to update', *charger* 'to load', *buguer* 'to bug' are quite frequent. As these examples show, the "negative influence" of one language (here English) on another (French) is mainly a question of lexicon. In specialised professions like computer programming, finance, and banking, for which English is used as a working language, this type of jargon is used very frequently.

When pervasive usage of Frenglish took off, a strong political reaction occurred in France, resulting in the 1994 Toubon Law, whose name refers to the then-Minister of Culture and Francophonie (defined as countries that promote French language, multilingualism, and cultural diversity, as well as peace, democracy, and human rights, based on (higher) education and research, economic cooperation, and sustainable development[25]). The Toubon Law stipulates that French must be used in public; in scientific conferences, French scholars may use French if all participants are not foreign speakers; and university theses must be written in French.[26]

---

24 https://fr.wikipedia.org/wiki/Franglais, accessed 8 November 2018.
25 https://www.francophonie.org/lorganisation-internationale-de-la-francophonie-81.
26 In fact, most PhD theses in scientific fields, including linguistics and philosophy, for instance, are written in English.

What were the effects of this law? French speakers certainly understood that the intrusion of the English lexicon had become increasingly pervasive in all aspects of public life, and that it was not possible to resolve the issue of foreign words.[27] Furthermore, we know that new words are introduced into ordinary language usages only if the things they denote are also adopted. Borrowed lexicon is not always adopted verbatim, with both its original pronunciation and meaning.[28] Some Frenglish words are not used in the same way in English. In England, for example, one does not say *WC* (*water closet*) as one does in France, but *toilets*; *smoking* does not mean a man's dress suit; *tuxedo* is used in North America, and *dinner jacket* is used in the United Kingdom; and *pressing* is not used for *dry-cleaning*. However, some lexical expressions have been copied: *like* has become *genre* in French, as in (20):

(20)　*Il est genre gentil garçon.*
　　　He is gender nice boy
　　　'He's, like, a nice boy.'

It is important to recall that lexical phenomena are passing fashions that do not last. The borrowed lexicon is used for the time it is necessary; in the technological domain, needs change very quickly. Does anyone still use a *walkman* (*balladeur* in French)? What company still has *brainstorming* (*remue-méninge* in French) sessions? Ten years from now new words will emerge because new concepts, new practices, and new objects will have appeared on the market, influencing people's behaviour.

What conclusion can be drawn from the above? Mainly that contributions from foreign languages to the lexicon are positive for the language that does the borrowing. French has borrowed many now-common words from other languages, though few native speakers are aware of this:

(21)　Nahuatl, Mexico
　　　cacao, chocolat, cacahuète, tomate
　　　'cocoa, chocolate, peanut, tomato'

---

27 Remember that this process is not unidirectional. Because of the Norman presence in England for more than four centuries in the Middle Ages, English imported more than ten thousand French words. Nowadays a lot of technical culinary terms have been imported from French into English: *vinaigrette, sauté, foie gras, croissant*, etc. It is also important to recall the creation of words like *courriel* 'email' which is used more in French Canada than in France.

28 There is a strong tendency in France to pronounce borrowed words according to French spelling conventions: the best example is the pronunciation of *Bruxelles*: [brysɛl] in Belgium, [bryksɛl] in France.

(22) Quechua, Peru
caoutchouc, pampa
'rubber, pampas'

(23) Arawak, The Antilles
maïs, ouragan, savane
'corn (maize), hurricane, savannah'

(24) Tupi, Brazil
acajou, ananas
'mahogany, pineapple'

(25) Tamul, India
mangue
'mango'

(26) Mandarin Chinese
typhon
'typhoon'

(27) Malay
jonque, bambou
'junk, bamboo'[29]

These words were borrowed at the same time as the things they refer to. To sum up, word borrowings are positive, and are not a threat.

5 One country, one language

The fifth commonplace assumption is the equation between one country and one language. When I was studying in the US in the early 1980s, I was asked by neighbours in West Hollywood, a higher-middle class suburb of Los Angeles, whether people in Switzerland spoke 'Swiss'? My attempts to explain the multilingual situation of this mountainous country – the only familiar things about it were banks, chocolate, and watches – were not very successful, especially when

---

[29] Most of these words are the same in English; the only difference is their spelling. The sole exception is *mahogany*.

they examined a map of Europe: "Wow, so many countries, and so many languages!" The contrast with the linguistic situation of the US was very clear, and the complex situation of Europe was difficult to fathom.

The equation 'one country, one language' is erroneous. First, not all European countries are monolingual. Besides Switzerland there are other well-known exceptions: in Spain, Castilian, Catalan, Basque and Galician, closely related to Portuguese, are all spoken; in Italy, French is spoken in the Aosta Valley and German is spoken in the north of the Veneto region; in France, apart from French, which is spoken by 80% of the population, Basque, Breton, Catalan, Corsican, Alsatian, Flemish, and Occitan are minority languages; in Belgium, German is spoken in the eastern part of the country, whose two official languages are French and Flemish; in the United Kingdom, Welsh is spoken in Wales, and Gaelic in Scotland. There are many varieties of Italian and German in Italy and Germany, with a typical situation of diglossia in Germany; that is, varieties of spoken German that differ from the standard common language. Finally, in Switzerland, four national languages are defined in the Swiss Constitution: German, French, Italian, and Romansh. Whereas French-speaking Switzerland is a rather homogenous dialectal region – the main differences are lexical and prosodic – a wide variety of German dialects are used in central and eastern German-speaking Switzerland. Most are mutually comprehensible, with the exception of one variety of Alemannic German in the Upper Valais; there are five varieties of Romansh and several varieties of Italian dialects in the cantons of Tessin and Graubünden.

Two issues must be addressed: firstly the erroneous equation "one country, one language", and secondly the reason why there are so many varieties of languages. We will begin by examining the question about varieties of languages.

We have already mentioned why North Americans speak English: it is the result of British colonisation of what are now Canada and the United States of America, with some French-speaking enclaves like Louisiana in the US, and Quebec and New Brunswick in Canada. A striking fact about North America – and the same is true for Central and South America – is the almost total disappearance of Amerindian languages. In the early 21st century there were only 949 Amerindian languages and 47 million speakers of Amerindian languages on the entire American continent. This is a very low ratio of speakers per language. There are still 210 living languages in Brazil, 240 in Mexico, and more than 100 in the US. It is very striking that in the National Museum of the American Indian in Washington, D.C., the topic of Amerindian languages is completely absent from the exhibitions and bookstore. As a comparison, there are 1,995 languages in Africa, 209 in Europe, 2,039 in Asia, and 1,341 in Oceania, with different repartitions in the number of speakers in the world: 11.8% for Africa, 0.8% for America, 61% for Asia, 6.3% for Europe, and 0.1% for Oceania, as shown in Table 1:

Table 1: Numbers of languages and speakers per continent.[30]

	Languages		Speakers	
	Nb	%	Nb (in millions)	%
Asia	2,034	31%	3,490	61%
Pacific	1,341	21%	6	0.1%
America	949	15%	47	0.8%
Africa	1,995	30%	676	11.8%
Europe	209	3%	1,504	6.3%

This table illustrates the pronounced difference between the number of languages and the number of their speakers: this difference correlates with the ratio speakers/languages worldwide, giving rise to a generalisation: the more languages there are, the less the number of their speakers, which explains why there is a serious risk of endangered languages, those with less than 10,000 speakers, of dying out. Crystal's data is presented below (Crystal 2010: 294):

Table 2: Ratio languages-speakers.

Number of speakers	Number of languages	% of languages
More than 1,000,000	283	4%
More than 100,000	616	9%
More than 10,000	1,364	21%
More than 1000	1,631	25%
More than 100	1,040	16%
Less than 100	455	7%
Known to be extinct	310	5%
No estimate	905	15%

Number of speakers: N = 5,022,648,000
Number of languages: N = 6,604

These data allow a new assumption to be made: the languages with the highest number of speakers are not many, only 13%. This means that the majority of languages (69%) have fewer than 100,000 speakers: these languages are potentially in danger.

It is clear that this macro-linguistic data, particularly for countries like Brazil (210 languages), Mexico (240), Cameroun (270), Democratic Republic of Congo

---

[30] Crystal (2010: 295), according to Ethnologue (Gordon 2005), based on 6,912 languages.

(210), India (380), Indonesia (670), New Guinea (670), and Australia (250), shows no correlation between country and language. But the question of why there so many languages remains.

One possible response is *geography*. In Amazonia the complexity of the river networks and the density of the forest are all factors of isolation. In Papua New Guinea the Highlands also isolate populations. Jared Diamond (2012: 2) describes a scene in 2006 at the airport of Port Moresby, the capital of Papua New Guinea, in comparison with what occurred in 1931 when the first contact between Highland people and Australian patrols took place:

> A linguist listening to the crowd would have distinguished dozens of languages, falling into very different groups: tonal languages with words distinguished by pitch as in Chinese, Austronesian languages with relatively simple syllables and consonants, and non-tonal Papuan languages. In 1931 one could have encountered individual speakers of several different languages together, but never a gathering of speakers of dozens of languages. Two widespread languages, English and Tok Pisin (also known as Neo-Melanesian or Pidgin English), were the languages being used in 2006 at the check-in counter and also for many of the conversations among passengers, but in 1931 all conversations throughout the New Guinea Highlands were in local languages, each of them confined to a small area.

We know that geographically isolated populations are differentiated in both genetic and linguistic terms (Cavalli-Sforza 2000). One extreme situation, which is well-known in the domain of Romance languages, is the case of Romansh*, which is spoken in the canton of Graubünden, a mountainous canton in eastern Switzerland. Five varieties of Romansh are spoken in five valleys of this canton: Surlivan in Disentis, Sutsilvan in Thusis, Surmiran in Albula, Puter in Samedan, and Vallader in Zernez. Geography – Graubünden is known as the canton of a thousand valleys – is correlated to this linguistic diversity.[31]

We will now return to the first issue, the inadequacy of the equation "one country, one language". We have observed that the geography of certain countries explains the extreme diversity of their languages and language varieties. The homogeneity of languages in Europe can be understood through the history of the countries in question. The unification of European countries in the 19th century also included the unification of language. Italy and Germany were defined as countries during this period, and the emergence of a strong centralised power explains why one language was attached to new political entities. In older countries like Spain, the United Kingdom, and France, the reasons are different. In France, the process of linguistic unification was triggered during the French revolution by the Abbot Grégoire's report, which recommended the eradication of

---

31 For a linguistic study about Romansh, see Anderson (2016).

French dialects and advocated the use of a single language in the French nation.[32] However, it was primarily the 1882 Ferry Law, which made attendance in school mandatory for children aged 6 to 13, that caused French to spread. French was the only spoken language allowed during schooltime, on the playground, and at home – pupils were punished if they were caught speaking their dialect or patois at home. This was not as successful as had been anticipated, however: in 1914, at the beginning of the First World War, only a quarter of young French soldiers understood the officers' orders given in French. French only became the main language of communication in France after World War I.

The political decision to eradicate all other languages in France shows that France is an exception in Europe: it has no other varieties like those in Italy and Germany.[33] In other words, variations in French are mainly prosodic, phonetic, or lexical, and contrast with the situations of diglossia* found in Italy, Switzerland, and Germany as regards Italian and German. The French situation is exceptional worldwide, and can elucidate some difficulties in the management of French society in terms of education and culture.[34]

To conclude, we have observed that historical and geographical factors cancel out the assumption "one country, one language". As we will see in chapter 3, the idea of national languages is an external language issue, which is not a central topic in linguistics. Internal language issues, on the other hand, are investigated by linguistics.

6 Children learn their mother tongue by imitating their parents' speech

Every parent has experienced the magical moment of their child's first word, his or her learning the lexicon, and then a continuous flow of speech. How does this happen? The French linguist Jean-Yves Pollock (1997: 13) has summarized this process well: "L'apprentissage du langage n'est pas quelque chose que font les enfants, mais quelque chose qui leur arrive" [Learning language is not something children do, but something that happens to them]. One of the best examples is given by Steven Pinker, a psycholinguist who studies lexicon acquisition, in his book *The Language Instinct* (Pinker 1995: 281)

---

[32] For the complete story of this unification process, see Certeau, Julia, and Revel (1985). It should be noted that French has been the official language for all administrative decrees in France since the Ordonnance de Villers-Cotterêt in 1539: all administrative texts, official acts, decrees and laws must be written in French, rather than in the Latin that was used until this time.
[33] See chapter 4 for a more nuanced description of variations in French.
[34] See chapter 7 for a discussion of a major societal issue in French society.

Indeed, when fussy parents or meddling experimenters do provide children with feedback, the children tune it out. The psycholinguist Martin Braine once tried for several weeks to stamp out one of his daughter's grammatical errors. Here is the result:

Child: Want other one spoon, Daddy.

Father: You mean, you want THE OTHER SPOON.

Child: Yes, I want other one spoon, please, Daddy.

Father: Can you say "the other spoon"?

Child: Other . . . one . . . spoon.

Father: Say . . . "other."

Child: Other.

Father: "Spoon."

Child: Spoon.

Father: "Other . . . Spoon."

Child: Other . . . spoon. Now give me other one spoon?

The acquisition of the mother tongue is thus not a learning process in the educational sense of the term. It is a natural process, which follows, as far lexicon is concerned, a regular curve: from 12 to 16 months, 0.3 words a day; from 16 to 22 months, 0.8 words a day; from 22 to 30 months, 1.6 words a day; from 30 to 72 months, 3.6 words a day; from 6 to 8 years, 6.6 days a day; finally; from 8 to 10 years, 12.1 words a day (Bloom 2000).

In a more general way, acquisition processes follow different steps. During the first year, the babble period, the baby exercises and adjusts her articulators with the sounds of her environment. An infant is born with the capacity to learn any language, but this ability is very quickly reduced to the phonetic characteristics of her mother tongue. Here is how Steven Pinker describes this period (Pinker 1995: 264–265):

> Babies continue to learn the sounds of their language throughout the first year. By six months, they are beginning to lump together the distinct sounds that their language collapses into a single phoneme, while continuing to discriminate equivalently distinct ones that their language keeps separate. By ten months they are no longer universal phoneticians but have turned into their parents; they do not distinguish Czech or Inslekampx phonemes unless they are Czech or Inslekampx babies.[35]

---

35 Inslekampx* is a Shalishan language spoken in Western Canada.

From 12 months utterances consist of single words like *mommy, daddy, no,* and *yes*. The period from 27–28 to 37–38 months is the most extraordinary period, known as the grammatical explosion, accompanied by the whole range of grammatical categories and constructions present in the child's environment. It is the period in which clauses expand from one to two or three words. The order of grammatical category acquisition is first nouns, then verbs, and lastly prepositions and determiners (functional categories). We can thus conclude that Brain's daughter was at a developmental stage in which verbs and nouns had been acquired, but not determiners. Here is how Pinker describes a three-year old child (Pinker 1995: 276–277):

> The three-year-old, then, is a grammatical genius – master of most constructions, obeying rules far more often than flouting them, respecting language universals, erring in sensible, adultlike ways, and avoiding many kinds of errors altogether. How do they do it? Children of this age are notably incompetent at most other activities. We won't let them drive, vote, or go to school, and they can be flummoxed by no-brainer tasks like sorting beads in order of size, reasoning whether a person could be aware of an event that took place while the person was out of the room, and knowing that the volume of a liquid does not change when it is poured from a short, wide glass into a tall, narrow one. So they are not doing it by the sheer power of their overall acumen. Nor could they be imitating what they hear, or else they would never say *goed* or *Don't giggle me*. It is plausible that the basic organization of grammar is wired into the child's brain [. . .].

The grammatical genius of children is not sociological, then, but biological: the child is programmed to acquire a language, whichever one she is exposed to. But this does not mean that the linguistic environment, the quality of the lexical entries provided by her parents, brothers and sisters and grandparents, do not have an important role, too. The linguistic environment is now seen to play a different role than what was believed in the 1960s.[36] The social and linguistic environment is indeed crucial: if this environment does not allow the faculty of language to be activated, learning will be differed, obtained with difficulty, or may not occur at all. Several cases of wild children have been observed since the 19th century, and their stories have been told in films by François Truffaut (*The Wild Child*, 1970) and Werner Herzog (*The Enigma of Kasper Hauser*, 1974). It is believed today that there is a *critical period* in childhood during which she must be surrounded by language.

This data allows for a second conclusion about the acquisition and development of language: children acquire the phonology, morphology, syntax, and semantics of their mother tongue with no difficulty, but these learning processes

---

[36] See Bernstein (1966) on his concepts of *restricted* and *elaborated* codes. See also Tomasello (2003) for a used-based theory of acquisition and Zufferey (2015) for the pragmatics of language acquisition.

do not depend solely on the quality of the stimuli in their environments: the *poverty of stimulus** thesis encapsulates this idea.[37] This thesis states that the quality of the linguistic competence* developed by a child cannot be explained by the nature, often limited and poor, of the speech of her parents and her environment.

7 Only words in dictionaries belong to languages

There is a remarkable belief shared by many speakers, especially in French-speaking Switzerland,[38] that only words found in the dictionary belong to a language. In other words, using these words is allowed, while words not in dictionaries are prohibited. What is to be made of this assertion? Is it acceptable or mistaken? In my opinion, this kind of reasoning mixes cause and effect: words are in a dictionary because they are used, and if some of them disappear from dictionaries it is because they are no longer in use. The introduction of regional words into language dictionaries only mirrors their importance in language use.

For instance, the Swiss French word *pive* 'woodpecker' appears in the 1993 edition of the French dictionary *Le Petit Robert*, because its usage was sufficiently widespread, especially in French-speaking Switzerland. The first occurrence of the word dates from 1661. It derives from the Latin *pipa* 'flute', and means "conifer fruit", resulting in words like *pive de pin* 'pine cone', which differs from the standard French version of the word: *pomme de pin*.[39]

We must now ask why the lexicons of languages change over time. Why do new words emerge? I already mentioned two reasons for such changes. First, lexicons include many borrowings. As noted above, the fact that French was spoken in England from the 11th to the 14th century resulted in around 10,000 words with French origins becoming part of the English lexicon, often creating duplicates like *liberty* and *freedom*, *people* and *folk*, *flower* and *blossom*, *to commence* and *to begin*, *to annoy* and *to bother*, *intelligent* and *clever*, *saintly* and *holy*, *in fact* and *indeed*, etc. (Walter 1994: 454).

The second reason why new words appear is because new things appear and must be labelled. One beautiful example of the creation of a new word occurred with the appearance of the machine called the *computer*, which was not trans-

---

[37] See Fodor and Crowther (2002) for a development.
[38] This population has a certain inferiority complex: for many of the French speakers in this linguistic area, French is not their native language, but a borrowed language, hence their greater or lesser degree of linguistic insecurity.
[39] Note that there is a conceptual motivation between the word's Latin root and its meaning: a *pive* resembles a flute because of its conical and elongated form. See Note 40 about motivation.

lated literally into French as *calculateur*,⁴⁰ but named *ordinateur* instead. The lexical root used for the French word corresponding to *computer* is not *calcul-* 'to compute' but *ordin-*, from *ordonner* 'to order'. This choice was made by the French Latin scholar Jacques Perret (1906–1992) in 1955, in answer to a request from IBM. The choice is interesting because it focuses on another function of the computer. Along with computing, it also orders. This example shows that there is a weak motivation between form and meaning, but does not refute the arbitrary relationship between form and meaning.⁴¹

Now, do new words always lack motivation? No, because in some morphological processes of word formation, especially words that are formed from proper nouns, motivation is present: terms like *sadiser*, *hollandiser*, *zlataner* all refer to the proper nouns of the people they are named after: the Marquis de Sade, François Hollande, and Zlatan Ibrahimovic.⁴² The meaning of these words derives from a particular characteristic associated with the person to whom they refer:

(28) *sadiser (someone)* = to behave in a sadistic manner

(29) *hollandiser* = to behave in an indecisive manner

(30) *zlataner (someone)* = to treat someone in a haughty and contemptuous manner

French is a language whose morphology is largely derivational: word formation begins with a root, to which prefixes and/or suffixes are added. This morphological process explains how verbs like *zlataner* can be formed:

---

40 Note that this word is used in French for very large computers such as the quantum computer, which is called *calculateur quantique* in French.
41 According to Saussure ([1916] 1968), there is no motivation between the *signifiant* 'acoustic image' and the *signifié* 'concept': the relationship between these two parts of a linguistic sign is arbitrary. In some cases, like in compounds such as the French *dix-sept* 'seventeen', there is some motivation because the number (17) is the sum of ten (10) and seven (7). Even in onomatopoeias, there is no clear motivation, since they vary from one language to another: the cock's cry is *cock-a-doodle doo* in English, *cocorico* in French, *kikeriki* in German, *kukeleku* in Dutch, *kukkokiekuu* in Finnish, *kokekokkoo* in Japanese, *gugugugu* in Koerean, *ü-ürü-üüü* in Turkish for instance.
42 The Marquis de Sade was an 18th-century French writer. The adjective *sadistic* was formed from his last name. François Holland is a former French president. Zlatan Ibrahimovic is a Swedish football player, who played for Ajax Amsterdam, Juventus Torino, Inter Milano, FC Barcelona, AC Milano, Paris-Saint-Germain, Manchester United, Los Angeles Galaxy, and currently AC Milano. Whereas Sade is well-known for imposing painful sexual relations, François Holland is described as an indecisive President, and Zlatan Ibrahimovic as an arrogant person.

(31) *Zlatan* + *er*   = *zlataner*
      Zlatan + verbal suffix = *to zlatan*[42]

Word formation processes are simpler in German. One example is composition. In German, a new word as well as a new philosophical concept, *Weltanschauung* 'vision of the world', was formed from the words *Welt* ('world') and *Anschauung* ('vision'). In English, the process is even simpler: a noun can be added before another noun, in a recursive way, as in (32):

(32) book > text book > department text book > math department text book > Harvard university math department text book

In French, compound nouns are not as productive as in English, because new nouns are not formed in the same way.[44] But new artefacts have given rise to new compound nouns in French:

(33) Verb-Noun compounds
      sèche-cheveux, sèche-linge, lave-vaisselle
      'hair dryer, clothes dryer, dishwasher'

(34) Compounds with prepositions
      Noun-P-Verb: *chambre à coucher, machine à laver, machine à écrire*
                     'bedroom, washing machine, typewriter'
      Noun-P-Noun: *machine à café*
                     'coffee machine'

Other processes of word formation go unnoticed because they generally concern frequently used words. For instance, *portemanteau* words are made by eliminating the duplicate syllables of two words:

---

43 In English, a simpler process occurs: *to zlatan* could be a verb as *to dog* is a verb derived from the noun *dog*. This simpler morphological process is limited in French to certain deverbalised nouns: *nager* 'to swim' gives rise to *nage* 'swimming'.
44 According to Fradin (2003), the most common word formation process in French is affixation (*personnel* = personne+*el* 'personal') rather than conversion (*orange* 'orange', from noun to adjective), replication (*guéguerre* 'war'), Verb-Noun composition (*tire-bouchon* 'corkscrew'), and Noun-Noun composition (*poisson-lune* 'moon fish').

(35) French
   a. *informatique* = **informa**tion + automa**tique**
      'computer science'
   b. *franglais* = **fran**çais + an**glais**
      'Frenglish'
   c. *courriel* = **courri**er + **él**ectronique
      'email'

(36) English
   motel = **mo**tor + ho**tel**
   smog = **smo**ke + **fog**
   modem = **mo**dulator + **dem**odulator

(37) German
   famillionär = **fa**miliär + **millionär** (Freud)
   'family of millionaires'

As these examples show, there are naturally more words in use than words included in the dictionary at any given time. I have not addressed the terminology issue, because it refers to specific areas of knowledge or professions, such as the extensive terminology used in aviation, medical science, fiscal and commercial law, banking, etc.

To sum up, the words belonging to a language are those that are used. The existence of dictionaries is, however, useful. The inventory of words in a dictionary constitutes a lexical and general common ground, and is also a resource about form (spelling) and meaning. Specialised lexicons on the other hand, are specific to their users, who are generally professionals, or members of younger generations. This is easy to understand. For younger generations, a specialised lexicon is a way to be different from and not be understood by their parents. French *verlan*, for example, is a youth jargon in which words are made by reversing the order of their syllables: *vénère* for *énervé* 'irritated', *teufe* for *fête* 'party', *ouf* for *fou* 'crazy', *chelou* for *louche* 'shifty'. Specialized jargon used by experts, especially scientists, allows for precise and unambiguous meaning. Jargon* therefore has two functions: first, it optimizes communication (experts), and second, it ensures obscurity of comprehension (younger generations).[45]

---

[45] The traditional sociolinguistic analysis attributes several functions to jargon. They consider it to be cryptic, playful, and an aid to creating one's identity.

8 Linguists are interested in word origins

The last assumption about language is etymology and its role in the analysis and comprehension of language. Although etymology is a science in and of itself and produces books of obvious documentary and historical interest,[46] I would like to show why etymology is not part of linguistics.

The explanation of why the origin of words does not play a role in their usage is simple: when a speaker uses a particular language, her brain is mobilised to access words and progressively build the continuation of the clause, but never to access information about the origin of the words which make up the clause.

Take the example of *garden-path sentences**, or sentences whose grammatical analysis leads to a dead end, like when one arrives at a dead end in a labyrinth. Here is a simple example of a garden-path sentence:

(38) *The old man the boat.*[47]

The grammatical analysis starts in the following way (the brackets indicate the first step of the syntactic analysis):

(39) [*the old man*] *the boat*

If the reader groups the words *the, old, man* to build the Noun Phrase (NP) *the old man*, he immediately comes to a dead-end: a Verbal Phrase (VP) is expected after the NP. However, he immediately encounters two problems. First, the following word, *the*, cannot be bound to a VP or be a verb. Moreover, the word following *the* is a noun (*boat*), and can be merged into an NP with the determiner (D) *the* to build the NP *the boat*. Furthermore, a sentence cannot be made up of two adjacent NPs, as in (40):

(40) * [*the old man*] [*the boat*][48]

What can the reader do now? The only solution is to retrace his steps, like in a labyrinth: when you come to a dead end in a labyrinth, you return to the most recent

---

[46] One good example for French is the *Dictionnaire historique de la langue française* (cf. Rey 1998).
[47] For French readers, I have included the original example, suggested by Gérard Sabah (personal communication):
   Le lac que l'écrivain décrit dans ce livre contemple est le lac de Côme.
   The lake that the writer describe-s/d in this book contemplates is the lake of Como.
Try to figure it out, you will be surprised! The answer is given at the end of this chapter in Note 55
[48] The asterisk * is used to mark a sentence as agrammatical.

intersection and take another path, repeating the process until you find the way out. So, the best thing to do with this sentence is to change the first grouping; instead of (39), you try a shorter grouping:

(41) [*the old*] *man the boat*

The old can be a *NP* (*old* being the head of the *NP*). Now, can the word *man* be a verb? Yes, *to man* means "to staff". So, if *man* is the verb (it needs to be in the 3rd person plural form), can the next words *the boat* be a complement of a verb such as *man*? Yes, and therefore the complete parsing of the sentence will yield (42), which means (43):

(42) [*the old*] [*man* [*the boat*]]

(43) *The old are the people who man the boat.*

I chose the example of a garden-path sentence to show that the speaker's and hearer's tasks are already complex enough – even with a sentence of just five words – without complicating things with issues linked to word origin. Etymology plays no role whatsoever in sentence production or in grammatical analysis.

That said, etymology is often used as an argument for criticising speakers' mistakes. Here is a typical example in French: the adjective *achalandé* 'crowed', whose origin is the noun *chaland* 'client' is generally used to mean "well supplied with goods". Now, when this word is used, as in (44), French purists[49] claim that the usage is incorrect because the adjective *achalandé* should be used only to mean "with a lot of clients". So, (44) should be used with meaning (45) and not with meaning (46):[50]

(44) *Ce magasin est bien achalandé.*
      'This shop is well supplied.'

(45) This shop is well supplied with clients.

(46) This shop is well supplied with goods.

An alternative analysis, which is non-normative, like the purists' analysis, consists of asking whether frequent use – *achalandé* meaning "well supplied with

---

49 See Pinker (1995: chapter 1 2) on English purists, and Leeman-Bouix (1994) on French ones.
50 For the complete argument, see Leeman-Bouix (1994).

goods" – can be explained according to linguistic principles. The answer is yes: this usage is indeed a classic case of *metonymy**, or a correspondence relationship. The "client-goods" relationship, as well as other connections, can easily be explained in pragmatic and cultural terms. For instance, the following correspondence relationships frequently occur in language usage:

(47) a. Cause-goal: *Pelé's head could not be stopped*
b. Meal-client: *The ham omelette left without paying.*
c. Author-book: *George Sand is on the left-hand shelf.*
d. Residence-government: *Downing Street has signed Brexit.*
e. City-government: *Paris has issues with Brussels.*

It is possible to understand the relationship between "client" and "shop well supplied with goods": clients go to shops that are well supplied with goods. We must then ask whether phenomena connected to a change of meaning are not more common. Here are two examples of such phenomena: first, the case of the preposition *chez* 'at, to' in French, which is an exception in Romance languages; second, the example of French negation, which is also an exception in Romance languages.

Let us start with the history of the preposition *chez* (Longobardi 2001). French has two spatial prepositions, one for places (*à*), the other indicating a building where a professional service is offered, or a social relationship:

(48) *Jacques va à Paris.*
Jacques go at Paris
'Jacques goes to Paris.'

(49) *Jacques va {chez le docteur, chez sa sœur}.*
Jacques go {to the doctor, to his sister}
'Jacques goes {to the doctor's, to his sister's}.'

Less standard usages use the preposition *à* instead of *chez*:

(50) *Jacques est allé {au docteur, à la boulangerie}.*[51]
Jacques is gone {at+the doctor, at the bakery}
'Jacques went {to the doctor's, to the bakery}.'

---

51 *Au* (contracted form) is the combination of the preposition *à* and the masculine determinant *le*: *à* + *le* = *au*. This is not the case with a feminine noun: *à* + *la* = *à la*.

What happens in these non-standard usages? Simply a generalisation of the usage of the locative preposition *à*. So, spoken French has the tendency to use the spatial preposition *à* for any type of location.

Why are there two prepositions in French? One recent hypothesis is that the preposition *chez* is historically derived from the noun *casa*, from Vulgar Latin, meaning "house", as opposed to the classical Latin *domus*, from which nouns like *domicile* are derived.[52] This process is known as *grammaticalisation** and results in the following generalisation: changes in grammatical categories always go from a lexical category (in this case a common noun) to a grammatical or functional category (in this case a preposition).[53]

The second example is French *negation*, which follows a different path from other Romance languages. The latter display a single preverbal negation, whose origin is the Latin *non*, whereas French negation is at once preverbal (with *ne*) and postverbal (with *pas*), as shown in (51) (Reinheimer and Tasmowski 1997):

(51) Latin: *Non plouet.*
     Italian: *Non piove.*
     French: *Il ne pleut pas.*
              'It is not raining.'

Where does this difference come from? The important point is that in Old French, negation is marked by *ne* (coming from the Latin *non*) followed by a noun denoting a small quantity, like *mie* 'crumb' (*miette* in contemporary French). Contemporary French still contains some traces of these small quantities, such as the words *point* 'a stitch' and *goutte* 'a drop'. What about *pas*? *Pas* indicates a small quantity, *un pas* 'a step' is a way of measuring a short distance. So the following negative sentences have these literal meanings:

(52) *Je ne marche pas* = I do not walk a step
     I neg walk step
     'I don't walk.'

(53) *Je ne couds point* = I do not sew a stitch
     I neg sew a stitch
     'I don't sew.'

---

52 English still uses the word *domicile* borrowed from French.
53 See Traugott and Dasher (2002) for generalisations about semantic changes, beyond grammaticalisation.

(54) *Je ne bois goutte* = I do not drink a drop
　　　I neg drink drop
　　　'I don't drink.'[54]

This process was described in the early 20th century by the French Indo-Europeanist linguist Antoine Meillet in these terms:

> Les langues suivent ainsi une sorte de développement en spirale: elles ajoutent des mots accessoires pour obtenir une expression intense; ces mots s'affaiblissent, se dégradent et tombent au niveau de simples outils grammaticaux; on ajoute de nouveaux mots ou des mots différents en vue de l'expression; l'affaiblissement recommence et ainsi sans fin.
> (Meillet 1912: 140–141)

> [Thus, languages follow a kind of spiral development: they add accessory words to obtain an intense expression; these words weaken, deteriorate and fall to the level of simple grammatical tools; new or different words are added with a view to expression; the weakening begins again and the cycle continues without cease.]

Five steps in the formation of negation have been described from the point of view of the history of the French language. This is called Jespersen's cycle (Jespersen 1917; van der Auwera 2009), and can be observed in the following sequence (Mosegaard Hansen 2018):

(55)　*ne > ne (pas) > ne pas > (ne) pas > pas*
　　　not > not (not) > not not > (not) not > not

(56)　*je ne dis > je ne dis (pas) > je ne dis pas > je (ne) dis pas > je dis pas*
　　　I neg say> I neg say (neg) > I neg say neg > I (neg) say neg > I say neg
　　　'I do not say.'

A precise table has been established for the removal of *ne* from negations: in old and middle French, *ne* is hardly ever removed, whereas in classical French (17th–18th centuries), *ne* is sometimes removed. In modern Quebec French, however, *ne* has been completely removed (Martineau and Mougeon 2003).

The negation has moved from *ne* to *pas* because the negative clitic *ne* has weakened so much that it has become almost non-existent. If Jespersen's cycle is correct, it would predict that the process will continue, that *pas* will also weaken,

---

54 Today, *goutte* is limited in its usage to the verb *voir* 'see', as in *ne voir goutte* 'to not see anything'.

and that a new negative word, called a *forclusive**, will indicate the negation. This is exactly what is happening in Quebec French today (Déprez and Martineau 2003):

(57) Quebec French
   J'ai pas vu personne.
   I have neg seen nobody
   'I have not seen anybody.'

(58) European French
   J'ai vu personne.
   I have seen nobody
   'I have seen nobody.'

What conclusions can we draw from these facts? That the observation of linguistic phenomena is not carried out to learn about the origins of word meaning; its goal is rather to understand the changes in the grammatical form of sentences. Negation is a good example, because it shows the dynamics of linguistic change.

9 Conclusion

The conclusion of this chapter is simple. The eight questionable assumptions we have examined can be replaced with the following alternatives:
1) non-written languages are real languages;
2) there are no languages that are more important than others;
3) logic, clarity, and beauty are not properties for defining languages;
4) languages do not change solely because of the influence of other languages;
5) there is no "one country, one language" equation;
6) children acquire their mother tongue naturally rather than by imitation, because they are programmed to do so;
7) the number of words in a language is higher than the number of words in the dictionary;
8) the main topic of linguistics is studying the processes of linguistic change rather than etymology.

In the next chapter, I will discuss the difference between language and communication, and will show that language is not communication and that communication is not language.[55]

---

55 The solution to the problem of the garden-path sentence is as follows:

Le lac que l'écrivain décrit dans ce livre contemple est le lac de Côme.
The lake which the writer described in this book contemplates is the lake of Como.

First attempt: [*Le lac* [*que l'écrivain décrit dans ce livre*] *contemple*] *est le lac de Côme.*
   The problem is twofold: first, the matrix clause *le lac contemple* 'the lake contemplates' does not make sense; second, *est le lac de Côme* 'is the lake of Como' is a VP, which is disconnected from the first clause. We have come to a dead end, and have to parse again.
   Second attempt: [*Le lac* [*que l'écrivain* [*décrit dans ce livre*] *contemple*] *est le lac de Côme*]
   The matrix clause is *le lac est le lac de Côme* 'the lake is the lake of Como'. The relative clause is *que l'écrivain contemple* 'which the writer contemplates', and *décrit dans ce livre* 'described in this book' is a parenthetical clause. The steps of parsing are as follows:

Le lac [*que l'écrivain* [*décrit dans ce livre*] *contemple*]
Le lac [*que l'écrivain décrit dans ce livre contemple*] *est le lac de Côme*

Chapter 2
Why is language not communication, and why is communication not language?

Although this is a simple question, the answer is complex: what is language used for? Try asking your family. You will get a practically unanimous answer: to communicate. The main function of language, if not the principal one, is indeed communication. However, as soon as the answer is given, further questions arise: what is the relationship between language and thought? Does language allow thinking or not? Moreover, if language is used for communication, what is the difference between language and other animal communication systems? Do other species have a language? If they do, why don't humans understand them, and why can't we learn these languages? There are many human languages, about 6,900, and we are able to learn and understand them without being taught them in school – this is the situation of most multilingual speakers, who form the majority of speakers on our planet.

It becomes clear that the case is more complex than we first imagined. This is good news. You may have thought that language was not a complex phenomenon, and here is proof to the contrary, which justifies my profession as a linguist. However, the bad news is that, if the relation between language and communication is not so simple, two things must be explained: first, what is language? In other words, what is the difference between human language and other animal communication systems? And second, what is communication? I will begin with the second question, which is seemingly simpler; a discussion of human and animal communication systems will take place later.

1 What is communication?

How can communication be defined? When one hears that a politician or a government "communicates", this is generally not understood as a compliment. Worse, what is conveyed through this type of "communication" is not information, but *elements of language*, or what is known as *political cant*.[56]

---

[56] The concept of *element of language* is recent in France, and was popularized for French audiences in Bernard Tavernier's film *Quai d'Orsay* (2010), in which the character of Dominique de Villepin (a former French Prime Minister) refers to Thucydides, the Greek historian from the 5th century BCE, in a series of quotations that were adapted to current situations on which they shed

Communication is thus concerned with information*. Technically speaking, we refer to communication* when there is a transfer of information from a source (sender) to a destination (reception) (Hauser 1996; Reboul 2007, 2017a). However, communication requires more than this: the transfer must travel through some type of conduit. A great number of metaphors express this idea, such as *I managed to get the idea across*, and *I hear you loud and clear*.[57] However, the ideas to be conveyed (the messages) must be rendered transferable in order to be communicated.

Think of something, anything, for instance what you are going to do next weekend: attending a movie, visiting an exhibition, walking along a river or a lake, etc. When you think of something, the idea is private: it is not transportable. But the idea can be conveyed through speech, and this is precisely the function of language. For instance, you can tell your family: *On Sunday afternoon, we're going to see an exhibition at Beaubourg*. This time, your message has been changed into a signal, which can be transported through the air if you are talking, on a sheet of paper if you are writing in your diary, and via the Internet if you're typing on your smartphone. The message will be received by your recipients, directly in the case of spoken communication, delayed if you have written your message and sent an email, immediately if you communicate on Facebook or another social network.

Now, how can we explain that communication is successful, that is, that your message has been understood? Your interlocutor must speak the same language as you do. If you hear *Ashita bōbūru de aimashou* ('Tomorrow we will meet at Beaubourg'), you may be surprised, as you will be if you receive the following Japanese ideograms on your smartphone: 明日ボーブールで会いましょう. Unless you can speak and write Japanese, you cannot understand these messages. Sharing the same code is thus a condition for comprehension. But is it a necessary condition for successful communication? A sufficient condition? We will see that, luckily for you, this is not the case.

Let's imagine that you are lost in the Tokyo train station. You are desperately looking for the Chūō line, which will take you to Musashi-Sakai, from where you take the train to the Tama station – you are visiting the Tokyo University of Foreign Studies. You are lost, because in your part of the station the names of the train lines are in Japanese ideograms. You try to speak English, but no one else around you speaks it. What do you do? You cannot mimic your destination, but you try with Musashi-Sakai. You say: *Musashi-Sakai*↗, with a rising intonation* – you think this is a universal feature for asking questions. Your pronunciation is not very

---

light. The concept of *political cant* refers to "hypocritical and sanctimonious talk of (...) political nature" (https://www.lexico.com/definition/cant, Accessed 9 July 2020).
57 See the well-known article by Reddy (1979). For a more comprehensive approach on metaphors, see Lakoff and Johnson (1980). See chapter 6 for a development.

good, but someone understands you and tells you the direction to take. Around the corner, you see bilingual signs and follow the directions for the Chūō line.

What happened here? Did you just take part in ordinary verbal communication? Certainly not, but your attempt to obtain information was successful, and you found your way again.

What can we conclude from this half-linguistic, half-gestural exchange? First, you showed your intention to receive an answer to a question, expressed in telegraphic language, assuming that your pronunciation of Musashi-Sakai could be understood – when coming back on the train, you are a little bit more careful with the intonation of Musashi-Sakai, and realize that your earlier pronunciation was poor. This aspect of communication is called, according to Sperber and Wilson, *ostension**, and is crucial to the success of communication: in this situation, in order to be understood you had to indicate that you were trying to find your way. But you did more than that, as did your Japanese interlocutor: she understood your intention because you showed it in your utterance, even when you only said *Musashi-Sakai*. As for you, you understood when she told you to retrace your steps: you thus inferred your interlocutor's intention.

In short, in order for communication to succeed, two intentions must be recognized: the speaker's communicative intention* and her informative intention*. You recognized both intentions without speaking Japanese, that is, without a linguistic code*. The sharing of a common code is therefore not a necessary condition for communication to succeed.

But is the presence of a shared code sufficient for communication to take place? Consider the following case. Is verbal communication between people speaking the same language guaranteed because the speakers speak the same language? Does it not happen sometimes that you are not understood, or incorrectly understood? We do not stop to correct our words, for instance by saying *That's not what I meant, You didn't understand*, or *I didn't want to offend you*, etc. Why does our speech transmit our thoughts and our intentions imprecisely? The answer is simple, but unfortunately rather hopeless: we do not communicate our thoughts explicitly, and if we did, we would make others' lives unbearable.

An example is now in order. My favorite one occurred in my family. Here is a short dialogue that took place between myself and my five-year old son Nathanaël, after he had finished supper:

(59) Jacques: *Nat, go brush your teeth!*
     Nathanël: *Dad, I'm not sleepy.*

What is the relationship between brushing one's teeth and sleeping? I'm sure you've figured it out: I told to my son to go brush his teeth in order to TO tell him to go to bed, and he told me that he was not sleepy TO tell me that he didn't want to go to bed then. Why did I not simply say:

(60) *Nat, go to bed.*

The answer is easy: I wanted him to brush his teeth and then to go to bed. So why did I not say:

(61) *Nat, go brush your teeth and then go to bed.*

Because if I had, I wouldn't have been precise enough, since I wanted him to go to bed IMMEDIATELY after brushing his teeth. So I should have said

(62) *Nat, go brush your teeth and then, immediately afterwards, go to bed.*

But would that have been precise enough? Should I not have told Nat to go to sleep in his OWN bed and not his brother's? What we are observing here is the impossibility of making our intentions explicit. This is not because they are ineffable, and I would like to convince you that they are not by elaborating on my son's answer.

Nathanaël began to speak very early, and quickly became accomplished at it: because of this, I would not have been surprised if he had answered:

(63) *Dad, look, you know very well that I'm not sleepy. You know, and you know that I know that you know, that you told me to go brush my teeth to tell me to go to bed. But is that reasonable, since I'm not sleepy, and even if I go to bed, I won't fall asleep right away? Don't you think it would be reasonable for me to go to bed when I'm really tired?*

Now, I'm exaggerating a little, but what I want to prove is that communicating explicitly or literally is not necessary for communication to be successful. This idea, developed over thirty years ago by Dan Sperber and Deirdre Wilson ([1986] 1995), states that our utterances are only clues to our intentions: we do not need to be explicit for communication to be successful, because communication is based on information belonging to the conversational common ground*, which is also known as the mutual cognitive environment*, that is, a set of facts mutually taken to be true or inferable.

Here is another example. Nathanaël was participating in a young firefighter's training program. One day I received the schedule of the appointments, which took place on Saturdays. Now, the information included only the dates of the meeting and the names of the villages. I picked up the phone and called the person in charge of the program, complaining about the lack of specific places and times. His answer was confusing:

(64) *But you see, everyone knows that in Salornay we meet at 10 AM, and in Cluny at 2 PM, and in Salornay we meet in the village square, and in Cluny at the fire station.*

Why should he have to point out what everyone knew? But at least one person, namely myself, did not know what I should have known. This presumably known information, which linguists call presupposition*, is very useful, because it lets us avoid saying unnecessary things. If I talk about my son, it is because I have a son: this was your immediate conclusion when I mentioned him, and you added this information to the common ground if you did not already know that I had a son. However, if I talk to you about my son when in fact I don't have one, I am deceiving you and making you believe something false.

These examples have shown that language is neither a necessary nor a sufficient condition for communication. But this does not really help us: how can we explain the fact that we use a mode of communication, namely language, that is different from other animal communication systems?

2 Verbal and animal communication

Members of other species manage to communicate among themselves, but they cannot communicate with members of other species. The same is true of the human species. Although 6,900 languages are spoken in the world, none of them are incomprehensible to the human species: to acquire a language one only needs to learn it or be in contact with it very early in life. On the other hand, living with a cat or a dog does not make it possible to speak cat or dog.

But one thing is certain. Despite intensive attempts to teach human language to chimps, bonobos, or gorillas, the results are unconvincing: even the most gifted chimps, after years of learning sign language or ideogram systems, have not gone beyond a lexicon of 200 words, which corresponds to the average lexicon of a two-year old child. Nor have primates succeeded in combining more than three words in an utterance, which also corresponds to the normal development of a two-year old child.[58]

---

[58] For a Synthesis, Lestel (1995); see also Reboul (2017a).

Primates to whom language has been taught exhibit the following linguistic behavior: they do not initiate any exchanges (unless they are to beg); they do not create any new sign sequences, and they are not able to speak about absent objects. In other words, there are major differences between primates' and humans' representational capacities. The second property shows their complete absence of creativity in learning, which also contrasts with human learning.

Here is a classic example of an interaction between an instructor (Cathy) and the female gorilla to whom sign language was taught (Koko) (Patterson 1978):

(65) *Manipulating hands and fingers, Cathy had asked Koko, "What's this?"*
"Gorilla," signed Koko.
"Who gorilla?" asked Cathy.
"Bird," responded a bratty Koko, and things went downhill from there.
"You bird?" asked Cathy.
"You," countered Koko.
"Not me, you are bird," rejoined Cathy, mindful that "bird" can be an insult in Koko's lexicon.
"Me gorilla," asserted Koko.
"Who bird?" asked Cathy.
"You nut," replied Koko, resorting to another of her insults. (For Koko, "bird" and "nut" switch from descriptive to pejorative terms by changing the position in which the sign is made.)
"Why me nut?" asked Cathy.
"Nut, nut," signed Koko.
"You nut, not me," Cathy replied.

Does this example show a true dialogue, like the kind human speakers have when they use language in a conversation? Indeed not: this excerpt is more like a dialogue with a two-year old child than an ordinary adult conversation.

What can we glean from this example? Beyond demonstrating the inability of large primates to learn what we call language, or a specific language, it shows that human language is an insurmountable barrier for other species. This proves the first claim of this book, namely that *language is specific to human species*.[59]

I hear you protesting. Are there not sophisticated communication systems among other animal species? The example most often suggested is the sonar com-

---

[59] This claim is neither new nor original. However, it is not shared by the linguist community or by most primatologists. Most of them try to reduce the distance between species. Language is a crucial argument for this issue.

munication system, or echolocation*, used by large marine mammals such as dolphins and whales. Actually, the extraordinary thing about this communication system is the method of communication rather than the system itself: these animals use sound waves that can hardly be detected by the human species, such as infrasound in the range of 100 to 150 kHz. This kind of communication is not specific to these mammals; hunters also use decoys that emit frequencies that are mostly imperceptible to our species. The echolocation communication system of large maritime mammals has a definite advantage: it enables the propagation of signals over long distances, up to several hundred meters away. This is significantly farther than human speech carries. Human sounds cannot be heard beyond 50 meters away – if you want them to, you have to shout. Whistling works better (150 meters), which explains why the archeologist Steven Mithen (2007), an expert on *Homo neanderthalis**, claims that Neandertals used a sung protolanguage, or at least communicated using a high-pitched voice, because their larynxes were placed higher than those of human males.

Another frequently given counterexample is the capacity of some birds, such as mynahs and macaws, to mimic human speech. Some cockatoos, like Alex,[60] have developed the ability, through lengthy and constant training, of recognizing shapes, colors, and object names. From more than a century ago come the examples of Clever Hans, a horse that could count,[61] and, more recently, Rico (Kaminski, Call, and Fischer 2004), a dog that understood more than 200 words. These animals are often mentioned to contradict human specificity for language. Should we not take the linguistic and cognitive talents of these animals seriously, and use them to gain a perspective on the position we give ourselves in the animal world? These topics are important, mainly because the place of other animal species in our world (food production, breeding issues, animal rights) has become a crucial societal issue.

3 Animal communication systems

Animal communication systems (Hauser 1996; Anderson 2004, 2017; Reboul 2007, 2017a) can be divided into three categories: signs, cues, and signals.[62] Signs* cor-

---

[60] https://www.youtube.com/watch?v=HskAElznEpg, accessed 18 October 2019.
[61] https://en.wikipedia.org/wiki/Clever_Hans, accessed 2 January 2020.
[62] This classification is inherited from the semiotic tradition (Peirce 1931–1935). "I define a sign as anything which is so determined by something else, called its Object, and so determines an effect upon a person, which effect I call its interpretant, that the later is thereby mediately determined by the former" (Peirce 1998: 478). Signs can be represented in different ways: as icons (like

respond to non-permanent traces left by animals, such as the tracks of a rabbit in the snow, bear claw marks on tree trunks, fur on a fence, or even faeces (urine and droppings). These signs are not permanently active (they disappear over time), and overall, they are factive*; that is, they describe something that is true. For instance, a rabbit can't pretend to go through a snowfield: it does so. In this context, the rabbit's tracks transmit information.

The crucial point here is that human beings also leave traces of their presence, such as footprints and wheel imprints. In some cases, as the readers of detective stories know, footprints can be left on purpose to make one think that the shoe-wearer was present at the scene of the crime. However, in the case of animals, signs are factive, even if their voluntary or intentional character can be questioned; for instance, we know that dogs have the disagreeable reflex of urinating to signal their presence. The message "I was here, this is my territory" is certainly a reflex. But what about tiger scratches on tree trunks? These signs don't only mean that a tiger has come by; they also give information on the size of the signer, like "I am tall", in addition to signifying his or her presence. As the philosopher Paul Grice[63] put it, signs correspond to *natural meaning**. According to his definition, if *x* naturally means *p*, then x implies *p*. For instance, if smoke naturally means fire, then smoke implies fire.

Natural meaning, according to Anne Reboul's reading of Grice (Reboul 2017a), has two properties: being factive – giving true information – and not being under the control of volition: the tuft of fur left by a goat on a fence is not put there voluntarily, whereas a criminal, using the boots of the person he wants to accuse as the culprit, does so voluntarily and communicates false and non-factive information.

A second type of animal communication is what Marc Hauser calls cues*. These include a butterfly's markings and the color of a snake's scales. A good example of a cue is the markings of the monarch butterfly, whose bright colors signal that it is not edible. A young bird ingesting the butterfly will be poisoned and will learn not to eat this prey again. But nature is surprising: there is an edible butterfly, the viceroy, which imitates the monarch butterfly. Its markings, which demonstrate aposemantism*, protect against predators, and in this case, deceive birds that are looking for insects to eat. When viceroy butterflies engage in Batesian mimicry*, the cue is not factive. But is it still a case of natural meaning? Certainly not. But it is not a case of non-natural meaning, either – for instance linguistic meaning.

---

portraits), as indices (whose relation to object is a factual correspondence) or as symbols (whose the relation to the object is an imputed character). See Atkin (2013).
63 Meaning. In Grice (1989).

The third animal communication category, signals*, can be illustrated by the alarm calls of certain apes such as vervet monkeys. These small Kenyan tree monkeys have three alarm calls: for threats coming from the sky (eagles), four-legged threats (leopards), and slithering threats (snakes). These signals are factive, but are they under voluntary control?[64] This is a plausible hypothesis, because the monkeys that sound the alarm are females, and the vervets' social structure is matrilineal. That means that the position of females in the group hierarchy depends on the number of their descendants: the more descendants a female has, the higher her position in the group. The choice of a female to sound an alarm call can be understood like this: if she does not sound the alarm, she herself will be safe, but the risk of losing her descendants will be high and, therefore increase the risk of being demoted in the group's social hierarchy. On the other hand, if a female sounds an alarm, she herself will be exposed, because in order to alert the others, she must go to the far end of the branches. By doing this, she risks becoming a target for the predator, but at the same time, she is protecting her descendants and thus her own position in the group hierarchy. If one imagines that such signals are voluntary, the question then arises as to whether an analogy can be made with humans engaging in verbal communication. I will answer in the negative later. Until then, another definition of linguistic meaning is needed.

4 Intentional systems and non-natural meaning

To show that animal communication is different from human language communication, Anne Reboul (2007) uses the concept of HOT* (higher-order thought), an intentional system devised by the philosopher of mind Daniel Dennett (1983, 1987). For Dennett, a system is intentional when it can entertain mental states, such as belief, desire, or intention. For instance, suppose that you want to drink a glass of orange juice (Jacob 2004): for your intention to be satisfied, you must entertain the belief that there is some orange juice in the fridge. If you know that there is no orange juice, then you must give up your desire to drink orange juice. But if you strongly entertain this belief, you have to perform a series of actions. At each step, you expect that a new issue will not arise:

(66) *You go to the kitchen, entertaining the belief that the kitchen door is open, and not locked.*
You open the kitchen door and suppose that there is a fridge.

---

64 See Reboul (2017a: 22) for a summary of properties of signs, cues, and signals.

You open the fridge door, thinking that there is some orange juice inside.
You grasp the orange juice bottle, believing that the bottle is not empty.
You move the glass of orange juice you have just filled to your lips, without dropping it.
You drink, avoiding choking by drinking too fast.

Intentional behavior supposes that someone engaged in this behavior entertains both beliefs and intentions. Thus one can suppose that the female vervet monkey who sounds an alarm call entertains the belief that a threat exists, and that she intends to warn her conspecifics. How can we prove this? Ethological studies have shown that conspecifics know how to distinguish between true and false alarm calls. If alarm calls are recorded and broadcast without the presence of predators, the signal will be obeyed the first time it is broadcast, but after the second time, conspecifics no longer react to the signal. This demonstrates that vervet monkeys know how to discriminate between true information and false information.

Now, are we in the presence of a true language here, and therefore something analogous to human verbal communication? A very strong argument in favour of this statement – despite the limitations of a system of only three alarm calls – is that these signals are part of young vervets' genetic material. In other words, these signals are pre-wired. We know this because young vervets do not have to learn them, but only to use them in an appropriate way. Mothers correct their young to reinforce the relationship between signals and type of predator.

This contrasts in an unusual way with language acquisition. As we saw in chapter 1, language is not part of the human genome: a language must be learned, and if Universal Grammar seems to be part of human genetic material, this is not the case for the lexicon.

This gives us an initial way of differentiating between systems such as vervet monkeys' alarm calls and natural languages. The former systems are not the same in terms of complexity. However, we can make a second argument based on Daniel Dennett's notion of intentional system*. Dennett set out four levels of complexity for intentional systems, from 1 to 4:

(67) First order: *x believes or wants [$_1$ that p]*
Second order: *x believes or wants [$_2$ that y believes [$_1$ that p]]*
Third order: *x believes or wants [$_3$ that y believes [$_2$ that x believes [$_1$ that p]]]*
Fourth order: *x believes or wants [$_4$ that y believes [$_3$ that x wants [$_2$ that y believes [$_1$ that p]]]]*

According to Dennett, verbal communication is fourth order, whereas vervet monkeys' alarm calls are first order. Suppose a female vervet, let us call her Julia, makes the eagle alarm call. This can be represented in Dennett's intentional system, as shown in (68):

(68) Julia wants her conspecifics to hide.

Now, Julia does not want her conspecifics to believe there is an eagle above the bushes: she wants them to return to the bushes.
 Suppose that Mary tells her children to go home immediately because of a thunderstorm:

(69) *Children, leave the pool and go home immediately.*

How can we represent what Mary means? According to Dennett, the verbal communication intentional system is fourth order. Accordingly, Mary's utterance should have the following meaning:

(70) Mary wants [$_4$ her children to believe [$_3$ that she wants [$_2$ that they believe [$_1$ that they must leave the pool and go home immediately]]].

In other words, meaning in verbal communication corresponds to what Paul Grice terms *non-natural meaning**. The concept of non-natural meaning in verbal communication is related to the usages of the verb *to mean*, which refer sometimes to natural meaning* (71) and sometimes to non-natural meaning (72):

(71) Natural meaning
 Those spots mean measles.
 The recent budget means that we shall have a hard year.

(72) Non-natural meaning
 Those three rings on the bell (of the bus) mean that the bus is full.
 The remark, 'Smith couldn't get on without his trouble and strife,' meant that Smith found his wife indispensable.

As we saw above, natural meaning is factive and not under the control of volition. On the other hand, non-natural meaning is not factive and under the control of volition. In other words, the speaker who means$_{NN}$ wants to say, in the first case, by ringing the bell, that the bus is full and in the second case, that Smith's wife is indispensable. Grice's examples show that sounds or a sentence are used to mean something, and that there is no correlation between the wording and what was meant: the bus driver could have decided that only ONE ring was enough, and the person talking about Smith could have used another expression to mean what she intended. In other words, the speaker says one thing in order to mean something else.

So, how can an addressee understand what the speaker means? Grice's answer sets forth his definition of non-natural meaning*: "'*A* meant$_{NN}$ something by *x*' is roughly equivalent to '*A* uttered *x* with the intention of inducing a belief by means of the recognition of this intention'" (Grice 1989: 219).

When meaning$_{NN}$ occurs, the addressee must recognize the intention to produce an effect – what Sperber and Wilson call *informative intention* – as well as the speaker's intention to produce this effect via the recognition of her intention to produce the effect. Sperber and Wilson term this *communicative intention*.

It is apparent that if the communicated meaning through language is non-natural, it is systematically non-literal, or implicit. It then becomes necessary to state how linguistic communication should be characterized: although language is a code, verbal communication goes beyond the usage of a code. How does this work?

5 Two models for communication

Verbal communication is unusual because it uses not one, but two models of communication. The first is a code model*: a natural language is a code that associates messages with signals. What is the second model?

The classic view of language entertains a semiotic conception of communication: in communication, several codes are used.[65] Let's return to the example with my son:

(73) Jacques: *Nat, go brush your teeth.*
      Nathanaël: *Dad, I'm not sleepy.*

Could not we say that, beyond the linguistic code, which assigns a meaning to every word spoken by Jacques and Nathanaël, there is another code, a social one, the social code of the Moeschler family, according to which one goes to bed after having brushed one's teeth? After all, such family routines are often made explicit if they have not been understood by being exposed over and over. In other words, non-literal communication uses innuendo, which is only possible if the participants in the exchange share all the social codes that allow

---

[65] The semiotic vision of communication is strongly argued by Eco (1976).

for communication. This view is strongly anchored in social sciences dealing with communication. When a misunderstanding occurs, the explanation is that the social codes necessary for communication were not shared. This shows that culture – the background information necessary to ensure the success of communication – is a set of codes. The case for the semiotic view of communication can be made through the following examples: religious communities are based on codes or rituals; sports activities imply common codes of behavior in addition to common knowledge of the rules; political meetings and unions obey well-known speech patterns and behavioral codes, and those who do not respect them are punished, in much the same way that hunter-gatherer societies used banishment (Diamond 2012).

A very good example is Italian bars. Suppose you arrive in Italy by car after having gone through the Fréjus tunnel (France). You feel relaxed, because in the Susa valley, French is spoken – you speak French, but not Italian – and you can place your order in French. So you go directly to the bar to order your coffee, and at this point you understand that you have to go to the cashier, place your order, pay, and then hand the receipt to the bar staff to get your coffee. The good news is that the same process is used in all Italian bars. So, you have just learned a new code, and now you can order coffee anywhere in Italy. But what happens when you arrive in Torino, at the Piazza San Carlo? There you don't go to the cashier first, but sit on the terrace and order your coffee. To pay, you have to ask for the bill, and at this point you understand that the waiter will not take your money; you must go inside the restaurant and pay, using your receipt, which generally indicates your table number.

Here, you begin to ask whether my first conclusion was right: it seems that for every new situation the rules change. What should be done? The answer is obvious: you use your mind and draw the correct conclusions. You have learned new things about Italian culture and bars, cafés, and restaurants, and have drawn the relevant conclusions. After all, you decided to visit a foreign country and are ready to encounter different rules. But are these rules codes?

Let's look at the situation in a more general way. If social relationships and cultures are codes, how can we explain that we manage to communicate in new contexts without knowing them beforehand? According to the code theory of communication, this should be impossible. Moreover, how would it be possible to explain the ability to change one's cultural context without too much difficulty, and to manage communication in different cultures? The code approach is clearly unable to these questions.

On the other hand, a strong argument was suggested by the linguist Deirdre Wilson and the cognitive anthropologist Dan Sperber (Sperber and Wilson [1986] 1995: 56). Peter and Mary spend an evening together. Peter says to Mary:

(74) Peter: *Do you want some coffee?*
Mary: *Coffee would keep me awake.*

How can we know if Mary's response is a refusal or an acceptance of a cup of coffee? No social code allows us to solve this enigma, simply because the relationship between Mary's answer and her refusal or acceptation is not based on codes, but on reasoning based on information about how the world works.

What can we gather from this example? Simply that understanding an utterance does not occur by adding social codes to the linguistic code, but through inference* and a set of premises* which define the context[66] and allow the listener to draw conclusions. For instance, if Peter knows that Mary has to work late that evening, he will draw the following conclusion:

(75) Mary said: "Coffee would keep me awake".
Coffee is a stimulant.
Someone who has to stay up late is going to take a stimulant.
<u>Mary has to work late this evening</u>.
So Mary will drink some coffee.

Briefly stated, Mary said to Peter that coffee would keep her awake TO mean she wants some coffee.

We now see how Mary's meaning – her informative intention, also known as *speaker meaning** – can be understood by Peter: he must draw an inference on the basis of contextual information and the utterance. We now understand that a misunderstanding might occur merely through an incorrect contextual assumption*, that is, by making a mistake in choosing how to interpret the context*.

If in (74) Peter thinks that Mary has to go to bed early, he will understand that she is refusing his offer of coffee:

(76) Mary said: "Coffee would keep me awake".
Coffee is a stimulant.
Someone who wants to go to be early is not going to take a stimulant.
<u>Mary wants to go to bed early.</u>
So Mary will not drink coffee.

---

[66] The notion of context has a precise and restrictive definition: a context is a set of information, which allows, when an utterance occurs, to draw a contextual implication, that is, what the speaker means.

This example shows another way that Peter could understand Mary's utterance. But we do not yet have an answer to the question of *why* Mary gives an indirect and implicit answer rather than a direct and explicit one.

6 Why communication is non-literal

One commonplace about language comes directly from Antiquity and the theory of two levels of language. The first level is the literal level: it is used to describe the world, but the words are not especially vivid; the second one (rhetoric), the level of non-literality, is primarily used to give colour and life to discourse. Here is how Roland Barthes (1970: 218) describes the way words work in ancient rhetoric:

> 1) il y a une base nue, un niveau propre, un état normal de la communication, à partir duquel on peut élaborer une expression plus compliquée, ornée, douée d'une distance plus ou moins grande par rapport au sol originel. (...); 2) la couche seconde (rhétorique) a une fonction d'animation: l'état « propre » du langage est inerte, l'état second est « vivant »: couleurs, lumières, fleurs (*colores, lumina, flores*); les ornements sont du côté de la passion, du corps; (...)

> [1) there is naked basis, a proper level, a normal state of communication, from which one can elaborate a more complicated, decorated expression, capable of a larger or smaller distance relatively to the original ground. (...) 2) the second (rhetoric) layer has as a function of liveliness: the "proper" state of language is inert, the second state is "vivid": colors, lights, flowers (*colores, lumina, flores*); ornaments are on the side of passion, body; (...).]

The theory of two levels of language considers *literal communication to be the normal state of communication*. However, as shown in Mary and Peter's dialogue, rhetoric was not used. Mary does not answer indirectly to add color: she communicates in a non-literal way because it is a more relevant way to communicate than a literal manner would have been.

Let's look at another example, which shows the importance of implicit communication. Peter and Mary spend an evening together, and Peter offers Mary a glass of wine. Mary refuses in this way:

(77) Peter: *Do you want a glass of wine?*
      Mary: *I'm driving.*

Mary's answer allows Peter to conclude that Mary does not want wine (one should not drink before driving), but overall Mary gives the reason why she refuses a glass of wine (planning to drive is a good reason for not drinking alcohol). If she had given an unjustified answer like *No*, she would not have mentioned the reason for her refusal – typically a refusal is a reaction that can be interpreted as impolite, and must be justified (see chapter 4). If she had answered *No, I'm driving*, she would have been explicit, but her answer would have been longer, and therefore less relevant than the simpler answer, *I'm driving*.[67]

This example allows us to partially answer the question *Why is communication non-literal?* Because an implicit answer is more economical and more relevant than an explicit one. It can therefore be said that we communicate in an implicit way for reasons of communicative and cognitive efficiency.

This can be proven by demonstrating how family communication takes place: in a family, everyone shares a great deal of information, and it is very rare to point out small details except when parents have to remind children about family rules. This mutual knowledge allows for great fluidity in family exchanges, and makes it unnecessary for everything to be spelled out. Imagine a dinner conversation in which every contextual assumption had to be explained: it would be pure hell!

7 What is language?

Up to this point I have shown how communication works. I have also demonstrated that communication cannot be reduced to language, and vice versa. Verbal communication takes place through a complex code (a language), used along with an inferential system, because we generally communicate in a non-literal manner. Now, in order to come full circle, we must define what a language is.

My definition of a language* is very simple: it contains a phonology*, a semantics*, and a syntax*. Let's look for the moment at a lighter version of what language is. Chapter 3 will explore a more complex version.

What we call a language is a combination of a string of sounds and a string of meanings. A language is made up of a lexicon*, and every word of a lexicon has a form (a string of sounds) and a meaning. A sentence is also a string of words yielding a string of meanings. A sentence is ambiguous when some words have several meanings, which results in multiple representations of its meaning, called *polysemy**. But a sentence can also be ambiguous because word groups inside a sentence, called *phrases*, give rise to different semantic representations. This type of situation occurs in the following examples:

---

[67] See, chapter 3 for a precise definition of *relevance*.

(78) *I saw her duck.*

(79) *Mary hit the man with an umbrella.*

Duck can be a noun referring to an animal, or a verb meaning to avoid. As far as *an umbrella* is concerned, does it describe the instrument with which Mary hit the man, or the accessory the man is carrying?

(80) a. *I saw [her duck_{<animal>}].*
      b. *I saw her [duck_{<avoid>}].*

(81) a. *Mary hit the man [with an umbrella].*
      b. *Mary hit [the man with an umbrella].*

If meaning can vary because grammatical organisation varies – we will see in chapter 3 how the grammar of language works – we can state that rules govern form and meaning in a language, whichever language it is.

We can now describe a language, for instance English, as a system of rules at the phonological level, that is, of the system of phonic units such as phonemes, a system of rules at the meaning level, words, and groups of words, and a system of rules governing the grouping of grammatical units.

As far as phonological organisation is concerned, it has been observed that, in English, not all theoretically possible combinations of three consonants in a word are the case. Only 9 of these combinations are actually used: *s+p+l,r,j*; *s+t+r,j*; *s+k+,l,r,j,w*, as shown below (Crystal 2003: 250):

(82) a. **spl**it, **spr**ite, **sp**u*me* (graphic *u* pronounced [ju:])
      b. **str**ict, **st**ew (graphic *ew* pronounced [ju:])
      c. **skl**erotin, **skr**it, **sk**ew [skju:], **squ**ish [skwiʃ]

Sequences of three consonants like [spw-] and [stl-] do not occur in English. Moreover, there are vowel restrictions on these consonants' clusters. For instance, only [u:] can occur after [stj] and [skj]. There are thus restrictions in the combinations of the English sound system on building phonemes, or clusters of sounds.

Semantic organisation, on the other hand, does not only occur at the level of the lexicon* – that is, in a language's repertory of words. It also occurs at the level of the sentence. In chapter 3 we will examine the principle that underlies the meaning of sentences – compositionality*. For the moment, though, let us examine some elementary semantic phenomena, which don't require any special technical knowledge. Some ready-made expressions, called *idioms**, have an overall meaning: this is true of compound nouns like (83), but also for verbal expressions like (84):

(83) *washing machine*
typewriter
bedroom

(84) *to kick the bucket*
to be a good egg
to be dressed to the nines

The meaning of *kick the bucket* is not the addition of the meaning of *kick, the,* and *bucket*. Moreover, the choice of the determinant is not free: it is not possible to say *kick a bucket* if one means *to die*, nor to use this transitive construction in the passive voice. *The bucket was kicked by John* literally means "John gave a kick to the bucket", rather than "John died", the idiomatic meaning.

In order for any system of communication to qualify as a language, therefore, it must possess a phonology, a semantics, and a syntax. Two consequences can be drawn from this definition, which are directly linked to the principal topic of this chapter.

First, this definition says nothing about the function of language, communication. Language therefore appears to be dissociated from its function. This assumption aligns with what we discussed earlier that verbal communication requires two systems, the code model* and the inferential model*. The code model explains how messages are associated, through a linguistic convention, with signals, whereas the inferential model explains how speaker meaning can be interpreted on the basis of the semantic content of the sentence and the context in which it is uttered. Using the definition of a language that implies a phonology*, a semantics* and a syntax*, we now have a strong argument for dissociating language from communication: language is not communication, and communication is not language.

Second, we can now explain why animal communication systems are not languages. Vervet monkeys alarm calls, for example, consist of a string of sounds – their phonic imprints are different, so a phonology is present – that also have a meaning – "there is a threat coming from the sky/with four legs/slithering on the ground" and thus a semantics – but they lack syntax. In other words, vervet monkeys cannot compose utterances with more than one communication unit, like humans do in their sentences – the one you are now reading contains 29 words! The minimal definition for language therefore excludes animal communication systems.

We now possess a working definition of a language, but we have not yet explored its relationship to communication.

8 The two functions of language: Communication and cognition

What are the functions of language? Certainly communication is one of them, since language is used in a special type of communication: human verbal communication. This type of communication is very different from animal communication. It is based on a complex code – a language – and on general inferential abilities specific to human cognition. Language thus ties together specialized knowledge of a specific language and the general reasoning abilities that allow us to understand one another.

The type of communication that uses both code and inference has been described as a special case of ostensive-inferential communication* (Sperber and Wilson [1986] 1995). Earlier we considered an example of ostensive-inferential communication when the Japanese passer-by gave information by pointing to the Chūō train line. In ostensive-inferential communication, the communicator shows her communication act through her communicative intention* and invites her addressee to infer her informative intention*, or what she wants to communicate. In verbal communication, the ostensive stimulus is the speaker's utterance, and the comprehension process is triggered by recognition of the speaker's communicative intention.

It may be that we are not vigilant enough, though, either because we did not understand the utterance addressed to us, or because we did not pay attention to an act of communication. Everyone has experienced drifting out of a conversation and being unable to answer a question in a meeting because he or she was not listening ... or we may have felt bored in class when we didn't pay attention to the speaker's acts of communication. On the other hand, if we do pay attention to a speaker's utterance in verbal communication, it is because we are able to suppose that it is worthwhile to mobilize our efforts to comprehend her. The next chapter will show why we feel interested, immediately and without thinking about it, in utterances addressed to us.

If language is used in communication, did it evolve for communication purposes? Some researchers in the domain of cognitive science and language science think so. The best known are Steven Pinker and Ray Jackendoff,[68] who argue for an evolutionary picture of language which, they believe, arose as a product of evolution. According to this perspective, the justification of the emergence of language was twofold: it basically concerned communication, but manipulation

---

[68] See Pinker and Jackendoff (2005), Jackendoff (2002), and Pinker (1995).

was also associated with it. As Steven Pinker explains in *The Language Instinct* (Pinker 1995: 369):

> Finally, anthropologists have noted that tribal chiefs are often both gifted orators and highly polygynous – a splendid prod to any imagination that cannot conceive of how linguistic skills could make a Darwinian difference. I suspect that evolving humans lived in a world in which language was woven into the intrigues of politics, economics, technology, family, sex, and friendship that played key roles in individual reproductive success. They could no more live with a Me-Tarzan-you-Jane level of grammar than we could.

Another assumption, which aligns with *biolinguistics** (Di Sciullo and Boeckx 2011) – research that combines biology and linguistics – conceives of language not as the result of evolution, but of exaptation*; that is, as the result of a feature of human cognition that was not initially devoted to communication, and which arose in a non-adaptive manner for communication (Hauser, Chomsky, and Fitch 2002; Reboul 2013, and 2017a). Here is how Anne Reboul introduces the issue of the function of language from the perspective of its evolution:

> That language is routinely used in human communication is not in doubt. However, what may be and should be discussed (though usually it is not) is whether language is a communication system in the strong sense (in which case it evolved for communication) or whether it is a communication system in the weak sense (in which case it evolved to fulfill another function, but was then exapted for communication). (Reboul 2017a: 4)

According to Hauser *et al.* the feature of cognition which appeared in a non-adaptive manner is *recursion**, a property that enables the embedding of a structure of any kind in a structure of the same type. It defines the *faculty of language in the narrow sense**, specific to human language. Recursion seems to have played a role in the development of the human species in terms of spatial representation, which is especially important for navigation, as well as in the development of mathematics, which includes the ability to count. We will return to the idea that language is based on recursion in the next chapter.

9 Conclusion

Defining language as a system of communication in the weak sense (Reboul 2017a) means that language did not appear for communication, but for another reason. The challenge is knowing what this reason was. The answer is obvious: the other function of language is *cognition*. Language, in other words, is directly linked to thought, allowing it to be externalized and then communicated.

But if language is the externalisation of thought, it follows that there is a language of thought* – known as *mentalese* – which every human being masters, and which allows for the representation of states of affairs, events, and situations, as well as reasoning about propositions and facts. As such, the language of thought is made up of the words of thought, called *concepts**, and *propositions**. The propositions are made up of concepts and operators, called *connectives**, which allow complex propositions such as conjunction, disjunction, conditional, and negation to be built (Reboul 2017a). For instance, using the concepts RAIN, COME, LEAVE, JOHN, MARY, we can build the atomic propositions [JOHN COME] and [MARY LEAVE], as well as the complex proposition [JOHN COME → MARY LEAVE], and then draw, from this last proposition and the proposition [JOHN COME], the proposition [MARY LEAVE] via the logical rule called *modus ponens*. These propositions are translated into English as follows:

(85) If John comes, then Mary will leave.
 John comes.
 So Mary will leave.

This approach, as we will see in chapter 3, strongly links *thought, language,* and *reasoning*. Chapter 3 will show why the language of thought is externalised, and how we can communicate our thoughts through natural language. Chapter 4 will explain why thoughts have a universal character, and are not specific to particular languages.

Chapter 3
Language structure and usage

Distinguishing between language structure and usage has been one of the most important discoveries in language science in recent decades, along with the difference between language and communication. The structural dimension of language is related to its properties as part of a system, while the usage dimension shows that language is an activity of communication. The necessity of separating language from communication was mentioned above: as we have seen, the main function of language is not communication, and communication can take place without language. That said, I will now expand on the reasons why the main function of language is not communication, demonstrating that the rules governing language structure are not the same as those that govern its usage.

1 Linguistic rules first

Since the emergence of what is now known as pragmatics*, the research field that investigates language usage in communication (and particularly speaker meaning*) rather than language itself, it has been acknowledged that language rules are not rules of usage.

This is a fundamental issue, because many phenomena are linked to language usage rather than to its structure. Examples of such phenomena include mother tongue acquisition, which is acquired through usage – language is not implemented in our brains; conversation, which is not something abstract, but is part of language usage and demonstrates types of grammatical structures that differ greatly from standard expressions; literature, which like all other types of textual production, frequently contains overt and explicit violations of grammatical rules; second language learning, which is more efficient in a total immersion environment than in a classroom; and personal identity, which is often associated with a person's prosodic imprint.

The most important thing about language is its usage, not its structure. However, the agenda of language science has not always looked at things this way. In a word, the study of language structure took precedence in linguistics for many years. In the early 20th century, Ferdinand de Saussure, a Swiss linguist who is recognized as the founder of European structuralist linguistics, gave priority in the study of language to the *langue** – a system of signs, defined by social conventions – as opposed to the *parole** – the individual usage of the *langue*. In the mid-20th century, Noam Chomsky, the founder of generative grammar, distinguished between *competence**

https://doi.org/10.1515/9783110723380-005

and *performance**, and prioritized the study of competence – the set of knowledge a speaker has about her language – over that of performance, or the working out of competence in verbal communication (Chomsky 1965). Chomsky's more recent research differentiates between internal language* (I-language) and external language* (E-language). The study of I-language, the linguistic knowledge of a particular speaker, takes precedence over the social and sometimes national phenomenon represented by E-language (Chomsky 1986, 1995).

In his introductory book on the minimalist program, the latest version of generative grammar, the French linguist Jean-Yves Pollock (1997), referring to Chomsky (1986), sets out linguistics' agenda in four questions (Pollock 1997: 1):

(1) Comment caractériser le savoir linguistique des locuteurs adultes, leur langue interne ou LI?
(2) Comment LI se développe-t-elle chez les locuteurs?
(3) Comment LI est-elle mise en œuvre dans la pratique langagière effective des locuteurs, leur performance?
(4) Quels sont les mécanismes physiques et neurologiques sur lesquels reposent LI et sa mise en œuvre?

[(1) How can one characterise the linguistic knowledge of adult speakers, their internal language or IL?
(2) How is IL acquired by speakers?
(3) How is IL put to use in speakers' actual practices and in their performances?
(4) What are the physical and neurological mechanisms on which IL and its implementation are based?]

Question (1) takes priority in the agenda of linguistic theory, and comes before question (2), which deals with language acquisition: indeed, how can one describe I-language acquisition if one does not know what I-Language consists of? Question (3), which is about the study of performance, is similar: one cannot study the implementation of I-language if one does not know what it consists of. The same is true of I-language implementation in the brain, although current research in neurolinguistics, especially in terms of the treatment of linguistic signals, has produced new hypotheses on this matter.[69]

As the above examples show, the study of abstract structures of language took precedence over the study of its usage for many years. Did this academic priority make sense? Let's take a look at its presuppositions. Suppose you decide

---

[69] See Gervain *et al.* (2016), Giraud Mamessier and Poeppel (2012).

to learn to drive. You certainly agree with the formal rules of modern society: to drive a car, you must take lessons with a driving instructor, pass an exam on the highway code, and take a driving test. These tests aim at checking whether the future driver masters both theory and practice: in other words, the driver should have sufficient knowledge and the ability to drive safely. But you know – and if you have children, you have certainly experienced this – that what the examiner tests is only performance, both for the highway code and the driving test. An anxious candidate may fail his exam, even though during his lessons he drives in a way that would allow him to pass the driving test.

This example makes an important point: that there can be a huge difference between competence and performance. Oral exams at university are living proof of this: many students have trouble giving answers during an oral exam, although their preparatory work was sufficient for them to pass the exam without any problem.

Let's look at another example about cars, which shows the reasons why linguistics differentiates between I- and E-language. When your car has a problem, you make an appointment with a mechanic, who has the knowledge to repair it. It's an interesting fact that in order to drive one doesn't need to know how a car works. If someone does know this, it has no impact on their driving – or perhaps knowing how an engine works would make drivers more careful. You can use your car without knowing how it works, and the same is true for many other artifacts: computers, lawn mowers, microwaves, ovens, water heaters, etc.

The same is also true of cognition: what we know can be in contradiction with what we do with this knowledge. For instance, every educated French speaker knows that the indicative mood is required by the temporal conjunction *après que* ('after'), whereas the subjunctive mood is required by *avant que* ('before'), as shown in examples (86) to (89):

(86) *Pierre s'est couché après qu'il a couché les enfants.*
Pierre himself is laid down after that he Indicative-have laid down the children
'Peter went to bed after he put the children to bed.'

(87) **Pierre s'est couché après qu'il ait couché les enfants.*
Pierre himself is laid down after that he Subjunctive-have laid down the children
'Peter went to bed after he put the children to bed.'

(88) *Pierre a donné le bain aux enfants avant qu'il les ait fait manger.*
Pierre has given the bath to the children before that he them Subjunctive-have made eat
'Peter gave a bath to the children before he gave them dinner.'

(89) *Pierre a donné le bain aux enfants avant qu'il les a fait manger.
Pierre has given the bath to the children before that he them Indicative-have made eat
'Peter gave a bath to the children before he gave them dinner.'

A French speaker may know this rule but not apply it, simply because the indicative/subjunctive alternation is specific to the conjunction *après que* 'after', and *avant que* 'before' does not behave in the same way. Similarly, subordination conjunction with *pour que* 'in order to', *afin que* 'in order to', and *bien que* 'although' also require the subjunctive tense.

2 Principle of linguistic organisation

We have just seen that implicit knowledge of linguistic rules can be in contradiction with how people use them. The next question is: what rules govern linguistic organisation? Modern theoretical linguistics identifies two principles at work: hierarchy and economy.[70]

Hierarchy: The idea is that the level of grammatical, or syntactic, organisation is hierarchical: a sentence is not simply a string of words, but obeys grouping rules. For instance, a simple sentence such as *Mary likes Lucy* results in a more complex description (90b) than the string of words that make it up (90a):

(90) *Mary likes Lucy*.
    a. *Mary*_{Subject} + *likes*_{Verb} + *Lucy*_{Object}
    b. [*Mary* [*likes* [*Lucy*]]]

The second representation results in an arborescent structure:

(91)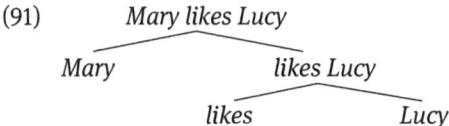

How can we justify this structure? The first representation (90a) makes it possible to distinguish between what traditional grammar terms the grammatical subject (*Mary*) and the direct object (*Lucy*). It is easy to show that nouns can be

---

[70] A third principle is often mentioned: the optimality of syntactic computations. Because of its complexity, I will not discuss this principle here.

replaced by pronouns whose form confirms their grammatical function – *she* for the subject, *her* for the direct object:

(92) a. *She likes her.*
     b. **Her likes she.*

Second, the subject cannot be grouped with the verb, which makes the following structure impossible in English: no other lexical unit can replace *Mary likes*:

(93)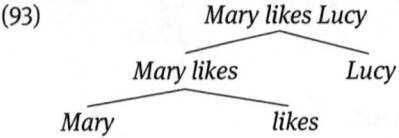

The important point is that a sentence, whether simple or complex, has a hierarchical organization rather than a linear one, as is shown in (94):

(94)   Mary likes Lucy
         ‾‾‾‾‾‾‾‾‾
         Mary   likes Lucy

Economy: The rules and principles of Universal Grammar must also satisfy a principle of economy: they must be minimal in number and as simple as possible. Current theoretical linguistics recognizes only two rules: *merge** and *move** (Rizzi 2013 for a development).

Move appears to be generalized in a language like English. It is found in relative clauses, interrogatives, indirect interrogatives, passives, cleft sentences, and left dislocation:

(95)   *The girl [whom John loves <the girl>] is a vet.*[71]

(96)   *Who does Mary loves <who>?*

(97)   *I wonder [who Mary loves <who>].*

(98)   *Mary is loved by her pupils <love> <Mary>.*

(99)   *Mary [<Mary> she loves her pupils].*

---

71 The words that have been moved are crossed-out and are between < >.

These sentences are the result of *derivation**, which moves the crossed-out elements from their origin position to their surface position in the clause.[72]

Suppose that you have a set of fridge magnets for putting together sentences. The set contains only French words – it was a gift from a French relative. You choose a few words: *la, le, belle, voile, ferme*. Since you speak some French, you understand each word: *la* is a feminine article ('the') or a direct object feminine clitic pronoun ('her'), *le* is a masculine article ('the') or a direct object masculine clitic pronoun ('him'), *belle* is a feminine adjective ('beautiful'), *ferme* is either a noun ('farm') or a verb ('to close'), *voile* is either a noun ('veil') or a verb ('to hide'). With these five words, if you try to build a meaningful sentence, you can only construct the sentence *la belle ferme le voile*. You accomplish this through three main operations, resulting in the two alternate meanings mentioned in (100) and (101):

(100) *la, belle, ferme: la belle ferme*
'the, beautiful, farm': the beautiful farm'
le, voile: le voile
'him, hides: hides him'
la belle ferme le voile
'the beautiful farm hides him'

(101) *la, belle: la belle*
'the, beautiful: the beautiful'
ferme, le, voile: ferme le voile
'closes, the, veil: closes the veil'
la belle ferme le voile
'the beautiful one closes the veil'

What have you done? You have merged lexical units, or words, into groups: *la belle* can be a complete group, consisting of an article (a determiner) and a noun: {{*la*}, {*belle*}} = {*la belle*}. But you can obtain a different result by adding *ferme* to this string: {{*la*}, {*belle*}, {*ferme*}} = {*la belle ferme*}. The same goes for *le voile*, where you can merge a pronoun and a verb: {{*le*}, {*voile*}} = {*le voile*}; or an article and a noun which merge with a verb: {*ferme le voile*}.

---

[72] In the traditional version of generative grammar, the concepts of *deep structure* and *surface structure* are applied. Rules that allow a speaker to go from one structure to another are called *transformation rules*. In minimalism, the current version of generative grammar, move is a syntactic operation intervening in a derivation, but is not a rule of transformation. On the current version of Chomskyan theory, see Chomsky (1995), Boeckx (2006), (2011), and Hornstein, Nunes, and Grohmann (2005). For a comprehensible grammar of the English language, see Quirk *et al.* (1985).

Now you have two groups, one with a noun as the central unit, the other with a verb: {{la belle ferme}, {le voile}} = {la belle ferme le voile}, or {{la belle} {ferme le voile}} = {la belle ferme le voile}. These different merges can be represented in the two following trees:

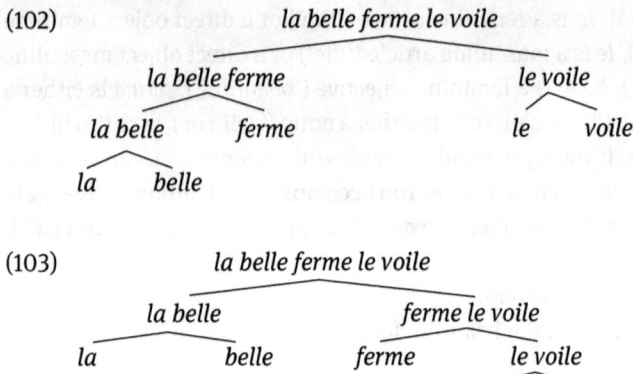

These examples show that syntactic computations prove the existence of a hierarchical organization of grammar, and that the operations implied in the derivations generating the sentences are limited to merge and move.

3 FLN and FLB

What is the architecture of grammar, the computational system responsible for sentence derivations? As we have seen, one constant in linguistic theory is to define language as a pairing of a string of sounds and a string of meanings.

Noam Chomsky hypothesized a human mind/brain component specific to language, which he termed the *faculty of language**. This component interacts with two other systems: the cognitive system, which stocks information, and the performance systems that are responsible for accessing and using information. How do these systems work? According to Chomsky (1995: 2)

> [. . .] the cognitive system interacts with the performances systems by means of levels of linguistic representations [. . .]. A more specific assumption is that the cognitive system interacts with two such "external" systems: the articulatory-perceptual system A-P and the conceptual-intentional system C-I. Accordingly, there are two interface levels, Phonetic Form (FP) at the A-P interface and Logical Form (LF) at the C-I interface. This "double interface" property is one way to express the traditional description of language as sound with a meaning, traceable at least back to Aristotle.

One way of representing the relationship between these two interfaces and the cognitive system (*narrow syntax*) is a T diagram. The terms used for the cognitive system are the *faculty of language in the narrow sense** (FLN), the *sensorimotor interface** for the A-P interface, and the *conceptual-intentional interface** for the C-I interface. These two systems correspond to the *faculty of language in the broad sense** (FLB). These interactions are represented below:

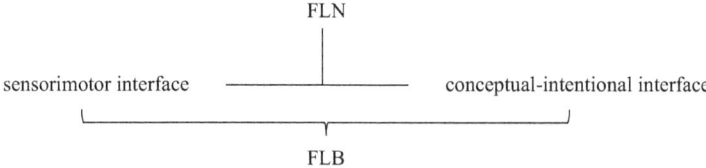

Figure 1: The architecture of grammar (based on Hauser, Chomsky, and Fitch 2002).

FLN is restricted to a single property, recursion*, or the property of natural language to embed expressions of the same type in one another. The clause is a recursive category, since one clause can contain another clause:

(104) a. *Paul told me that John said to him that he wanted to go to Norway.*
 b. [₁ *Paul told me* [₂ *that John said to him* [₃ *that he wanted* [₄ <~~John~~> *to go to Norway*]]]

In (104), three subordinate clauses are embedded in the matrix clause. The nominal phrase is also a recursive category, since it can contain a phrase of the same type: phrases 1 and 3 are Nominal Phrases (*NPs*):

(105) a. *the school of the village*
 b. [NP1 *the school* [PP *of* [NP2 *the village*]]]

FLB thus contains both sensorimotor and conceptual-intentional interfaces. These systems are specific to the human organism, along with memory, respiration, digestion, and blood circulation (Hauser, Chomsky, and Fitch 2002). They contrast with external, ecological, physical, cultural, and social environments.

The most important question asked by Hauser et al. is whether FLN and FLB are specific to human species. They discuss three hypotheses in their seminal article: (H1) FLB is strictly homologous to animal communication; (H2) FLB is a derived adaptation, specifically human, for language; and (H3) only FLN is uniquely human.

According to H1, FLB is strictly *homologous** to animal communication. Since a homologous feature is inherited from a common ancestor, systems that are homologous to FLB (including FLN) should also exist in non-human animals. This hypothesis is not probable if we suppose that FLN is specific to the human species. According to H2, FLB is a derived *adaptation**, specifically human and highly complex, for language. FLB has a communication function and a genetic component: natural selection played a role in FLB formation because this process has no parallel in non-human animals. Finally, according to H3, only FLN is human. The question of whether FLB is shared with other species like primates must therefore remain open.

According to H3, the largest part of FLB is based on mechanisms shared with non-human animals, while FLN – the recursion computational mechanism – is due to recent evolution that is specific only to our species. On the other hand, the largest part of the complexity exhibited in language seems to derive from the sensorimotor and conceptual-intentional interface complexity (FLB), combined with sociocultural and communicative contingencies. Briefly stated, according to Hauser et al., FLB has an ancient evolutionary history that is significantly earlier than the emergence of language, whereas FLN is limited to recursion* (narrow syntax) and its interplay with interfaces.

If we return to the first two hypotheses, we can observe that they define a direct correspondence (via descendants and modifications) between a feature implied in FLB in humans and a similar feature in other species. We must then ask whether a series of gradual modifications led to language skills that result in an infinite capacity for linguistic generativity: the capacity of generating an infinite set of sentences from a limited set of elements (the lexicon).

On the other hand, the issue of whether humans' unique language ability is an adaptation differentiates between H2 and H3 is. The hypothesis of Hauser et al. is that FLN is anatomically composed of several independent features that interact with one another. Each has its own evolutionary history and was fashioned by natural selection, which implies a small connection with communication.

It is also important to know which conditions FLN must fulfil. Syntactic computations which are derived from FLN must be efficient. Chomsky hypothesized that, in addition to being efficient, FLN is an *optimal* solution for satisfying the interface conditions with FLB. According to Hauser et al., some linguistic problems, such as *wh-* movement (for interrogative pronouns) and garden-path sentences (as in the example of *the old man the boat*) are by-products of this assumption, generated by FLB's neuronal and computational constraints.

A final point must be addressed: neither FLN nor FLB can be justified by reasons related to language usage, or communication. But this is not the conclusion of Hauser et al., whose article ends in the following way:

Why did humans, but no other animal, take the power of recursion to create an open-ended and limitless system of communication? Why does our system of recursion operate over a broader range of elements or inputs (e.g., numbers, words) than other animals? One possibility, consistent with current thinking in the cognitive sciences, is that recursion in animals represents a modular system designed for a particular function (e.g., navigation) and impenetrable with respect to other systems. During evolution, the modular and highly domain-specific system of recursion may have become penetrable and domain-general. This opened the way for humans, perhaps uniquely, to apply the power recursion to other problems. This change from domain-specific to domain-general may have been guided by particular selective pressures, unique to our evolutionary past, or as a consequence (by-product) of other kinds of neural reorganization". (Hauser, Chomsky, and Fitch 2002: 1578)

In other words, there is not only something specifically human about FLN, but also in the history of our species: humans took advantage of a feature of our cognition that is specific to areas such as spatial representation and numbers and applied it to the general domain that is language. This could provide an explanation for the uniqueness of FLN in relation to other animal species. It would also explain why the faculty of language is, for Noam Chomsky and his co-authors, a trait of human cognition that no other species share. And that in turn would explain why Chomsky's article led to great scientific controversy, especially as related to Steven Pinker and Ray Jackendoff, for whom modern language is a prolongation of an early state of language known as *protolanguage**, which in their opinion was shared by Homo erectus and Neanderthals.

4 Protolanguage and modern language

Derek Bickerton, an American linguist at the University of Hawaii who specializes in pidgins* and creoles*, has hypothesized two levels of language (Bickerton 1990, 2009): a protolanguage, existing at the time of Homo erectus 1,7 million years ago, and a modern language, spoken by *Homo sapiens* between 300,000 and 50,000 years ago.[73]

Bickerton defines protolanguage as a modern language minus its syntax. In his opinion, traces of protolanguage are found in *pidgins** (contact languages like

---

[73] Researchers on language evolution do not concur on the date of modern language emergence. It is accepted knowledge today that modern language resulted from a genetic mutation that affected only the brain. This fact is based on recent research on the FOXP2 gene, the cultural explosion during the Neolithic period, particularly the cave paintings created 40,000 years ago, and the expansion of Sapiens over the entire globe, which began between 60,000 and 50,000 years ago.

the Chinook Jargon, used in the past for trading with American Indians in the north-eastern United States), in agrammatic aphasia,[74] in the language of young children (utterances with two or three words), and in sign language learned by primates.

In the book he published in 2002, Ray Jackendoff gives further arguments showing that today's languages contain linguistic fossils of protolanguage, and particularly fossils of the "one-word" step in language evolution:

(i) *Interjections*: they have no syntax and are specific to a certain type of situation: *oops* to signal a mistake, *damn* to signal discontent, *ouch* to signal pain, *shh* to ask for a lower volume, and *psst* to call attention to something.
(ii) *Pro-sentences*: Pro-sentences like *yes* and *no* do not have a syntax, but they have a meaning: that of a positive or a negative answer.
(iii) *Greetings*: *Hi*, *bye*, and *farewell* have no syntax: they are single word expressions, or idioms.

How is it possible to bring together signals made by primates, protolanguage, and modern language as seen from an evolutionary perspective? Ray Jackendoff (2002: 238) defines four layers that led to modern language: primate conceptual structures, the decontextualised use of symbols, protolanguage, and modern language. In order for protolanguage to emerge, two things were required: an unlimited number of symbols,[75] and especially a word order with basic semantic relationships. The rule suggested by Jackendoff (2002: 248), which appears to be universal, is "Agent first, Focus last". Here are two examples that illustrate this rule. Suppose that you and I speak proto-English, in which word order determines semantic relationships such as the Agent (the entity that performs the action described by the verb). How can sense be made of the following proto-English sentences?

(106) *John apple.*

(107) *Hit tree John.*

---

[74] Steven Pinker (1995: 307) gives the following example of aphasia, attributed to the patient Peter Hogan: "Yes . . . ah . . . Monday . . . ah . . . Dad and Peter Hogan, and Dad . . . ah . . . hospital . . . and ah . . . Wednesday . . . Wednesday nine o'clock and ah Thursday . . . ten o'clock ah doctors . . . two . . . two . . . an doctors and . . . ah . . . teeth . . . yah . . . And a doctor and a girl . . . and gums, and I".

[75] In her books on the evolution of language, Anne Reboul (2007) and (2017a) assumes that this step is crucial for the emergence of syntax.

In the first sentence, the Agent is *John*, and *apple* is the Theme of the verb, which is not made explicit. This is not surprising, because there are many grammatical structures in English with a coerced verb, i.e. one that is semantically constrained. For instance, there is have no difficulty in inferring the coerced verb in these sentences:

(108)   *Mary wants a baby = Mary wants to* HAVE *a baby*

(109)   *Juliet wants chocolate = Juliet wants to* EAT *chocolate*

(110)   *John wants a new car = John wants to* BUY *a new car*

In (107), the sentence contains an Agent and a Focus, or new information. It is thus possible to understand that this proto-English sentence corresponds to the modern English *the tree hits John*, in which the Agent is *tree* and the Focus is *John*.

Finally, according to Jackendoff, protolanguage, though it has no syntax, does have a protosyntax, which consists of a grouping of lexical units. How can the words in (111) be grouped?

(111)   *Cat brown eat mouse.*

Is *brown* grouped with *cat* or *mouse*? The most probable grouping is between *cat* and *brown*, not between *brown* and *mouse*, simply *because cat* and *brown* are adjacent. The grouping is therefore:

(112)   [*cat brown*] *eat mouse = the brown cat eats the mouse*

Now, what is required for protolanguage to become modern language? According to Jackendoff the necessary elements are a set of *grammatical categories** such as Noun, Verb, and Adjective; a set of abstract semantic relations known as *Thematic Roles** and including Agent*, Patient, and Theme; a set of grammatical functions* such as Subject and Object; and finally, *inflexion**, or a *morphology**.

For Jackendoff (2002: 261), modern languages go beyond the relationship between sounds and meaning, mediated by auditory structures (audition) and motor control structures (production): they are composed by additional components responsible for the complexity of the linguistic architecture languages, that is, a phonology, a syntax, and a morphology.

In other words, modern language is defined as the relationship between strings of sounds (phonology) and strings of meaning (semantics) organized by syntax. The crucial point for Jackendoff is that "grammar is not a single unified system, but a collection of simpler systems" (Jackendoff 2002: 264).

The two visions of the evolution and architecture of language examined so far are difficult to reconcile. In the first model suggested by Hauser et al., language is not a product of evolution, but the result of an adaptive change of a feature of cognition that was originally associated with a function other than communication. The relationship between language and communication is not direct in this case, because language is the externalization of thought. In the second model, the Jackendoff-Pinker approach, modern language is the result of evolution and a set of autonomous systems (phonology, semantics, and syntax). The relationship between language and communication is straightforward because one of language's functions is communication.

How is it possible to explain human communication and particularly utterance meaning? Do linguistic rules come into play, or can other rules explain language usage? We have already partially answered this question. As we observed in chapter 2, language is not communication, and communication is not language. But this answer does not tell us what communication rules actually are. We will now explore two key responses to this issue, one based on the concept of *cooperation*, the other based on *relevance*.

5 Cooperative principle and maxims of conversation

The comprehension of verbal communication has changed radically since the William James lectures given at Harvard University by the philosopher of language Paul Grice (U.C. Berkeley). Grice is probably most famous for his article *Logic and Conversation*, which was published for the first time in 1975 (Grice 1975).[76] It presents the main assumption that speakers' behaviour in conversation is governed by the acceptance of a cooperative principle and of rules or maxims of conversation. The notion of *cooperation** is central to current research on human cognition as well as in primatology research. Most species, particularly primates and species that live in groups, must cooperate for simple reasons of survival.[77]

Suppose that you go for a hike with a group of friends. At the halfway point an accident happens: one of the hikers falls and breaks his leg. You have no phone coverage and the weather is changing quickly – you are hiking in the mountains. You have no chance of finding shelter nearby. What do you do? No one would say

---

76 All of Grice's lectures are collected in Grice (1989).
77 See Tomasello (2008) for an evolutionary approach to cooperation.

to the injured person: "OK, I'll go on without you!". Why?[78] One answer is that if you acted like this, your behaviour would be judged as selfish as well as illegal, in terms of failing to assist a person in danger. Now, do you decide to stay and find a solution because you do not want to spend several months in prison? Of course not. You stay simply because you are naturally interested in others, for reasons related to feelings you share with them, such as their pain (empathy). Generally speaking, you are able to represent others as having the same mental states as you do: your cooperative behaviour is directly related to your cognition. This cognitive property, known as *theory of mind** (Dennett 1987, Baron-Cohen 1995), allows one to ascribe mental states such as belief, wish, and intention, to others.[79,80]

This reflexive capacity is central to verbal communication, particularly to what the speaker means with her utterance. In order to understand her intentions, in particular her informative intention*, the addressee must ask why the speaker said what she said and what she wanted to mean with what she said. To reach this answer, Grice (1975: 45) uses his well-known cooperative principle*: "Make your conversational contribution such as is required, at the stage at which it occurs, by the accepted purpose or direction of the talk exchange in which you are engaged".

The speaker must therefore follow the direction of the exchange in which she is engaged, and do what is expected of him: answer a question, pass the salt when it is requested, and so on. Refusing to answer a question is non-cooperative behaviour (114), as is answering *No!* to a request to pass the salt (115):

---

[78] This question seems odd, but one must consider the many situations in which people witness an accident or attack and leave without helping the victims. Such occurrences are legion in the subway and on the train.

[79] Jean-Baptiste van der Henst (personal communication) remarked to me that theory of mind is not enough: a torturer can have a very robust theory of mind. The faculty that comes into play in this particular case is *prosociality*. See Pfaff (2014).

[80] Theory of mind became a central thesis in developmental psychology when its role in autism was demonstrated (Frith 1989). The test that shows the role of the theory of mind in cognitive development is the test of false belief. The ability to attribute false beliefs to others corresponds to a developmental stage – around the age of 5 for children with typical development, and later for verbal autistic children. Here is the test: Sally and her grandmother are in the kitchen. Sally puts her doll in a toy chest, then leaves the room. Her grandmother decides to put the doll in the cupboard. The test question is "where do you think Sally is going to look for her doll?" The correct answer is "in the toy chest". Autistic children answer "in the cupboard". The correct answer implies that one can attribute a false belief to Sally: Sally believes her doll is in the toy chest because she put it there. But this belief is false, because her grandmother moved Sally's doll to the cupboard. The crucial point is that the scope of the question is about what Sally believes, not about where the doll is.

(113) Passer-by 1: *Can you give me the time?*
      Passer-by 2: *No, I can't.*

(114) Jacques: *Can you pass me the salt?*
      Axel: *No!*

How can a speaker be cooperative in a conversation? This does not mean answering *yes* to everything or accepting rather than refusing an invitation. Cooperating supposes that a speaker will respect or exploit – that is, violate in an ostensive manner – one of the conversational maxims. Grice introduced nine conversational maxims divided into four categories: quantity, quality, relation, and manner.

The maxims of quantity enjoin the speaker to give as much information as required, and no more. The maxims of quality can be resumed by "speak truthfully" and "do not say what you believe to be false or for which you lack evidence". The maxim of relation requires the speaker to be relevant, i.e. that he speak on the subject of the conversation. The four remaining maxims of manner, which can be summed up as "be perspicuous", require the speaker to avoid obscurity and ambiguity, and to be brief and orderly. These nine maxims can be respected or violated.

Here are some well known examples of respecting these maxims. If you choose a term that is semantically weak (115–116a) instead of one that is semantically strong (115–116b) – the strong expression entails the weak one – it is because you cannot say more (quantity). Similarly, if you use a loose (117a) expression instead of a precise (117b) one, you implicate that you do not know where the person in question lives:

(115) a. *Some students passed.*
      b. *All students passed.*

(116) On a restaurant menu
      a. *Cheese or dessert.*
      b. *Cheese and dessert.*

(117) a. *Mary lives somewhere in the South of Burgundy.*
      b. *Mary lives in Cluny.*

An indirect answer must be relevant, and must contain the reason for the answer (relevance), as in (118):

(118) Peter: *Are you going to pragmatics class?*
      Mary: *I have a dentist appointment.*

Using the conjunction *and* allows for the conclusion "and then" (submaxim of order).

(119) a. *They got married and had a baby.*
b. *They had a baby and got married.*

Ostensive violations of maxims also occur. The speaker may voluntarily not give enough information, in order to show that she does not want to provide the asked-for information. By answering *Mary lives somewhere in the South of Burgundy*, the speaker means that she does not want to say exactly where Mary lives. One can also violate the maxim of quality in a figure of speech by using a metaphor to say that Mary is a marvellous person who is reliable and hard-working:

(120) *Mary is a pearl.*

Finally, one can ostensively be unclear in order not to be understood, for instance by ones' children:

(121) *We're going to the beach, but we aren't stopping for i-c-e c-r-e-a-m on the way back.*

Briefly stated, Grice's central idea is that the speaker says something in order to mean something else: what she means is called a *conversational implicature**because it is obtained via one of the maxims of conversation.[81]

How are conversational implicatures obtained? Grice describes the manner in which the addressee draws an implicature in the following way:

> He has said that p; there is no reason to suppose that he is not observing the maxims, or at least the CP; he could not be doing this unless he thought that q; he knows (and knows that I know that he knows) that I can see that the supposition that he thinks that q IS required; he has done nothing to stop me thinking that q; he intends me to think, or is at least willing to allow me to think, that q; and so he has implicated that q. (Grice 1975: 50)

According to Grice, the grasping of an implicature is the result of *reasoning*. This type of reasoning is an ex post-facto reconstruction, typical of philosophical argumentation in which there is no a priori cognitive justification. That said, we

---

[81] Grice identifies another type of implicature, known as *conventional* implicature; in this case a particular word triggers the implicature. Certain discourse connectives like *therefore* and *but* always trigger the same type of conclusion. If Peter says *John is an Englishman; he is, therefore, brave*, he does not say that Englishmen are brave: he *conventionally implicates* it.

know that the computation of an implicature takes time and is costly in cognitive terms. In other words, going beyond literal meaning implies an extra effort in cognitive processing. One of the most important questions is why we agree to mobilize mental energy to understand an implicature's meaning.

One answer is that if the hearer does not do this, he may not grasp what the speaker means (speaker meaning*). The interesting point is that we agree to spend energy on understanding what utterances mean. This is surprising, because we might think that cognition is lazy, and that it seeks the path of least effort. We will return to this point in the next section. For the moment, let's take a detour into the sporting world.

In the 1980s there were two types of slalom skiers in the Alpine Ski World Cup: those, like Gustavo Thoeni and Ingemar Stenmark, who made wide turns around the slalom gates – a series of poles around which the skier must weave in and out – and those who cut close to each pole.[82] The first category skied in wide curves that were far from the poles, whereas the second, represented by the Yugoslavian skier Bojan Križaj, took a shorter and more direct path, twisting his body suddenly during changes of direction. One way of skiing was supple, smooth, and harmonious, while the other was choppy. Which way did the winners ski? Bojan Križaj fell a lot, because his technique was riskier, while Thoeni and Stenmark almost always finished both rounds and won frequently. In other words, Thoeni and Stenmark's method was better than Križaj's. What can we conclude here? Simply that the shortest path was quicker but riskier. The longest path, which was also the smoothest, guaranteed satisfactory results in terms of both safety and time.

Can we make a comparison between this example and utterance comprehension? Definitely. First of all, the most direct path is not necessarily the shortest. This paradox must be explained, and we will see that the most important dimension is the context in which utterances are understood. Secondly, a longer but smoother path can be more efficient than a more direct path.

Let's return to the example about passing the salt. An answer such as *Yes, I can* to the question *Can you pass the salt?* supposes that the hearer has stopped at the literal meaning of the question. This response doesn't make sense: at table, a speaker doesn't ask whether her neighbour is capable of passing the salt; she just wants him to do it. Stopping at the literal meaning amounts to going only halfway. We must explain why we go beyond literal meaning in utterance comprehension without making a big cognitive effort.

---

[82] I remind young readers that skis in the 1980s were not parabolic and were longer (about 2 meters long) and thinner than those of today.

Can Grice's approach answer the question of why we go beyond literal meaning? If we return to the process of working out implicatures, we can say that a literal reading of the question is uncooperative: an addressee who answers that he is capable of passing the salt does not contribute to the conversation in a cooperative way, or is showing his inability to understand what the speaker meant. It is clear that the maxim of relation is involved in this example.

We might ask why the speaker does not phrase her question in a way that makes her request clear, by saying (122) or (123):

(122) *I order you to pass me the salt.*

(123) *Pass me the salt, please.*

I have already given a partial answer to this question: verbal communication functions in an economic manner, and non-literal communication is the best way to achieve this. The traditional answer is to say that implicit communication is *more polite* than explicit and direct communication. We will examine the relationship between politeness and implicit communication in chapter 4, and show that it is more complex.

One might ask whether the Gricean approach to communication can answer questions about the origins and evolution of language. Anne Reboul has given an initial answer (Reboul 2013, 2017a) about the role of implicit communication in language evolution. According to her theory, implicit communication plays a fundamental role in the evolution of language. In implicit communication, the speaker leaves it up to the addressee to draw the conclusions he wants him to draw, without imposing this through explicit communication. When this occurs, there is an obvious risk of the speaker manipulating the addressee, and the advantages of communicating through language are not apparent. Indeed, if there is a risk that the verbal communication will involve the speaker's manipulation of the addressee, then the advantages of being able to exchange information and the efficiency of using a rich yet imperfect code do not compensate for the risk of manipulation.

The role of implicit communication can be illustrated in two ways. In Anne Reboul's first example, Bob, the boss, tells Bill that he has decided to give the manager's position to Bill's competitor, John (Reboul 2013: 263):

(124) Bob: *I have decided to give the job of manager to John.*
       Bill: *That's an excellent choice, especially now that he has stopped drinking!*

Bill's utterance presupposes that John used to drink too much, and implicates that Bob's decision is not a good one. But no one can accuse Bill of explicitly communicating the fact that John used to drink too much. By using a mode of implicit communication, in this case a presupposition*, Bill is able to communicate to Bob that his choice was wrong, as well as telling him in an implicit way that John used to be an alcoholic. But Bill leaves it up John to draw this conclusion.

Now, affirming something through a false presupposition often leads to clashes in conversation. This is well-known: a journalist can include a false presupposition in his question, making it impossible for the interviewee to give an answer and forcing her to talk about the presupposition; a police detective, when questioning a suspect, can insert a presupposition whose veracity is not known to him:

(125) Journalist: Why are you _resigning_?
PRESUPPOSITION: You are _resigning_.

(126) Detective: _Where_ have you hidden your wife's body?
PRESUPPOSITION: You have hidden your wife's body _somewhere_.

The example of Bill and Bob shows that the role of implicit communication is to place the responsibility for comprehension on the hearer. In this way the speaker cannot be accused, rightly or wrongly, of manipulation.

Anne Reboul's second example is about a businessman, Mr. Bronston, correctly accused by the American IRS of having a bank account in Switzerland. The following dialogue occurred during his first trial (Zufferey, Moeschler, and Reboul 2019: 77):

(127) Judge: Do you have a bank account in Swiss bank, Mr. Bronston?
Bronston: No, Sir.
Judge: Have you ever?
Bronston: The company had an account there for about six months, in Zurich.

In his first answer (_No, Sir_), Bronston is not lying, since it is true that he did not have a Swiss bank account at the time of his trial. In the second answer _(The company had an account there for about six months, in Zurich)_, Bronston does not say he himself did not have an account in Switzerland, which would have been the case if he had said (128):

(128) _I have never had an account in a Swiss bank._

However, in his answer *The company had an account there for about six months, in Zurich*, Bronston implicates that he never had a bank account in Switzerland, because of the maxim of quantity "Make your contribution as informative as is required" (Grice 1975: 45). The important point here is that the judge accused Bronston of perjury. However, in a second trial, the judge's decision was dismissed, because Bronston had never said, in the sense of an explicit communication, that he had not had a Swiss account.

The important point is the following: how did the judge reach the conclusion that Bronston was not sincere? He assumed that Bronston respected neither the maxim of quantity – he did not give all information – nor the maxim of quality – his implicature "I never had a bank account in Switzerland" was false.

But the implicature cannot be obtained here through the supposition that Bronston was respecting Grice's cooperative principle. Indeed, the comprehension of implicatures is achieved through the supposition that the speaker is cooperative. According to Anne Reboul, this results in an important dilemma: the judge understood the implicature ("Bronston never had a bank account in Switzerland") perfectly well, but he felt Bronson was lying because he was convinced that the implicature was false. If the implicature was false, Bronston was not being cooperative in the sense of Grice's second maxim of quality: "Do not say that for which you lack adequate evidence" (Grice 1975: 46). The judge understood the implicature and evaluated it as false on the basis of another principle, rather than on the basis of the cooperative principle. Which principle did the judge use for his evaluation?

6 Principles of relevance

We have observed that the cooperative principle is not the principle that allows an implicature to be understood. If this is the case, how then are we able to draw the correct conclusion about what the speaker wants to say?

In their book *Relevance*, Dan Sperber and Deirdre Wilson ([1986] 1995) suggest an alternative to the Gricean explanation. Their version leads to an explanation of the reasons why verbal communication is both encoded – it uses a rich though imperfect code – and inferential – it uses general inferential competences that allow conclusions to be drawn on the basis of the utterance and the context in which it was produced. Briefly stated, Relevance Theory is a contextualist approach to utterance comprehension: if the context changes, the interpretation changes.

Imagine the following situation: if you hear Anne say in response (130) to Jacques' question (129), you know that Anne wants to say that it's the time when the postman usually comes, eleven o'clock:

(129) *What time is it?*

(130) *The postman has just come.*

If Anne produces her utterance just after a car has gone by, then she is either asking Jacques to let the dog out, because the routine is to do this after the postman comes, or to fetch the post. One might imagine other contexts, but we can see that a linguistically unambiguous sentence can have different meanings that depend on context. This illustrates that *context* plays a fundamental role in utterance comprehension. But how do we manage to make the correct hypothesis about the meaning of the utterance? How does Jacques know that it is eleven o'clock, that he should let the dog out or fetch the post?

Dan Sperber and Deirdre Wilson's central assumption is that verbal communication, like human cognition, is governed by a *principle of relevance*. From the point of view of cognition, evolution has given humans the ability to discriminate between relevant and non-relevant information. In other words, human cognition is driven by the search for maximal relevance. We seek relevant information instead of irrelevant information. Sperber and Wilson have termed this principle the *cognitive principle of relevance**.

If we apply the principle of relevance to utterance comprehension, the hearer is seeking relevant information; an interpretation whose effects will balance the efforts made in processing the utterance. These effects are *positive cognitive effects**, defined as relevant information for the addressee. For instance, if Jacques understands that he should fetch the post when Anne says *The postman has just come*, he will draw a relevant conclusion, and can strongly suppose that his conclusion corresponds to what Anne wanted to tell him.

There is a communicative counterpart to the cognitive principle of relevance. This is the *communicative principle of relevance**, which enables the addressee to presume that the speaker produced the most relevant utterance under the circumstances. This means that the addressee may suppose that the utterance is optimally relevant, and that it is worth the effort of processing (the effects obtained balance the effort made in processing) in keeping with the hearer's capacities and preferences.

A *presumption of optimal relevance** is hence associated with every utterance: as an act of communication, it implies that the speaker has a communicative intention, and the recognition of this intention explains why the addressee pays attention to the utterance and why he automatically agrees, without asking whether it will be worth the effort or not, to mobilize mental energy to understand what the speaker means – her informative intention.

It is therefore for reasons of *relevance* that we agree to process speakers' utterances. But how is relevance defined? The idea is that relevance is not something that requires questioning: when a speaker says something, one does not ask whether it is relevant or not. On the contrary, the communicative principle of relevance enables one to suppose that the utterance is optimally relevant. This does not mean that the results achieved always balance the processing efforts: when we are no longer interested in a conversation, when we stop listening to a lecturer, and when we turn off the radio or television during the President's speech, it is because our expectations of relevance are not satisfied. The child who yawns in class merely shows in an ostensive way that the information being conveyed is irrelevant to him.

We can draw two conclusions from the above. First, that utterance comprehension is not an infinite process: it ends as soon as our expectations of relevance are satisfied. If they are not satisfied, processing is abandoned – this is what happens for the yawning child. This means that a relevant interpretation yields enough effects to balance the effort of processing, and that processing stops as soon as an effort-effect balance is reached. The comprehension strategy of relevance is thus a simple one: "Follow a path of least efforts in computing cognitive effects (. . .). Stop when your expectations of relevance are satisfied" (Wilson and Sperber 2004: 613). Secondly, we can conclude that *relevance** is a comparative notion rather than a quantitative one: relevance is relative to the individual who is processing the utterance. In other words, an utterance is relevant in terms of the cognitive effects it yields and the processing efforts it requires: the more cognitive effects are obtained, the more relevant the utterance is; the more cognitive efforts are required, the less relevant the utterance is.

Four situations help to understand the relations between effect and effort:

(i) An utterance yields many effects but requires many processing efforts: this is typically the case for a scientific text: it is difficult to read but contains a lot of information.

(ii) An utterance yields many effects but requires few processing efforts: this what all authors seek to achieve. One can also suppose that the media try to minimize the treatment costs in order to maximise effects.[83]

(iii) An utterance yields few effects but requires many processing efforts: this is the situation experienced by lots of students, for whom many efforts yield few results.

---

[83] The electronic versions of some newspapers mention the reading time for their articles.

(iv) Finally, one might imagine a situation in which an utterance requires few efforts and produces few effects: the typical example given is that of the soap opera, whose situations are predictable because they are highly stereotypical.

We have now obtained a theory of comprehension. The interpretation of an utterance is the result of an inference – a positive cognitive effect – that the speaker invited her addressee to draw. But one might ask to what extent the speaker encourages her addressee to draw conclusions in order to obtain the informative intention.

To illustrate this question, Sperber and Wilson (1986: 195) set out the following exchange between Mary and Peter:

(131)　Peter:　*Would you drive a Mercedes?*
　　　　Mary:　*I wouldn't drive ANY expensive car.*

It is clear that Mary meant she would not drive a Mercedes, because Mercedes are expensive cars. Now, is it possible to say that Mary meant that she would never drive a Porsche or a Rolls-Royce, which are also expensive cars? The same question could be asked for Maseratis, Lamborghinis, Bentleys, etc. Did Mary want to mean all this? And couldn't we say that she meant that she doesn't like displays of wealth and that she wouldn't go on a cruise? All of the following contextual assumptions in (132) can be attributed to Mary, which would lead to the implicated conclusions below (133):

(132)　Contextual assumptions
　　　　Porsches, Rolls-Royces, Maseratis, Lamborghinis, and Bentleys are expensive cars.
　　　　People who refuse to drive an expensive car disapprove of displays of wealth.
　　　　People who would not drive an expensive car would not go on a cruise.

(133)　Implicated conclusions
　　　　Mary would not drive a Porsche, a Rolls-Royce, a Maserati, a Lamborghini, or a Bentley.
　　　　Mary disapproves of displays of wealth.
　　　　Mary would not go on a cruise.

In other words, the issue of the limits of interpretation has reared its head again. There is no easy answer here: the original question to Mary was about a Mercedes, not about a Rolls-Royce. So, it is probable that what Mary wanted to communicate was limited to the implicature "Mary would not drive a Mercedes". But it is also clear that it is not worth Peter's while in the next few minutes to ask the same question about a Porsche, or to produce two tickets for a Caribbean cruise!

Without meaning that she would not drive any other expensive cars besides a Mercedes, Mary has invited Pierre to draw this conclusion. We can conclude that, given the context, she *weakly* communicated these conclusions.

7 Relevance and implicit communication

We can now state Relevance Theory's solution to the question of why verbal communication is implicit. Let's return to the Mercedes example. We can imagine that Mary might have answered (134) or (135):

(134) *No*.

(135) *I wouldn't drive a Mercedes*.

Why does Mary mention *expensive* cars? We could imagine that this is Mary's way of giving the reason for her negative answer. It is a well-known fact (see chapter 5) that non-preferred answers that are negative must be justified. If this does not occur, the risk for Mary is that Peter, the questioner, will ask a *why*-question, as shown in (136):

(136) Peter: *Would you drive a Mercedes?*
       Mary: *No.*
       Peter: *Why?*
       Mary: *I wouldn't drive ANY expensive car.*

If verbal communication and conversational exchanges in particular are governed by a principle of communication such as the communicative principle of relevance, it is legitimate to suppose that communicating in an implicit way must be advantageous. We have observed that the main advantage of implicit communication is that it gives the responsibility of drawing the conclusion – which corresponds to the speaker's informative intention or the speaker meaning – to the addressee.

However, we might ask how implicit meaning is advantageous for both the speaker and her addressee. If the speaker gives the addressee the choice of drawing a conclusion about her meaning, the speaker cannot be accused of manipulating her addressee. However – and since the main property of implicatures is cancellability – implicatures are said to be *non-truth-conditional**. In other words, if the addressee draws the conclusion the speaker invited him to draw by himself, the speaker can deny that he wanted to communicate this implicature.

Here is another example. A client in a restaurant is hesitating between two menus:

(137) Menu at 30€: *Cheese and dessert.*

(138) Menu at 25€: *Cheese or dessert.*

The head waiter sees the client hesitating and suggests:

(139) *If you take the Cheese or dessert menu, I will give you both.*

How is this possible? The client understood that if he chose *cheese* OR *dessert* he could not have both. But this conclusion has no logical foundation: it is a cancellable conclusion, because it is an implicature, and implicatures are defeasible.

8 Conclusion

We now have an initial answer about why verbal communication is preferentially implicit: it can be enriched in terms of information – it can provide a reason, for example – and it is cancellable – the speaker can deny having meant what the addressee thinks he is allowed to conclude.

We must now ask how an addressee can trust a speaker who can opt out by denying the implicit content she has invited her addressee to process. The answer to this question must be processed through the following paradox: the addressee must be able to trust the speaker, but he must also be epistemically vigilant – he cannot be naïve. As Hugo Mercier and Dan Sperber (2017) have shown, however, verbal communication is subject to another paradox: in order not to be manipulated, the addressee must be vigilant – he must be able to assess the relevance of the speaker's utterance – but on the other hand, the speaker tends to be lazy.[84] In

---

[84] Other research in Relevance Theory, like that of van der Henst *et al.* (2002), shows that the speaker can make efforts to decrease the addressee's effort and subsequently increase relevance. Their article describes the authors' research on how time is read on analog and digital watches in a variety of settings. See also for new developments Scott, Clark, and Carston (2019).

other words, different behaviours occur according to whether one is a speaker or an addressee: as a speaker we are lazy, and as an addressee we must be vigilant.

We now know that rules governing language structure are not the rules that govern its usage. This conclusion confirms the conclusion of chapter 2: language and communication are two different things. These two chapters have insisted upon the cognitive nature of language and communication. It is now time to investigate their social dimension in chapter 4.

Part II: **Language, society, and discourse**

The second part of this book is devoted to issues that are generally treated outside the domain of linguistics. It is a surprising fact that the traditional agenda of pragmatics does not include three issues that are central to language: first, *language and society*, which sociolinguistics studies second, *discourse*, which encompasses independent areas of language science such as *text linguistics* (van Dijk 1977, de Beaugrande and Dressler 1981) and *discourse semantics* (Kamp and Reyle 1993); and third *literature* – an exception to this trend is the syntactic approach to free indirect style in the research Banfield (1982).

Pragmatics has, however, been used in recent decades to investigate issues that involve society, discourse, and literature. The next three chapters will not present an exhaustive discussion of all possible approaches to such topics as politeness, discourse, and literature. Nor will they deal with new issues like impoliteness (Culpeper 2011), critical discourse analysis (Fairclough 2010), and traditional literary issues such as dialogism and polyphony (Holquist 2002).

In chapters 4, 5 and 6 I will adopt a pragmatic approach to the relationship between language and society, addressing the issues of culture, linguistic variation, politeness, and the pragmatic approach to discourse, as well as discussing a general approach to non-ordinary usage of languages in literature, including narration and free indirect style. These topics are extensions of cognitive pragmatics' departure in new directions like discourse comprehension, discourse connectives, and tenses (Reboul and Moeschler 1998a), narration and causality (Moeschler 2019), the pragmatics of time (Wilson and Sperber 2012: chapter 8), and free indirect style (Reboul, Delfitto, and Fiorin 2016).

In chapter 7, I will expand the domain of pragmatics to explore societal issues including the media, political discourse, and messages on the Internet, adopting a *superpragmatic* approach to verbal communication in order to account for areas that go beyond meaning.

Chapter 4
The social dimension of language

The vision of language presented up to this point is not unanimously accepted in language science. Nor do the social sciences adhere to it.[85] One of the dogmas of certain currents in the social sciences embraces the primacy of culture over nature, and in terms of language of the primacy of cultural facts over biological ones.

The scientific community is divided on the issue of the human and social sciences, particularly as concerns their status as true sciences. In the 1990s a book by Alan Sokal and Jean Bricmont (1999) caused a major controversy when the authors demonstrated that certain areas of the humanities and social sciences were willing to publish anything and everything that adhered to the dogma of post-modernist ideology.

The issues are different in 2021: they imply different positions on questions of language. Two major orientations have emerged. These have led to disagreement in the human and social sciences as well as in linguistics: the social science approach lies on one side of the divide, and the cognitive science approach on the other. In the former case language is defined as a social phenomenon, and in the latter as a biological fact.[86]

The roadmap seems clear in terms of what has been discussed so far in this book, but things are actually more complicated. The Chomskyan approach is aligned with the biology side, as illustrated by the biolinguistics program. But what about Pinker and Jackendoff's alternative approach? At first glance it would appear to belong to the same paradigm – it gives crucial weight to cognition and its specific relationship to language.[87] However, the social dimension is also part of their approach, although this is not explicitly mentioned. Finally, from the pragmatics point of view, the Gricean approach has no cognitive justification, unlike Relevance Theory, which is open to social phenomena – Relevance

---

[85] I here refer to traditional orientations in the social sciences, and not to recent approaches to sociology and anthropology, which aim at the naturalisation of social processes. For this perspective, see Sperber (1996).
[86] See Scott-Phillips (2015) as well as Dan Sperber's research on cognitive anthropology (Sperber 1996).
[87] See Pinker (1995) on language, Pinker (2013), and Jackendoff (1983), (1996), (2002), (2012) on the relationship between language and cognition.

Theory contains all the conceptual material necessary to address the relationship between language and society.[88]

In this chapter I will discuss Edward Sapir's approach to language, which centres on the notion of culture. This will enable me to introduce an anthropological and more radical version of language popularized in the *Sapir-Whorf hypothesis*. I will subsequently introduce the concept of linguistic variation, particularly the difference between a language and its dialects, and the chapter will end with a discussion of the role of politeness in language usage.

1 Language as a social phenomenon

What defines human beings? If you are starting to be convinced by the arguments in this book, you might be tempted to answer that it might be that language is an inherently human characteristic. However, this answer is not generally given. Other answers, all of them serious, are usually mentioned. These include reason, consciousness, laughter, society, tools, and religion.

The argument for reason is certainly the most plausible of all, and is in fact the argument put forward in a book written by Mercier and Sperber (2017). There is little to say about this viewpoint, except that we cannot reason without language: we use language to communicate, convince, and argue in favour of, which is the main theses of Mercier and Sperber's book. For these authors there is no gap between language and reason, only a continuum linked to the properties of human cognition. The argument for consciousness, based on biological knowledge (Edelman 1992), is also a strong one, but it does not explain the relationship between consciousness and language. It is important to realize that, in the domain of contemporary philosophy, philosophy of mind goes hand in hand with philosophy of language.[89] Is laughter specific to human beings? The French Renaissance writer Rabelais thought so, stating in his preface to *Gargantua* that "le rire est le propre de l'homme" [laughter belongs to humankind]. However, large primates also laugh, especially when they are tickled. As far as society is concerned, research by primatologists and ethologists has shown that other species live in societies, often with sophisticated systems of political regulation.[90] The use of tools cannot be used as a criterion, either, because chimps know

---

[88] We must recall that Dan Sperber is an anthropologist, and that his approach stems from the social sciences.
[89] A very good example is given in John Searle's book on intentionality (Searle 1983). For a philosophical approach to consciousness, see also Chalmers (1996). For a general overview of philosophy of language, see Hale and Crispin (1997) and Lepore and Smith (2006).
[90] See de Waal (2002) and (2007).

how to use twigs as tools to catch termites. Finally, the sophisticated belief system that is religion (Boyer 2001) could not have emerged without language.

Language has emerged as a strong candidate for defining the human species. When we take alternatives answers into account, though, language does not appear to be an isolated phenomenon when approached from the cognitive and sociological viewpoints. We know, for instance, that brain areas that are mobilized for the treatment of language largely overlap with those that treat music.[91] On the other hand, language is not restricted to one individual, but shared by all members of humankind. Collective and social dimensions cannot be dissociated from language, though for much of its history the field of linguistics has done everything it can to eliminate them, in keeping with reductionism*, the most widely used scientific method.

In terms of the two main approaches that fashioned language science in the 20th century – Saussure's structuralism and Chomsky's generative grammar – only Noam Chomsky explicitly raised the cognitive and social issue by distinguishing between I- and E-language. That said, his definition of external language has always been more negative than positive: "It's [E-language] a study of how that language faculty is put to use – which makes it external to I-language by definition" (Andor 2004: 101).

We must bear in mind that internal language is the set of linguistic knowledge of an individual, defining what is known as his *idiolect*. The fact that members of a linguistic community share certain aspects of their internal language, which allows them to communicate, is transferred to the domain of external language, or the transfer systems of narrow syntax, via sensorimotor and conceptual-intentional interfaces.

One of the issues in language science, therefore, is to understand how this knowledge, which is specific to individuals because it is specific to their mind/brain, makes it possible to use external language, which in turn permits communication to take place. The traditional answer, given by Ferdinand de Saussure, is that the members of a speech community share a *langue**, defined as a system of signs*, which is composed of a *signifiant** (acoustic image) and a *signifié** (concept) – a social convention –, and termed a treasure, a principle of classification by Saussure:

> Language [*langue*] – and this consideration surpasses all the others – is at every moment everybody's concern; spread throughout society and manipulated by it, language is something used daily by all. Here we are unable to set up any comparison between it and other institutions. The prescriptions of codes, religious rites, nautical signals, etc., involve only a certain number

---

[91] For the relationship between language and music, see Frauenfelder and Delage (2013). For a cognitive approach to music and language, see Arbib (2013).

of individuals simultaneously and then only during a limited period of time; in language [*langue*], on the contrary, everyone participates at all times, and that is why it is constantly being influenced by all. (Saussure 1977: 73–74)

Language [*langue*] is therefore a social institution based on a convention. The stability of the linguistic code over time can be explained by the "collective inertia toward innovation": because the *langue* is a social institution it is stable in social and temporal terms.

At this stage, two questions arise: first, if social inertia generates a stable linguistic system how can we explain that languages evolve and change? Second, how can we explain that a social institution, defined as passive, a treasure, and a principle of classification, may be used in communication? Here is Saussure's answer: the putting into play of the *langue* takes place in the *parole** ('speech'): "The study of speech [*parole*] is then twofold: its basic part – having as its object language [*langue*], which is purely social and independent of the individual – is exclusively psychological; its secondary part – which has as its object the individual side of speech, i.e. speaking, including phonation – is psychophysical" (Saussure 1977: 18).

A paradox arises here: the social part of language, *la langue*, is passive – it is merely a principle of organization, not a set of rules for usage – whereas the active part of language, speech (*la parole*) at the origin of the speech acts, is individual. The American linguist William Labov has formulated this paradox, called the *Saussurian paradox*, in the following way (Labov 1972a: 185–186):

> Saussure conceived of linguistics as one part of "une science qui étudie la vie des signes au sein de la vie sociale". Yet curiously enough, the linguists who work within the Saussurian tradition (and this includes the great majority) do not deal with social life at all: they work with one or two informants in their offices, or examine their own knowledge of *langue*. Furthermore, they insist that explanations of linguistic facts be drawn from other linguistic facts, not from any "external" data on social behavior.

> The development depends on a curious paradox. If everyone possesses a knowledge of language structure, if *langue* is "un système grammatical existant virtuellement dans chaque cerveau" (p. 30), one should be able to obtain the data from the testimony of any one person – even oneself. On the other hand, data on *parole*, or speech, can only be obtained by examining the behavior of individuals as they use language. Thus we have the *Saussurian paradox*: the social aspect of language is studied by observing any one individual, but the individual aspect only by observing language in its social context. The science of *parole* never developed, but this approach to the science of language has been extremely successful over the past half-century.

Labov means that *the study of language in its social context*, which should have resulted in a true science of language, did not emerge until the 1960s. Labov's research attempted to fill this gap, and it was the first time a sociolinguistic approach to language, known as *variationist sociolinguistics**, was used. Before discussing the variationist approach, I must mention an earlier approach, which was borrowed from anthropology and resulted in hypotheses about language that differed greatly from Saussure and Chomsky's traditional approaches.

2 The Sapir-Whorf hypothesis and linguistic relativism

A commonplace about the relationship between language and culture stems directly from ethnolinguistic research, and particularly from the work of linguists Edward Sapir (1884–1939) and Benjamin Lee Whorf (1897–1941), who made a major impact on 20-century language studies. Their approach contrasts with traditional methods in linguistics represented by Saussure and Chomsky. The issues implied by *linguistic determinism**, and its weaker form, *linguistic relativism**, address the relationship between language and culture in a precise way, as well as focusing on language and society.

For Sapir, language is a feature possessed by all human groups. Its link to culture appears to be causal: "Of all aspects of culture it is a fair guess that language was the first to receive a highly developed form and that its essential perfection is a prerequisite to the development of culture as a whole" (Sapir 1931: 155).

What are the aspects of language that demonstrate its interaction with culture? Language, according to Sapir, is a symbolic system consisting of a phonetics, a grammar and a vocabulary. Of these three features, vocabulary is the best candidate for expressing the relationship with culture.

> It is the vocabulary of a language that most clearly reflects the physical and social environment of its speakers. The complete vocabulary of a language may indeed be looked upon a complex inventory of all the ideas, interests, and occupations that take up the attention of the community, and were such a complete thesaurus of the language of a given tribe at our disposal, we might to a large extent infer the character of the physical environment and the characteristics of the culture of the people making use of it. (Sapir 1912: 228)

The fact that vocabulary allows access to the physical and social environment of a community (its culture) should lead us to wonder about the relationship between the meaning of a word and its reference. According to Sapir, cultures are differentiated by their lexicons, and the difference in the lexicons of languages can be explained by their cultures. At this point the obvious circularity between language and culture becomes apparent: language determines culture and culture determines language. Whorf's version, which popularised *linguistic relativism**, provides an explanation of this issue. Steven Pinker cites a well known passage by Whorf, which explicitly shows the relationship between language and culture:

> We dissect nature along lines laid down by our native languages. The categories and types that we isolate from the world of phenomena we do not find there because they stare every observer in the face; on the contrary, the world is presented in a kaleidoscopic flux of impressions which has to be organized by our minds – and this means largely by the linguistic systems in our minds. *We cut nature up, organize it in concepts, and ascribe significances as we do, largely because we are parties to an agreement to organize it in this way – an agreement that holds throughout our speech community and is codified in the patterns of our language.* (italics are mine) (Benjamin Lee Whorf, quoted by Pinker 1995: 59–60)

If we replace *patterns of our language* by *vocabulary*, we can summarise the so-called Sapir-Whorf hypothesis in this way:

(140) The Sapir-Whorf hypothesis
    (i) The vocabulary of a language organises speakers' concepts of that language.
    (ii) The function of concepts is to dissect reality and to give access to representations of the world that are linguistically determined.

This approach gives rise to the two theses:

(141) (i) Languages are different not only in their lexicon, their phonology, and their grammar, but also in their way of organising the world through concepts, which are the mental counterparts of lexical units.
    (ii) The lexical variation in languages can be explained by the variation in how linguistically determined cultures dissect reality.[92]

Steven Pinker, like Pullum (1991), reminds us of the inaccuracy of linguistic determinism by citing the example of the Inuit language's snow vocabulary:

> Speaking of anthropological canards, no discussion of language and thought would be complete without the great Eskimo Vocabulary Hoax. Contrary to popular belief, the Eskimos do not have more words of snow than do speakers of English. They did not have four hundred words for snow, as it has been claimed in print, or two hundred, or one hundred, or forty-

---

[92] Frederick Newmeyer remarked that the Sapir-Whorf hypothesis can be represented in a different way, by taking into account functional categories (*closed lexicon*, such as tenses, prepositions, determiners, pronouns, etc.) rather than lexical units (the so-called *open lexicon*) which vary from one language to the other and are presumed to build thought. Steven Pinker wrote an outstanding summary of Whorf's analysis of the Apache language (Pinker 1995: 61): "His assertions about Apache psychology are based entirely on Apache grammar – making his argument circular. Apaches speak differently, so they must think differently. How do we know that they think differently? Just listen to the way they speak".

eight, or even nine. One dictionary puts the figure at two. Counting generously, experts can come up with about a dozen, but by such standards English would not be far behind, with *snow, sleet, slush, blizzard, avalanche, hail, hardpack, powder, flurry, dusting*, and coinage of Boston's WBZ-TV meteorologist Bruce Schwoegler, *snizzling*. (Pinker: 1995: 64)

Despite these reservations, the radical version of the Sapir-Whorf hypothesis has had an enormous impact on the social sciences and the humanities. One of its strongest implications is the thesis that claims that speakers of one language think in a different way from those of another language.[93]

Now, if language determines culture, it should be possible to observe a difference in ways of reasoning. We ought, for instance, to see a difference in the way Western cultures and Asian cultures solve problems. The possibility of such a difference is significant in certain anthropology research – this is the *culturalist* thesis – which has recently been challenged from an *evolutionary* cognitive perspective. Jean-Baptiste van der Henst and his French and Japanese colleagues have experimentally tested groups of French and Japanese students on their capacity to solve contradictions (van der Henst et al. 2006). The researchers hoped that either the culturalist or the evolutionary thesis would be confirmed by the experiment. According to the culturalist point of view, Asian people seek a compromise between two contradictory points of view, while Western people tend to follow the logical principle of non-contradiction – either a proposition is true or it is false, but it cannot be both true and false at the same time. In other words, "it is false that *p* is true and *not-p* is true" is a tautology, or a proposition that is always true. The evolutionary thesis, on the other hand, stipulates that when a contradiction arises in a communication context, there is a universal tendency to give more weight to one's own beliefs than to the beliefs of the other, to avoid falling into the trap of deceptive information. The data obtained in the experiment tends to confirm the evolutionary approach and therefore to refute the culturalist thesis.

This type of experimental research is crucial to serious examination of important issues such as the hypotheses implied by linguistic determinism. These relativist theses are so strongly anchored in our culture that only empirical and experimental data is able to contradict them. But even when this data is cited, scepticism still occurs. I will now mention several complementary elements that allow the veracity of the relativist theses to be called into question.

One consequence of the Sapir-Whorf thesis is the idea that some words and expressions are *not translatable*. According to this line of thought, translation

---

[93] Fortunately, there are less radical versions of relativism, represented by the research of Stephen Levinson (2003) on space.

is merely a process of interpretation, because there can be no correspondence between the meaning of the terms in one language and their counterparts in other languages, at least for some of them. This thesis, which makes literal translation impossible, is worth spending some time on.[94]

Firstly, it supposes that sentences in a given language that have been translated necessarily have a complete semantic and literal representation, and that access to this interpretation is necessary for accessing its non-literal meaning. But we have already seen that the relationship between what the speaker says and what she means is more complex than that, and especially that interlocutors need not access identical representations of their utterances' linguistic meaning.

Secondly, the relativist thesis implies a biunivocal correspondence between the lexicon of a language and its corresponding concepts. Put in another way, concepts that correspond to words in one language are necessarily different from concepts associated with the "corresponding words" in another language. A great number of linguistic arguments have been given to support this claim. One of them, about the many words for snow in Inuit, was mentioned above, although critical studies have shown that these many words do not exist. A second type of argument cites the differences in colour terms from one language to another. A frequent example is about the colours blue and green: Russian has two words for blue, and Korean has two words for green. This fact gives rise to the following question: do Russian and Korean speakers see colours that are different from those seen by speakers of other languages? A positive answer, which would legitimate the causal relation between lexicon and concept as well as the strong version of linguistic relativism, would then lead to another question: are these speakers physiologically different from the speakers of other languages? The question is obviously absurd. English also contains many colour terms: *carmine, vermilion, Sienna*, etc. for *red*, and numerous variants for *blue*, including *sky blue, dark blue, navy blue, light blue*, etc. We also know, thanks to the research of Brent Berlin and Paul Kay (1969), that the human perceptive system can distinguish eleven colours, even if languages do not all have the same number of colour terms. The most important finding about colour terms is that they make up a system: they are ordered in relation to one other. Berlin and Kay observed that the 98 languages investigated have between two and eleven basic colour terms. English contains *black, white, red, yellow, green, blue, brown, purple, pink, orange,* and *grey*. Moreover, when a language has only two colour terms, one designates light colours (*white*), and the other dark colours (*black*). When a third term appears, it is always *red*. The fourth term is either *yellow* or *green*. Then come first blue and

---

[94] Vladimir Nabokov is known to have preferred word for word translations of his works.

then *brown*. *Orange, pink, purple,* and *grey* make up a series that exists only if other colours (*white, black, red, yellow, green, blue, brown*) exist in that language.

This example leads to the conclusion that the relativist hypothesis cannot be applied to colour terms. Colour terms do not determine colour perception: our overall system of perception of colours determines how we classify the world in terms of colours.

3 The reasons for the success of the relativist thesis

We can now legitimately wonder why the relativist thesis resists the counterarguments and evidence that refute it. The relativist thesis endorses a very strong thesis about language, about which I have already expressed doubt. This thesis is an extreme formulation of the code model, which is known as *autonomy of meaning**:

(142) Autonomy of meaning
       Meaning is in words.

According to this hypothesis, words contain meaning within themselves, and this meaning does not vary from one speaker to another or from one context to another. This thesis contradicts another thesis, termed *contextual dependency**:

(143) Contextual dependency
       Meaning depends on context.

As you may have guessed, if we believe that verbal communication uses two models of communication, the code model and the inferential model, we must lean towards contextual dependency, because complete sharing of semantic representations is not necessary to ensure successful communication.

I will give one example that favours autonomy of meaning, and another that favours contextual dependency. As you will see, both explanations contain logic and are a priori acceptable. You will see why the argument in favour of autonomy of meaning is familiar to us. We will begin with the example that allows us to understand contextual dependency. The linguist George Lakoff imagined the following example: on the breakfast table there are three place settings that include an orange juice, and one that includes an apple juice (Lakoff and Johnson 1980: 12). The hostess says to her guest:

(144) *Please sit in the apple-juice seat.*

The next morning the place settings no longer include fruit juice. However, the guest's seat from the day before can still be called *the apple-juice seat*, even though there is no apple juice there to identify it.

We can now generalise Lakoff's intuition in a way that includes words and their semantics: in the example of the apple-juice seat, the seat in question is still referred to with this expression, even though there is no apple juice on the table, because a salient context, the one in which a glass of apple juice was present, continues to determine the interpretation of the expression.

Now, think about the multiple meanings that a word can have, for instance the noun *bachelor*. You certainly know that if someone is referred to as *a bachelor*, the utterance entails that he is not married:

(145)   a. *The Pope is a bachelor.*
        ENTAILMENT: the Pope is not married
    b. *My sons are bachelors.*
        ENTAILMENT: my sons are not married
    c. *Madonna is a bachelor.*
        ENTAILMENT: Madonna is not married

Now, the ordinary usages of *a bachelor* have other meanings. If Louise says (146) to Julia, she certainly does not want to talk about a man whose only characteristic is that he is unmarried. If that were the case, Louise could have talked about Mary's sixty-year-old neighbour, who has lived in the same apartment with his mother since he was born:

(146)   *Mary is happy: she finally met a bachelor.*

What does Louise mean? She certainly means that the person Mary met, Luke, is young, unattached, and even interested in getting married, in short, an ideal partner for Mary. But none of these properties can be implied by the lexical item *bachelor*: these are contextual meaning extensions, also known as pragmatic enrichments. Deirdre Wilson calls these extensions *ad hoc concepts**. These conceptual representations are constructed in each new context (Wilson 2003). To return to our example, the word *bachelor* is the lexical entry of a lexically encoded concept BACHELOR, which, in the context of the dialogue between Louise and Julia, gives rise to a new ad hoc concept BACHELOR*:

(147)   BACHELOR* = YOUNG, UNATTACHED, INTERESTED IN MARRIAGE

The phenomenon of ad hoc concepts is generalised, and essentially concerns two types of enrichment: *narrowing** and *broadening**. Narrowing consists of understanding a concept in a more precise and more restrictive manner, whereas broadening is the opposite process: understanding a concept in a larger or looser way. For instance, BACHELOR* is a case of narrowing, while usages of words such as *rectangle, raw, Kleenex* are cases of broadening:

(148) a. *My garden is a rectangle* ≠ my garden has four right angles
b. *This steak is raw* ≠ this steak is not cooked
c. *Give me a Kleenex* ≠ give me tissue made by the Kleenex brand.

The theory of ad hoc concepts is a version of Relevance Theory that expands ideas about the relationships between language and communication. The vision of meaning it advocates is radically contextualist – it differentiates between linguistically encoded concepts and contextually inferred concepts – and also tells us something important about language: that the value of a word only makes sense in its usage in context.

We must now answer the question as to why the autonomy of meaning thesis so strongly resists the alternative contextualist thesis: what argument can give credibility to and justify the autonomy of meaning thesis? The answer lies in the repertoire of metaphorical expressions used to describe communication, which strengthen the vision of language according to which "meaning is in words". These metaphorical expressions form a conceptual structure called *conduit metaphor* (Reddy 1979).

The conduit metaphor* consists of a repertoire of frozen metaphors that define communication as the transmission of a message encapsuled into signals: these messages (meanings) are autonomous and individuated, are inserted into words, phrases, clauses, and texts, and are defined as containers. Containers are conveyed from a sender to a recipient, and then are decoded in a process similar to the encoding process. The conduit metaphor corresponds to a "railway" vision of communication. The train travelling from one station to another corresponds to the process of transferring that defines communication. The train is made up of cars, which correspond to containers, and the train cars contain goods and people, which correspond to meanings.

The conduit metaphor is not merely a repertoire of expressions in English, French, and most other Indo-European languages. Its structure can be summarised in three propositions (Lakoff and Johnson 1980: 10):

(149) (i) IDEAS (OR MEANING) ARE OBJECTS.
(ii) LINGUISTIC EXPRESSIONS ARE CONTAINERS FOR MEANING.
(iii) COMMUNICATION IS SENDING.

The first proposition – IDEAS (OR MEANING) ARE OBJECTS – presumes that meanings are autonomous entities; they are not abstractions or words, but things that populate the world. This is the hypothesis of most semantic models, which presume the existence of a relationship of denotation* between a word and the object in the world to which it refers, and in which this mediated relationship is the relationship of meaning.[95]

Secondly, the conduit metaphor presumes that words are containers, or envelopes, for the individuated entities that are meanings. According to this approach, meanings correspond to this apparently simple operation, which combines words and entities in the world. In the end communication is reduced to a transfer of information: nothing is said about the manner of communication, whether it is verbal or not, or whether it acts upon its addressees. The conduit metaphor is therefore a model of communication reduced to its simplest possible form. Some examples follow here (Lakoff and Johnson 1980: 11):

(150) a. *To get an idea across to* someone = an idea is an object, put into words, which is transferred from one individual to another.
 b. *To give someone an idea* = to give an object implies a transfer from one individual to another.
 c. *To put an idea into words* = one gives a linguistic form to one's ideas, identified as objects, and once on paper, they can be transferred to an addressee.
 d. *To capture an idea in words* = one can capture only material entities; ideas are objects that can be put into containers such as words and sentences.

What is the conduit metaphor used for? According to this metaphorical structure, natural languages cause us to think of communication as a conduit, and words are defined as autonomous entities in terms of their meaning. In other words, the above-mentioned English expressions, which are used to speak about communication – and the same is also true of French – confirm the postulate of autonomy of meaning. Michael Reddy (1979: 290) explains the conduit metaphor as follows:

> (1) language functions like a conduit, transferring thoughts bodily from one person to another; (2) in writing and speaking, people insert their thoughts or feelings in the words; (3) words accomplish the transfer by containing the thoughts or feelings and conveying them to others; (4) in listening or reading, people extract the thoughts and feelings once again from the words.

---

95 This version of meaning was popularised in the semiotic triangle by Ogden and Richard ([1923] 1989).

A great number of metaphors discuss communication with terms that are similar to the conduit metaphor. Another example is the *alimentary conduit metaphor* in French (Moeschler 1991). According to this metaphorical system, the sender of the communication is assimilated to a cook, the recipient to a consumer, and the communicated message to the meal that is eaten. These propositions are exemplified by the following alimentary conduit metaphors:

MESSAGES ARE FOOD

(151)   *Sa conférence était une vraie <u>salade</u>.*
        His lecture was a real salad
        'His lecture was incomprehensible.'

(152)   *La discussion a <u>tourné au vinaigre</u>.*
        The discussion has turned to vinegar
        'The discussion soured.'

(153)   *Ses arguments <u>ne manquent pas de goût</u>.*
        his arguments neg lack neg of taste
        'His arguments are interesting.'

THE SENDER IS A COOK

(154)   *Il nous a <u>mitonné</u> un discours <u>aux petits oignons</u>.*
        He us has simmered a discourse with little onions
        'His discourse was excellent.'

(155)   *Il a <u>alimenté</u> la conversation de plaisanteries douteuses.*
        he has fed the conversation with jokes questionable
        'He told bad jokes during the conversation.'

(156)   *Marie nous a <u>concocté</u> un projet original.*
        Mary us has concocted a project original
        'Mary concocted an original project.'

THE RECIPIENT IS A CONSUMER

(157)   *Elle <u>buvait</u> ses paroles en l'écoutant.*
        She drank his words in him listening to
        'She drank his words as she listened to him.'

(158)   *J'ai dû ingurgiter les Principia Mathematica pour l'examen de logique.*
        I have had ingest the Principia Mathematica for the exam of logic
        'I had to read *Principia Mathematica* for the logic exam.'

(159) Coluche a <u>craché dans la soupe</u> lorsqu'il a reçu le César du meilleur acteur.
Coluche has spat in the soup when he has received the César of the best actor
'Coluche bit the hand that fed him when he won the César prize for best actor.'

This first system, which is known as the major framework, is complemented by a second one, the minor framework, which addresses the process of ingesting food:

INGESTION CAUSES PLEASURE

(160) Les nouvelles de Sciascia doivent <u>se déguster</u> lentement.
the short story of Sciascia must themselves taste slowly
'Sciascia's short stories must be read slowly.'

(161) Je <u>me</u> suis <u>régalé</u> de ce poème.
I me am regaled of this poem
'I took pleasure in reading this poem.'

(162) Jean <u>buvait du petit</u> lait en écoutant la conférence.
John drank some whey in listening the lecture
'John took pleasure in listening to the lecture.'

INGESTION CAUSES DISPLEASURE

(163) J'ai dû <u>avaler</u> son explication sans répondre.
I have had swallow his explanation without answering
'I had to swallow his explanation without answering.'

(164) Elle n'a pas <u>gobé</u> son excuse.
she neg has swallowed his excuse
'She didn't accept his excuse.'

(165) Ce qu'il m'a dit m'est <u>resté sur l'estomac</u>.
what he me has told stayed on the stomach
'What he told me troubled me.'

What do these utterances mean? Simply stated, these ordinary metaphors, whose literal meaning is not taken into consideration – one property of idioms is to give direct access to non-literal meaning – make the code model familiar and acceptable as a way of representing how communication and meaning work. These frozen metaphorical structures also help us become familiar with the idea that meaning is located in words. If this idea is acceptable, then we can draw the conclusion that it is indeed language that compels our vision of the world.

This is not my conception of the relationship between language and our representations of the world. Idiomatic expressions and conventional metaphors, however, remind us that linguistic relativism is generated by the representation of the world that language gives us. Given these conditions, it is not surprising that the relativist approach appears both familiar and acceptable.[96]

4 Linguistic variation: The example of French

What is a language? The following formula is attributed to Maréchal Lyautey (1854–1934): "Une langue nationale est un dialecte qui dispose d'une armée et d'une marine" [A national language is a dialect that has an army and a navy].[97] As we have seen above, a national language is at best what Chomsky referred to as an E-language. One may wonder whether there is middle position between the extreme view of a non-linguist like Maréchal Lyautey and that of an influential linguist like Noam Chomsky. As we observed in chapter 1, a language is not associated with a country or a nation: it is merely the history of the 19th and 20th centuries that causes us to think so.[98]

We know that French is spoken outside France, and if French speakers tend to forget that other languages are spoken in France (Arabic, African languages, Basque, Alsatian, Turkish, etc.), this is because only French is a national language in France.[99] Now, does this imply that homogeneity is necessary, and that only French should be spoken in France? Of course not. Varieties of French do exist, though they are mainly phonetic and lexical. We will now examine two examples of phonetic variation.[100]

---

96 I will return to relativism in chapter 6 as part of a discussion on metaphors.
97 The American tradition in the history of linguistics attributes this quotation to Uriel Weinreich.
98 For an accessible history of the French language, see Rey (2007).
99 We should recall that France only signed the European Charter for Regional or Minority Languages in 1999, and that it stated a certain number of reservations about the Charter. One of these concerned the equality of all of citizens in the eyes of the law, and the recognition of only one French people, which in turn implied only one language.
100 See the webpage https://francaisdenosregions.com/2017/07/06/ces-mots-qui-ne-se-prononcent-pas-de-la-meme-facon-dun-bout-a-lautre-de-la-france/, consulted on the 7th of October 2020. This example is taken from the webpage https://www.swissinfo.ch/fre/multiculturalit%C3%A9_

The first is the pronunciation of the round and velar vowel *o*. A phonetic distinction can be made between two kinds of pronunciation: one is open (this is known as a semi-open vowel), and the other is closed (known as a semi-closed vowel). The interesting point here is that this difference occurs in two different geographical areas of France. *Rose*, for instance, has an open *o* in south-eastern France – [ɔ] in IPA – whereas in the rest of the country the pronunciation is closed – [o] in IPA. These two variants have no phonological effect: [o] and [ɔ] are not phonemes* in French: they work as phonemes only in areas where speakers distinguish between the two – for instance in regions where the words *seau* [o] 'bucket' and *sot* [ɔ] 'stupid' are pronounced differently and have different meanings. This is the case in French-speaking Switzerland, for example. A similar example in another geographical area concerns the pronunciation of a consonant that is unpronounced elsewhere. French speakers pronounce *vingt ans* 'twenty years' as [vɛ̃tɑ̃] – the consonant [t] is audible though it is generally unpronounced: this is a typical example of what is called *enchaînement* 'sequencing' in French (Encrevé 1988). We might now wonder how *vingt francs* 'twenty francs' is pronounced, with or without a [t]? Almost all French speakers in France would say [vɛ̃fʀɑ̃], without the [t], whereas in north-eastern France, including French-speaking Switzerland, the pronunciation is [vɛ̃tfʀɑ̃], with a pronounced [t].

Because the two geographical areas of these phonetic contrasts are different – and this is true of all phonetic contrasts in French – this means that the French language is not only phonetically non-homogeneous, but that this non-homogeneity is caused by a variety of factors: each phonetic contrast corresponds to a different map.

Now, one might wonder whether these phonetic variations result in different languages. Certainly not. A criterion that defines the difference between languages and varieties of languages is needed in order to make this answer valid. The French-speaking world is not a good example, because the differences among varieties of French spoken in France, Switzerland, Belgium, Canada, and West Africa are only superficial, and are primarily lexical, phonetic, and prosodic; the grammars of these varieties have few differences from one another. Quebec French is an exception, and contains some grammatical patterns that are not used in Europe: doubling the subject pronoun in *yes/no* questions (166), and the inclusion of a forclusive* adverb to mark negation (167):

---

la-suisse-un-pays-avec-toujours-plus-de-langues/43087612. See Avanzi (2017) for a cartography of regional French.

(166) *Tu connais- tu Simon?*
You know you Simon?
'Do you know Simon?'

(167) *Je connais pas personne.*
I know neg nobody
'I know nobody.'

These varieties exist and are often an important part of their speakers' identity, but unlike French West Indian creoles, for example, they are not different languages, because they satisfy the traditional criterion for defining a language, inter-comprehension.[101]

To illustrate this criterion, imagine that you are an English speaker, that you speak and understand French as a second language, and that you are going to Geneva, in French-speaking Switzerland. Do you think you will have problems conversing with French-speaking people in Geneva? If you answer yes, it is due to your belief that differences in pronunciation – what is informally called an *accent* – and lexicon – French speakers in Switzerland say *septante* 'seventy' instead of *soixante-dix*, for instance – are insurmountable obstacles to verbal communication. I imagine you will be amused by the Swiss accent, but your ability to understand words and sentences will be unaffected, and you will only notice a few differences in the lexicon, but none in grammar. The internal language of Swiss French-speaking speakers is practically identical to the internal language of speakers from France. To use the terminology introduced in chapter 3, the differences between the two are situated in the interface, or the faculty of language in the broad sense (FLB), rather than the faculty of language in the narrow sense (FLN). A language's homogeneity is thus the result of standardisation, and the long history of French has almost completely removed variational differences.

The statement above is not totally accurate, however: there are indeed varieties of French. Because they are not officially acknowledged, however, they have no institutional space in which to express themselves. Varieties of speech used by those who live in suburban ghettos (*banlieues* in French) are both a social and a professional handicap (Bentolila 2007).[102] However, the situation in France is not one of diglossia*, which means that such varieties are generally assessed as unacceptable from the social, cultural, and even political points of view. Indeed,

---

101 Note that some movies made in Quebec are subtitled in standard French in France. Certain series made in Quebec and broadcast in France are also dubbed in standard French.
102 This variety of French is generally termed as *parler des banlieues* 'suburban ghetto speech'.

the contrast between varieties of French and standard French remains problematical, especially because these varieties are not in competition with a standard language like they are in German-speaking Switzerland, where standard German is used as a *lingua franca*.

The sociolinguist William Labov has demonstrated that the relationship between linguistic innovations and solidarity within a social group leads to differentiated linguistic behaviour: "Any group of speakers of language X which regards itself as a close social unit will tend to express its group solidarity by favoring those linguistic innovations which set it apart from other speakers who are not part of the group" (Labov 1972a: 314). Is the linguistic situation of varieties of the French language comparable to that of Afro-American English Vernacular (AAVE) (Labov 1972b)?[103] This question is difficult to answer because of insufficient data about the situation in France. While Labov has done major research on AAVE, very little variationist research has been carried out on the French used by those living in suburban ghettos.[104] The best way to answer our question, therefore, is to explore Labov's conclusions.

5 The example of AAEV as a linguistic variety

The research Labov carried out in 1965 was generally considered as a serious alternative to the Chomskyan paradigm, which was introduced through the publication of *Syntactic structures* in 1957 and *Aspects of the theory of syntax* in 1965, and hence began to develop in American and European universities.

As we will see, Labov's research was not anti-Chomskyan. On the contrary, it attempted to influence sociolinguistics, the study of language in its social context. Here is how Labov described his research (Labov 1972b: xiv):

> In 1965, we began research supported by the Office of Education into the differences between the vernacular language of south-central Harlem and the standard English of the classroom (...). Our major concern was the reading failure that was painfully obvious in the New York City schools. Did dialect differences have anything to do with it? [. . .] But as we proceeded, it seemed ever clearer that the major reading problems did not stem from structural interference in any simple sense, and our concern with the uses of the vernacular increased. One major conclusion of our work (...) is that the major causes of reading failure are political and cultural conflicts in the classrooms, and dialect differences are important because they are symbols of this conflict.

---

103 Labov's original publications in the 1970s used the acronym BEV for Black English Vernacular.
104 One exception is the corpus *Multicultural Paris French*, written under the supervision of Françoise Gadet and her colleagues, whose results are presented in Gadet (2017).

The reading failure of a well-defined population of students had more than one cause, but the dialect of young blacks, Black English Vernacular or BEV, known as AAEV or Afro-American English Vernacular today, played a role. Indeed, Labov (1972b: xiii) identified this well-defined dialect through linguistic description techniques: "By "black English vernacular" we mean the relatively uniform dialect spoken by the majority of black youth in most parts of the United States today, especially in the inner city areas of New York, Boston, Detroit, Philadelphia, Washington, Cleveland, Chicago, St. Louis, San Francisco, Los Angeles, and other urban centers".

Labov's research addressed two main questions: (i) is BEV [AAEV] a different language from standard English? (ii) is BEV [AAEV] the main cause of the reading failure of young blacks? The first question was formulated in this way: "Is BEV [AAEV] a separate language, so that standard English has to be taught to black children as a different system with the same techniques that are used to teach French and Spanish? Or is BEV [AAEV] system basically a variant of other English systems, that can easily be placed in relation to it?" (Labov 1972b: 36). Labov chose the second response, which addresses the status of language varieties traditionally known as *dialects**. However, Labov observed in his study of spontaneous discourse, especially ritual insults, which resulted in an important chapter of *Language in the Inner City*, that some aspects of BEV [AAEV] belonged to a distinct system, especially in terms of time and aspect categories, those grammatical categories that enable the expression of narration in discourse: "BEV [AAEV] is a distinct system from other dialects in several important grammatical categories of the tense and aspect systems" (Labov 1972b: 61). We will return to this issue in chapter 5.

Labov addresses the second question ("is BEV [AAEV] the main cause of the reading failure by young black people?") in sociological and cultural terms (Labov 1972b: xvi): "the major problem in reading failure is the political and cultural conflict within the classroom". The problem is therefore not simply linguistic – this situation is close to diglossia – but is linked to social and cultural issues and even with ethnic identity: "In the development of the New York city vowel system, we find that ethnic identity plays an important role – more important than the socioeconomic class, for some items" (Labov 1972a: 297).

How is it possible for a speaker, whatever her social status and culture, to be confronted with several linguistic varieties? The first and obvious answer, which makes the question trivial, is that the speaker must be in an environment where several linguistic varieties coexist. For Labov, whose approach on this point is compatible with Chomsky's, the question is not categorized as performance, but as competence: "We will argue that nativelike command of heterogeneous structures is not a matter of multidialectalism or "mere" performance, but is part of a unilingual linguistic competence" (Weinreich, Labov, and Herzog 1968: 101).

If there is an innate capacity to master several dialects, or several variants of the same language, then this capacity does not only play a role in the manner in which speakers manage the mastery of several languages in variable social and cultural contexts – we should recall that the situation of the majority of speakers in the world is multilingualism – but also in terms of our general cognitive capabilities. It is interesting here to measure the dimensions of the questions addressed, which involve both cultural and biological evolution: "(...) I am inclined to believe that the development of linguistic differences has positive value in human cultural evolution – and that cultural pluralism may even be a necessary element in the human extension of biological evolution" (Labov 1972a: 324).

In other words, variation is a fact that stems from culture as well as from biology – we know that variation in nature is a biological fact, caused by mutations. This fact strongly impacts the manner in which we can retrospectively think about linguistic variation, both in contexts of diglossia and of non-diglossia.

6 A question of politeness

A major area of research in language science focuses on the phenomena of politeness*, which stems from sociolinguistics. We will look at where interest in politeness originated later. First, however, I will explain how this issue is framed.

When I addressed language usage in chapter 3, I introduced the idea of cooperation to explain verbal communication. But I did not go into the social rules that regulate our behaviour. Firstly, except in certain cases brought on by exhaustion, stress, and feelings of injustice, our behaviour in verbal interactions is polite and civilised.[105] Secondly, politeness rules exist in every culture, but differ from one culture to another: we have all acted in a way we thought was polite and respectful only to find it had counterproductive results. And lastly, is politeness in human societies governed by universal principles? We will learn that this is indeed the case, despite the variety of politeness rules in different cultures.

Here are two examples in which behaviour considered in one culture as polite can be interpreted as impolite or rude in another. The cultures in these examples are French culture and the culture of Maghreb countries.

---

105 Trump's behaviour towards Joe Biden during the debate broadcast on 30 September 2020 was harshly criticised because he did not respect any rules of interaction and politeness. Since it was the first time that such disrespect for social rules had occurred during a presidential campaign, Trump's behaviour gave rise to a good deal of commentary from analysts, journalists, and people all over the world.

In the late 1970s, some friends and I took a holiday in Tunisia to visit a Tunisian friend. Ahmed had spent several years studying and working in Switzerland. He was a civil servant in the Tunisian Ministry of Finance and was supporting his mother and younger brother. Tunisia was a relatively liberal country then (Bourguiba was its President), and overall the strongest restrictions were social – for instance, women could not live alone without being thought of as prostitutes. We did not arrive empty-handed, because at this time it was usual to offer gifts to one's host. We gave him a bottle of Swiss wine and a bottle of whisky, thinking these gifts would remind him of Switzerland. We were very surprised to see our host's panic: alcohol was not allowed in a Muslim home. Our error was to believe that Swiss rules of politeness would also apply to someone living in North Africa who had spent two years in a European country. In other words, we were very far from thinking that our friend would now follow Tunisian rules of behaviour. It suddenly dawned on us that we couldn't behave in a Muslim country like we did in an occidental Christian country.[106]

The second example is similar. I was invited to give a series of lectures in another Maghreb country, and asked for some help at the airport, which was far from my final destination, especially because I was arriving late in the evening. Here is my email exchange with my host (Moeschler 2004: 64–65):

(168) Jacques: *Can you tell me how to get from X airport to Y?*
Maghreb colleague: *Concerning travelling from the airport to Y, you can take a train at the airport, with a change at Z station and you will arrive at Y downtown station, 2 minutes from the hotel.*

I was surprised to realize that my colleague responded to the literal meaning of my speech act, a question, rather than to its implicit meaning, a request for help, in other words a request for a ride at the airport. The situation was resolved when I explicitly asked for help.

Why was my request not understood? In fact, it *was* understood correctly, but another rule of politeness, which was not made explicit, came into play: my colleague could not drive at night, and it was impossible for him to pick me at the airport. But it was also impossible for him to confess this. We were faced

---

106 A more recent similar example occurs in the Netflix TV show *Emily in Paris*, in which a young American woman who works for a marketing company transfers to Paris to work in a French company recently taken over by Americans. Emily experiences many difficulties in social situations and situations of personal interaction, until her French colleagues tell her that her behaviour is rude and impolite from a French perspective: she lives in order to work whereas her French colleagues work in order to live.

with a communication conflict: for reasons of politeness, I could not make my request explicit, and for reasons of politeness it was impossible for my colleague to explain why my request could not be granted.

The notion of politeness is not completely removed from the notion of cooperation, however. In his well-known article *Logic and Conversation*, Grice refers to other aesthetic, social and moral maxims, including the maxim of politeness "Be polite" (Grice 1975: 47). But for Grice, this type of maxim gives rise to non-conversational implicatures, because conversational implicatures result from using a conversational maxim. Although Grice does not give examples of how this maxim is used in verbal communication, we can hypothesise that the alternation of the French second person pronouns *tu/vous* 'you', referring to the addressee, results from this maxim. A speaker who uses *vous* '2pl-Pro' is more polite than a speaker who uses *tu* '2sg-Pro'. Now, we know that the rules are more complex in French: the use of *tu* vs. *vous* is associated with such principles as proximity and solidarity. Colleagues at work use *tu* because there are close and experience solidarity for one another; hierarchical relationships, on the other hand, imply distance and non-solidarity, and trigger the use of *vous*, as in (169):[107]

(169) Dean: *Professeur Moeschler, je vous remercie de vos années de service.*
        'Professor Moeschler, I thank you for your years of service.'

Grice's idea has been developed by linguists, who suggest a linguistic justification for the concept of politeness. Robin Lakoff was one the first to postulate a Politeness Principle, which she presented in three maxims (Lakoff 1973):

(170) Maxims of politeness (Lakoff 1973)
    a. Distance: "don't impose": maintain a distance from your audience.
    b. Deference: "give options": allow the audience to accept or refuse.
    c. Camaraderie: "make the audience feel good": be familiar, nice and friendly.

These maxims allow one to understand why indirect speech acts are used in requests, for example. By asking a question like the one in (171) rather than giving an order like in (172), the speaker does not impose herself. She does not present herself as an authority figure (distance): she allows the address to choose

---

[107] To pursue this point, it is always surprising but pleasant to receive emails from African students using my first name and the use of the familiar form *tu*, as in (i):

(i) *Professeur Jacques, voudrais-tu diriger ma thèse de doctorat?*
    'Professor Jacques, would you supervise my PhD thesis?'

whether to make a positive or a negative response (deference), and she does not make him uncomfortable (camaraderie), like an authoritarian father might do at table by giving orders rather than polite requests:

(171) *Could you pass the salt?*

(172) *Pass the salt!*

At almost the same time, the English linguist Geoffroy Leech presented two maxims of politeness in his article *Language and Tact* (Leech 1980: 110–111): the maxim of tact and the meta-maxim of tact:

(173) Tact maxim
       ASSUME THAT YOU ARE THE AUTHORITEE AND THAT YOUR INTERLOCUTOR IS THE AUTHORITOR.

(174) Tact meta-maxim
       DON'T PUT YOUR INTERLOCUTOR IN A POSITION WHERE EITHER YOU OR HE HAVE/HAS TO BREAK THE TACT MAXIM.

The tact maxim is another way of explaining the usage of indirect speech acts such as (175), which contrasts with (172) and (176). The tact meta-maxim also explains why imperative or affirmative forms are not tactful:

(175) *Will you give me the salt?*

(176) *I want you to give me the salt.*

We have reached the temporary conclusion that the social usage of language implies principles such as politeness. But none of these three approaches (Grice's, Lakoff's, or Leech's) explains why social interaction is governed by politeness, or whether maxims of politeness are complementary to maxims of conversation. The emerging picture is somewhat confusing, and needs clarification.

The adoption of Ervin Goffman's concept of *face** resulted in a universal theory of politeness at the end of the 1970s and in the 1980s. All current research on politeness refers to the model developed by Penelope Brown and Stephen Levinson (Brown and Levinson 1987), mainly because this model presents itself as universal and independent of any particular culture.

7 Face and face-work

The sociologist Erwin Goffman (1922–1982), who initiated the micro-sociological approach to human interaction, greatly influenced dialogue and conversation analysis* by introducing the notions of *face** and *face-work**. Here is his definition of face (Goffman 1972: 5): "The term *face* may be defined as the positive social value a person effectively claims for himself by the line others assume he has taken during a particular contact." The notion of face is commonly used in a non-technical way to describe the position of a participant to an interaction: *to lose face* means "to be in wrong face, to be out of face or to be shamefaced" (Goffman 1972: 9). *To save one's face* on the other hand means not losing face; that is, "the process by which the person sustains an impression for the others that he has not lost face" (Goffman 1972: 9). In a more general way, *face-work* "designate[s] the action taken by a person to make whatever he is doing consistent with face" (Goffman 1972: 12) and refers to all of a participant's actions that aim at not losing face.

How do face-work processes intervene in verbal interaction? Goffman was one of the first scholars to propose a method of analysing verbal interactions that led to an understanding of how face-work processes intervene in dialogue. Goffman distinguishes between two types of interchanges in conversation, which he labels *supportive* and *remedial*.[108] Supportive interchanges* intervene in supportive rituals like greetings. In the following interchange, when *A* asks *B* how he is doing, this is not a question, but a salutation. In a parallel way the answer given is not an answer, but another independent greeting (Goffman 1971: 109):

(177) A: *How are you?*
B: *Fine, thanks.*
 And how are you?
A: *Fine, thanks.*

The second type of interchange is called *remedial**. It consists of repairing a virtual offense caused by a territorial intrusion. Face-work intervenes in situations like this one. According to Goffman (1971: 139), "The function of remedial work is to change the meaning that otherwise might be given to an act, transform-

---

108 "The sequence of acts set in motion by an acknowledged threat to face, and terminating in the re-establishment of ritual equilibrium, I shall call an *interchange*" (Goffman 1972: 19). *Interchange* has often been labelled *exchange*. See chapter 5 for a development.

ing what could be seen as offensive into what can be seen acceptable". Remedial activity typically takes place in what Goffman calls a remedial interchange, or "The total set of moves made in connection with a particular virtual offense" (Goffman 1971: 151). Here is a typical example of remedial interchange, organised into two remedial cycles and four moves – *remedy, relief, appreciation,* and *minimization.* These two cycles (remedy-relief and appreciation-minimisation) make it possible to progress from the violation of a norm (offense) to the resolution of the infraction:[109]

(178) Deed: A virtually offends B
remedy A: *Can I use your phone to make a local call?*
satisfaction B: *Sure, go ahead.*
appreciation A: *That's very good of you.*
minimisation B: *It's okay.*

Because they bring together the processes of face-work, politeness, and communication, remedial interchanges are a way of managing a speaker's territorial offense with implicit communication, because by asking a question, the speaker intrudes into the addressee's territory: "Tact in regard to face-work often relies for its operation on a tacit agreement to do business through the language of hint – the language of innuendo, ambiguities, well-placed pauses, carefully worded jokes, and so on. [. . .] *Hinted communication,* then, is *deniable communication*; it need not to be faced up to" (Goffman 1972: 30; emphasis is mine).

We have now obtained a new explanation for implicit, or indirect, communication. Following Grice's explanation, which introduced the notion of cooperation, and Sperber and Wilson's example, which lends implicit communication more relevance than literal communication, we now possess an interpretation that involves ritual processes of interaction, which include remedial interchanges.

The concepts of face and face-work are a starting point for explaining social and interactional phenomena. What we need, however, is a more consistent and more linguistically grounded conception of the concept of *face*, which is central to explaining the politeness phenomena.

---

[109] "A social norm is that kind of guide for action, which is supported by social sanctions, negative ones providing penalties for infraction, positive ones providing rewards for exemplary compliance" (Goffman 1971: 124).

8 Face and politeness

In the 1980s, a new approach that had an enormous impact on linguistics and pragmatics capitalised both on Grice's theory of meaning, which implies a reflexive process of the speaker's intention recognition, and on Goffman's face-work process, which is based on the notion of face. This approach is the politeness theory set out by Penelope Brown and Stephen Levinson (1987), whose strength lies in its crosslinguistic and intercultural dimensions.[110] Two premises must be stated at this point. The first is about the place of politeness in social relationships, and the second about the role of politeness. For Brown and Levinson, the main issue encountered by social groups is how to control internal aggression and external aggression towards other groups. Concerning the second premise, the place of politeness in verbal interaction, Brown and Levinson state that "politeness, like formal diplomatic protocol (. . .), presupposes that potential for aggression as it seeks to disarm it, and make possible communication between potentially aggressive parties" (Brown and Levinson 1987: 1).

The authors define this approach as a combination of Grice's theory of conversational implicatures, which assumes a cooperative principle and maxims of conversation on one hand, and politeness principles on the other. It is also an alternative to the dominant pragmatic approach in the 1970s, speech act theory, which was developed in particular by the philosopher of languages John Searle (1969, 1979). Searle's speech act theory, which originated in John Austin's William James lectures given in 1955 at Harvard (Austin 1962), hypothesises that utterance comprehension – access to speaker meaning, in other words – occurs through the access of the illocutionary force* of the utterance, which is defined as its value as a speech act such as an order, a promise, an assertion, an excuse, a declaration, etc.[111]

In contrast to speech act theory, Brown and Levinson first began by claiming that verbal communication is principally governed by a type of speech act called *face-threatening act* (FTA*), or acts which threaten face. Secondly, they also divided the concepts of *face* into a *positive face** and a *negative face**: "the desire to be unimpeded in one's action (negative face), and the desire (in some respects) to be approved of (positive face)" (Brown and Levinson 1987: 13). Thirdly, although the notion of face is universal, it results in a wide variety of cultural elaborations.

Here is a brief presentation of Brown and Levinson's model of what a speaker-hearer is (from Brown and Levinson 1987: 59–60):

---

110 The first version of their work was published in Goody (1978).
111 This process is termed *uptake* in Austin (1962).

(179) (i) Every speaker-hearer has a positive and a negative face and is a rational agent.
(ii) The speaker's and hearer's mutual interest is to maintain each other's face.
(iii) Some of their acts threaten face (FTAs).
(iv) The speaker, unless he wants to realise in a maximally efficient manner (bald on record), would minimise the face threat implied by the FTA.
(v) Given that this strategy is known by both the speaker and the hearer, the speaker will choose the less risky strategy.

Negative face therefore corresponds to personal territory, whereas positive face corresponds to the personality, the self-image. More generally speaking, negative face is "the want of 'every adult member' that his actions be unimpeded by other", and positive face is "the want of every member that his wants be desirable to at least some others" (Brown and Levinson 1978: 67).

What are the main threats to face? Brown and Levinson distinguish between acts that threaten positive face and those that threaten negative face. Acts that threaten the *hearer's negative face* are acts which predicate a future act of the hearer and exert pressure on him, such as *orders* and *requests*, *suggestions* and *advice*, *reminders*, *threats*, and *warnings*. But the speaker can also carry out acts that predicate his or her future action, such as *offers* and *promises*, as well as those that predicate a speaker's desire vis-à-vis the hearer, such as *compliments* or the expression of a negative emotion like *hate* or *anger*.

Acts threatening the *speaker's positive face* are those that evidence a speaker's negative evaluation of the hearer's positive face (*disapprobation, criticism, complaint, accusation, insult, challenge*), or the speaker's indifference to the hearer's positive face, such as *irreverence*, the *announcement of bad news*, the introduction of a *dangerous topic*, whether it be emotional or political, or the *interruption of a speech turn*, which clearly shows the speaker's uncooperativeness.

How is FTA used? Brown and Levinson delineate a hierarchy of strategies that explain FTA usage. In a normal context, the one implying vulnerability of face, the speaker will try to avoid face-threatening acts, or will use strategies to minimise the threat. In this case, the speaker does not perform an FTA.

Second, if the speaker chooses to perform an FTA, he can do so overtly, *on record*, or covertly, *off record*. The contrast here is between direct speech acts (180) and allusions (181), in which the FTA is accomplished non-overtly (*off record*). Finally, an *on record* FTA can be *with* or *without redressive action*. A badly-realised FTA, with no redressing action, corresponds to emergencies (182), minimal danger to the hearer's face (183), and situations in which the speaker is hierarchically superior (184):

(180) *I promise to come tomorrow.*

(181) *Damn, I'm out of cash, I forgot to go to the bank today.*

(182) *Go out immediately: there's a fire!*

(183) *Sit down, please!*

(184) *In my office, immediately!*

Third, the speaker can do an FTA *on record* but *with redress*: the speaker does the FTA through an act directed towards the hearer's positive face. This is defined as *positive politeness*. In such cases, the speaker wants what the hearer wants, as in (185):

(185) *If I were you, I would not trust Luke.*

But the speaker can also perform an FTA with a redressive action directed towards the hearer's negative face: *negative face* is based on avoidance, and in this case, negative politeness is equivalent to self-effacement. The FTA can be redressed with apologies (186), deference (187), hedges (188), non-personalisation as passives (189), and softening mechanisms (190):

(186) *Sorry for having been so rude.*

(187) *Can I ask you a question?*

(188) *Do you mind passing me the salt?*

(189) *You're fired!*

(190) *I would like to ask you a question.*

Brown and Levinson observed tension in negative politeness between the desire to communicate overtly (*on record*) and the desire not to impose oneself (*off record*). According to these authors, politeness strategies solutions use conventionalised indirect speech acts, such as *Can you pass the salt?*[112]

This approach to politeness explains human behaviour in social interactions that obey universal rules. For Brown and Levinson, politeness strategies are universal for all languages and cultures.[113] Although their work has produced many examples in a large number of languages, I would like to address the issue of the compatibility between the politeness model and the Gricean model of meaning and communication.

One crucial issue is the blocking of scalar implicatures in politeness contexts. Normally, the usage of the quantifier* *some* implicates *not all*: according to Grice's maxim of quantity – "Make your contribution as informative as is required" (Grice 1975: 45)[114] – a cooperative speaker, by choosing *some*, implicates that she cannot say *all*, and thus implicates *not all*:

(191) Anne: *How was your pragmatics exam?*
      Jacques: *Some students did not pass.*
      IMPLICATURE: not all students passed

The important point is that in a face-threatening context, in which the hearer's positive face is threatened, the scalar implicature *not all* is not drawn, and the hearer has a strong preference for the logical reading *some if not all*. This issue was discovered by Bonnefon, Feeney, and Villejoubert (2009: 251, 255), based on the results of their experiments:

> Imagine that you have joined a poetry club, which consists of five members in addition to you. Each week one member writes a poem, and the five other members discuss the poem in the absence of its author. This week, it is your turn to write a poem and to let the others discuss it. After the discussion, one fellow member confides to you that 'Some people hated your poem.' (…)

---

[112] For the traditional version of indirect speech acts see John Searle's article *Indirect speech acts* (Searle 1979). According to Searle's analysis, indirect speech acts are motivated by their relationship to semantic rules that define speech acts. Acts of request, for instance, can be carried out by questioning a hearer's condition, or his ability to do the requested action. In *Can you pass the salt?*, for example, the question is about the hearer's ability to perform the action. The idiomatic dimension of this formula is due to the conventional relationship of the rule that connects the ability to perform an action and the request to perform it.
[113] The universality of politeness principles in terms of FTAs has been abundantly contested for many decades by research on politeness. See for instance Eelen (2001), Linguistic Politeness Research Group (2011). See also Pinker (2007), and Zufferey, Moeschler, and Reboul (2019), and Reboul (2017a) for a discussion of Pinker's argument.
[114] A simpler version of the first maxim of Quantity is "Give the strongest information".

When X in 'some X-ed' threatens the face of the listener, individuals are less likely to infer that the speaker meant or knew that not all X-ed – and this is because they consider the possibility that the speaker might want to be nice more than to be precise".

In other words, the scalar implicature interpretation (*not all*) is ruled out in favour of the logical reading (*some if not all*) for reasons of politeness.[115]

How can we explain that in face-threatening contexts, the pragmatic meaning of logical words like *some* is cancelled? It is obvious that face-work, which implies minimisation to preserve the hearer's positive face, or his self-image, wins over the process of the working out of the implicature triggered by *some*. This is a situation in which two types of logic clash: the logic of rationality and reasoning is ruled out by the logic of politeness.

This leads to further issues. How do these two types of logic interact? And why are two types of logic necessary? One possible answer can be found in the usage of language in dialogue and discourse.

9 Conclusion

In this chapter, we have seen that, no matter which theory of language is adopted and no matter which theory of communication is employed to understand language usage, the social dimension of language must be taken into account. The central question is whether this dimension is anchored in the linguistic code or whether this dimension is linked to language usage. Sociolinguistic answers tend to adopt the first alternative, while recent research in pragmatics goes in the other direction. I will go in the second direction myself for the remainder of this book.

---

115 See Mazzarella (2015) for a detailed analysis, and Feeney and Bonnefon (2012) for similar results about *or* scalar implicature. For a critical discussion of threatening and boosting contexts, see also Terkourafi, Weissman, and Roy (2020).

Chapter 5
Language and discourse

Everyone has experienced strong contrast between linguistic competence* and discourse competence*. The most striking example for French readers is Patrick Modiano, winner of the 2014 Nobel Prize in literature, who was interviewed on a literary talk-show in 1995.[116] Patrick Modiano is universally recognised as a great writer, but is incapable of speaking in a fluent and consistent manner. We all know people who are extremely good at writing but poor at speaking, as well as good speakers who are unable to write in an intelligible and coherent way. Under no circumstances do these people suffer from a linguistic handicap – their linguistic competence is not at stake – but they do have difficulties in their discursive performances.

Such extreme divergence between competence and performance leads us to the issue of discourse, and in particular to what some scholars call *discourse competence**. Is there, along with the faculty of language, an ability to organise, plan, produce, and understand discourses?

Before going into this question, I would like to contextualise the discourse issue with a little story. About twenty-five years ago, a French journal in applied linguistics, *Pratiques*, asked me for a research article on philosophy papers written by high school students before and after they attended classes on discourse connectives such as *mais* 'but', *parce que* 'because', *donc* 'therefore', and their roles in written discourse (Moeschler 1994). My job was to determine whether these discourse connectives improved the quality of their texts (called *dissertations* in French educational terminology). The assumption to be tested was the following: the insertion of discourse connectives in students' texts would improve their discursive quality.

It was of course impossible to accomplish this task in a serious way, but I was at least able to show one thing: the insertion of connectives like *mais* 'but', *parce que* 'because', and *therefore* 'therefore', etc. only emphasised the argumentative weakness of the texts I examined. Why? Simply because connectives imply precise instructions, and these instructions suppose that the contents expressed in the sentences can be connected by the connective as required. The utterances (192) and (193) are comprehensible with or without a connective, but the connective creates a shorter path between expressed and inferred contents (Moeschler 2018a):

---

[116] Apostrophes, by Bernard Pivot, on Antenne 2. See https://www.ina.fr/video/I05124124 for one minute of this interview.

(192) *John fell: the pavement was icy.*

(193) *John fell because the pavement was icy.*

On the other hand, the insertion of a connective does not make things clearer in the following examples:

(194) # *John fell. His car broke down.*[117]

(195) # *John fell because his car broke down.*

(196) # *John fell but his car broke down.*

(197) # *John fell; therefore, his car broke down.*

These examples show that connectives do not play a role in discourse quality: if the connected sentences do not make sense, connectives are incapable of improving anything. As filmmakers say, you can't save a movie during the editing process: if the rushes aren't any good, the editing won't improve anything.

The question of the relationship between language and discourse is an important one. One of the most frequent affirmations in *discourse analysis** is that verbal communication does not consist of sentences, but of utterances, and that speakers only rarely produce a single utterance to express their intentions. Conversation analysis has studied certain routines in turn taking, and we can now ask whether these routines have a grammar – a different one from sentence grammar – and whether this grammar is part of a specific competence.

1 Some conversational rules

In traditional *conversation analysis*, which originated in the ethnography of communication (Gumperz and Hymes 1972, Gumperz 1982) and in ethnomethodology (Sacks, Schegloff, and Jefferson 1974, Heritage and Atkinson 1984, Garfinkel 2002), researchers aim to understand the rules of social behaviour through conversation analysis, which Harold Garfinkel calls *ethnomethods**. Here are three rules that conversation analysis has observed.

---

[117] The pound sign # indicates the semantic vs. syntactic oddness of an utterance.

Turn-taking rules: The units of conversation are called *turns*. The issue under consideration is when a speaker can take a turn, or contribute to the conversation. Several rules have been elucidated: (i) a speaker can give the next turn, or select the next speaker; (ii) if the turn is not given, and in order to minimise the risk of gaps and overlaps, the addressee can take his turn, or self-select as the next speaker at a specific moment, which is described as the *transition-relevance place*; (iii) if the turn is constructed in such a way that the current speaker does not select the next speaker, this procedure applies recursively (Sack, Schegloff, and Jefferson 1974: 704).

Here is an illustration of turn-taking which also shows a cultural variation. During my first dinner at my future in-law's house in Paris, the conversation was lively. Everyone contributed to it, generally by interrupting the current speaker. As a French-speaking Swiss citizen living in Paris as a post-doctoral student, I politely waited for the moment when the current speaker had finished in order to self-select. Unfortunately, another speaker always self-selected before I did, and I didn't get a single chance to speak. At the end of the meal I told my fiancée how surprised I was by the conversational rules of her family. Her answer amazed me: "Come on, you shouldn't wait for your turn, you just have to take it!" It dawned on me that in a Parisian family's conversation, the relevant transition place did not have the same location as in a Swiss conversation: the Parisian relevant transition place occurred much earlier than in French-speaking Swiss conversations: the Swiss were slower than the French! What I wrongly believed to be impolite behaviour was merely a difference in conversational rules. This example in variation leads us to an initial conclusion: conversational rules are rules of social behaviour. They are not rules of politeness or linguistic rules.

Adjacency pairs and conditional relevance: Turn-taking in conversation is organised. Some turns form an adjacency pair, or a sequence of turns that are (i) adjacent, (ii) produced by different speakers, (iii) ordered – there is a first and a second part – and (iv) typed – the first part of the turn requires a specific second part. The criterion that governs adjacency pairs is known as *conditional relevance** (Schegloff 1972, Levinson 1983): in an adjacent pair, the first part of the pair creates the expectation and the relevance of the second part. In other words, if the second member of a pair does not occur, and if a first member of a new pair is uttered next, it is understood as the preliminary of the second member of the first pair, whose relevance is presumed. Typical examples are sequences of the Question$_1$-Question$_2$-Response$_2$-Response$_1$ type:

(198) Q$_1$: *Are you going to pragmatics class?*
Q$_2$: *Why?*
R$_2$: *Because I want to talk with you after class.*
R$_1$: *Yes, of course.*

We might wonder why such sequences occur. Why is the answer not reached directly? The model of adjacency pairs does not really provide answers: it is a behavioural routine that does not falsify the principle of conditional relevance. The cooperative principle and the principle of relevance do offer a response, however. A question generally requires an answer that the information available to the speaker does not contain.[118] A *why*-question typically signals that the addressee does not understand why the question was asked. An alternative strategy for a speaker is to immediately give the reason for his question, as in (199). This alternative strategy is also the case for answers that may lack justification, especially when they are negative (200). Note that the addressee can answer negatively by giving the reason for her refusal (201):

(199) Q_1:   *Are you going to pragmatics class? Because I want to talk with you after class.*
         R_1:   *Yes, of course.*

(200) Q_1:   *Are you going to pragmatics class?*
         R_1:   *No.*
         Q_2:   *Why?*
         R_2:   *I have a dentist appointment.*

(201) Q_1:   *Are you going to pragmatics class?*
         R_1:   *I have a dentist appointment.*
         IMPLICATURE: the speaker is not going to pragmatics class

These examples show that conversational routines are about information rather than conversational organisation.

Preference organisation: The third example of conversational rules is *preference organisation**: in an adjacency pair, the second expected part is the preferred and unmarked part. The idea behind markedness theory (Comrie 1976, Levinson 1983) is that one member of a pair (for example in lexical units or morphology) "is felt as more usual, more normal, less specific than the other" (Comrie 1976: 111).[119] In this case it is known as *unmarked*. The other less usual,

---

[118] I exclude rhetorical and exam questions here: rhetorical questions are assertions, and for exam questions the questioner knows, in principle, the answers to the questions.
[119] An application of the markedness theory is the M(anner)-heuristics, given rise to M(anner)-implicatures (Levinson 2000). See the difference between *Bill stopped the car*, implicating "in in a stereotypical manner" and *Bill causes the car to stop*, implicating "in an abnormal way, for instance by the use of the emergency brake".

less normal, and more specific member is known as *marked*, and generally bears formal features (feminine gender in French, and plural inflection in English and French for instance). The same phenomenon has been observed in adjacency pairs: the second, expected part is unmarked and is known as the *preferred* part. The unmarked criterion is satisfied in the following pairs: request-acceptance, offer-acceptance, and invitation-acceptance. When a negative answer is given, however, it is considered to be *dispreferred*. A dispreferred member of a pair is marked: it does not consist, in the request/offer/invitation-refusal sequences, of a simple negative answer like *no*. It has indeed been observed that the dispreferred part has the following features: it is delayed by a pause; it is introduced by a preface (dispreferred markers like *well* and *uh*), by apologies, or by accounts that explain why the dispreferred part was selected (Atkinson and Drew 1979, Pomerantz 1984, Pomerantz and Heritage 2012, Bilmes 2014). A typical dispreferred answer to the pragmatics class example would be (202):

(202) Q_1: *Are you going to pragmatics class?*
R_1: *Well, you know, it's complicated: I have an appointment with my dentist.*

The rule of preference organisation is therefore as follows:

(203) Preference organisation
"Try to avoid the dispreferred action – the action that generally occurs in dispreferred or marked format". (Levinson 1983: 333)

The turn-taking system, adjacency pairs, and preference organisation are all well-attested facts. But are they rules of behaviour, linguistic rules, or discourse rules? Conversational analysis does not only address issues that are traditionally seen as a grammar of conversation; it also addresses the construction of dialogue and conversation. What defines conversation is that at least two contributors are engaged in the process. One concept that has emerged along these lines is *joint action*, which Herbert Clark (1996) defines as an action that requires collaboration and cooperation in order to be successful. Although conversation analysis originated in microsociology (see the role of scholars like Goffman, Sacks, and Garfinkel), in principle there is no mismatch between a Gricean approach to conversation, based on the notion of cooperation and implicature, and issues of conversation analysis,[120] mainly because Gricean pragmatics was developed as a theory of utterance comprehension.

---

[120] Arnulf Deppermann, in response to my question during the online conference *Rethinking pragmatics*, Universities of Bern, Fribourg, Neuchâtel, and Lausanne, Switzerland, 2 November 2020.

The question is whether these rules are rules of behaviour, linguistic rules, or discourse rules. If they are discourse rules, then discourse must first be defined as a linguistic unit. I will show that this cannot be done. My answer will explain why speakers have expertise about the quality of discourse: they have the ability to assess a discourse as good, relevant, and worthy of mobilising their attention, i.e. their time and mental energy.

2 Is discourse a linguistic fact?

All linguistic approaches to discourse share a strong presupposition: discourse is a linguistic unit, and language must be understood from the perspective of discourse. Discourse is the principal unit of language, rather than sentences, as syntactic approaches to language – those inspired by the Chomskyan paradigm – claim.

This vision of language, known as *text linguistics* (de Beaugrande and Dressler 1981), presents certain difficulties. An alternative response based on pragmatics[121] follows. The method used to define a unit in keeping with scientific procedure is *reductionism**. This method consists of looking for the smallest possible unit. In order to do this, the unit in question must not be (i) decomposable or (ii) able to be explained by causal relationships between units that compose it (Searle 1992). Which are linguistic units? Are they sentences, or are they morphemes and/or phonemes? A possible answer follows.

First of all, phonemes cannot be decomposed into smaller units, except into their distinctive features, which are not linguistically realised. A phoneme is therefore a linguistic unit. Second, the combination of phonemes enables the construction of morphemes, but can only explain their form, not their meaning. Therefore phonemes have no causal power over the meaning of morphemes.[122] A morpheme, which is decomposable, but which cannot be explained by the causal relations among its parts, is therefore a unit. And finally, combining morphemes results in sentences, whose syntactic and semantic rules are defined in terms of morphemes. The sentence may therefore be decomposed, and can be explained by the causal relationships between its parts. A sentence is therefore not a unit.

Fundamental linguistic units are therefore phonemes, which cannot be decomposed, and morphemes, which can be decomposed, but which cannot be

---

[121] This explanation is based on Reboul and Moeschler (1998a). For a shorter version, see Reboul and Moeschler (1997), and Moeschler (2010).
[122] This thesis, central to the theory of grammar, is challenged by the phonological symbolic approach, which postulates that there should be a relationship between phonetic form and meaning type. See Lakoff (1987).

explained by the phonemes that make them up. Sentences, on the other hand, are not units, since they can be explained by the causal relationships between the morphemes that constitute them. Viewed from this perspective, it is not surprising that phonology and morphology were the first areas to benefit from scholarly linguistic investigation in the 20th century.

The crucial question is to determine the status of discourse. If discourse were composed of sentences, a great number of linguistic facts, such as the interpretation of pronouns, could not be explained. Anaphoric pronouns* (third-person pronouns), obtained through a reference to another sentence, can only be interpreted contextually, or pragmatically. For instance, in the following discourse, the pronoun *he* in interpreted as referring to the proper name *Fred*, because the individual FRED has been added to the context, and the meaning of the pronoun *he* carries the instruction to retrieve the entity stored in the context:

(204) *Fred is drunk. He drank schnaps.*
     a. The individual FRED is added to the context.
     b. *he* = ?
     c. *he* = FRED

If a discourse is not made up of sentences, what does it consist of? My answer, developed in Reboul and Moeschler (1998a), is that discourse is made up of *utterances** rather than *sentences*. An utterance is a sentence that comes into being in a context. It implies a speaker, an addressee, and a time and place of speech. But the context also contains information that can be inferred from the cognitive environment shared by the speaker and her addressee. So, if a discourse is made up of utterances, can it be explained by the causal relationships between utterances? The second question to be asked is whether an utterance can be explained by the sentence that makes it up.

Let's begin with the second question: an utterance cannot be reduced to a sentence, because an utterance is a sentence that is uttered in a context. Furthermore, an utterance is not a linguistic unit but a pragmatic unit.[123] What about the first question? It is obvious that a discourse, from the point of view of its meaning, is more than the succession of utterances that compose it. Here is an initial explanation. You attend a lecture, which you listen to very carefully. After ten minutes, you stand up and leave the room. Why? Let us suppose that you understood all

---

[123] The question of its possible decomposition is not addressed here: according to traditional pragmatic approaches, an *utterance* is a *speech act* formed by an *illocutionary force* and a *propositional content*, both of which are semantic units (Searle 1969, 1979).

the utterances, and are not in a situation in which you are incompetent; on the contrary you are quite competent. So why do you leave the room? One answer is that you have UNDERSTOOD: you have perfectly understood what the speaker meant. You were able, quickly and without attending the entire lecture, to infer its overall meaning.

Here is a second example: you stop in front of the TV where your fifteen-year-old son is watching a soap opera. You watch it for five minutes and leave the living room. You are obviously not interested. Why not? Again, you quickly understood, and what you understood went far beyond the dialogues and situations you saw on the screen.

These examples have shown that more is involved in the comprehension of discourse than in the comprehension of utterances. But what does "more" mean? Let us first give a definition of what a discourse* is: *a discourse is a sequence of non-arbitrary utterances* (Reboul and Moeschler 1998a: 157).

3 Are there discourse rules?

The examples given up to this point do not support the idea of discourse rules. However, this position is quite counter-intuitive: we have all experienced good and poor discourses, coherent and incoherent discourses, and well-constructed and inadequately constructed discourses. Are there any discourse rules that corroborate our intuitions on the quality of discourse and its rules?

Let us take two extreme examples, which will lead us in a more comprehensive way to the issue of the possible existence of discourse rules. The first example is negative (it is not a well-formed discourse) while the second is positive (it is a perfect, well-formed discourse). The first one is not what one would call a discourse: it was produced by a patient in a psychiatric hospital, the Burghölzli, near Zürich, and was transcribed by the psychiatrist Eugen Bleuer at the beginning of the 20th century (Bleuler [1913] 1987). The second and positive example of a discourse is a short story by the French writer Stendhal.

(205) *Then, I always liked geography. My last teacher in the subject was Professor August A. He was a man with black eyes. I also like black eyes. There are also blue eyes and grey eyes and other sorts, too. I have heard it said that snakes have green eyes. All people have eyes. There are some, too, who are blind. These blind people are led by a boy. It must be terrible not to be able to see. There are people who can't see, and, in addition, can't hear. I know some who hear too much. There are many people in Burgholzli; they are called patients.* (Frith 2015: 83)

This discourse gives an impression of incoherence, though not in terms of the relationships between the utterances: it mentions geography, a geography teacher, his eyes, eye colour, snakes that have green eyes, blind and deaf people, and patients. In other words, each utterance is "logically" connected to the previous one. But we have the impression of a flow of thoughts skipping from one idea to the next.

What is missing in this discourse? The main thing is that it does not give access to the speaker's *global* intention; to what she means with HER discourse.

In contrast, here is a text in which access to a global interpretation is not only possible but indeed required if the reader hopes to understand why Stendhal is telling it:

(206) *Oserai-je raconter l'anecdote que l'on m'a confiée en prenant le frais à l'ombre du mur d'un cimetière dans une pièce de luzerne à la verdeur charmante? Pourquoi pas? Je suis déjà déshonoré comme disant des vérités qui choquent la mode de 1838:*

Le curé n'était point vieux; la servante était jolie; on jasait, ce qui n'empêchait point un jeune homme du village voisin de faire la cour à la servante. Un jour, il cache les pincettes de la cuisine dans le lit de la servante. Quand il revint huit jours après, la servante lui dit:

"Allons, dites-moi où vous avez mis les pincettes que j'ai cherchées partout depuis votre départ. C'est là une bien mauvaise plaisanterie."

L'amant l'embrassa, les larmes aux yeux, et s'éloigna.[124]

[Dare I tell the anecdote related to me while I was sheltering from the heat in the shadow of a cemetery wall among the charming green alfalfa? Why not? I am already notorious for telling truths which shocked the mindset of 1838:

The curate wasn't old at all; the maid was pretty; but the gossip about them was not enough to stop a young man from the neighbouring village courting the maid. One day, he hid the kitchen tongs in the maid's bed. When he came back eight days later, the maid said to him: "Come on then, tell me where you've put the tongs I've been looking for everywhere since you left. The joke's gone on long enough." Her lover kissed her, teary-eyed, and left.] (translated by Alasdair Gunn, from Moeschler 2019: 124)

The story's implicit meaning is obvious: the curate slept with the maid. Stendhal wanted to say that the clergy behaved in an amoral way – "truths which shocked the mindset of 1838".

---

[124] Stendhal. 1930. *Voyage dans le midi de la France*, 115. Paris: Le Divan.

Both discourses are clear illustrations of what a discourse is: *a sequence of non-arbitrary utterances that seeks a global interpretation*. This definition allows us to conclude that discourse is neither a linguistic nor a pragmatic unit. Discourse comprehension is thus not only compositional, but is also driven by the search for a global interpretation.[125] As we observed above, when you leave a lecture after ten minutes, it is because you quickly accessed the global interpretation, too soon in terms of the speaker's discourse planning; in the soap opera example, you understood the overall intentions (characters) in five minutes, primarily because they were easily inferable.[126]

Now, we must ask how the addressee, or the reader, can access a global interpretation. We will ascertain the necessary ingredients for a global intention to be constructed. But first I would like to discuss the linguistic approach to discourse through the concepts of cohesion* and coherence*.

4 Cohesion and coherence

One way of salvaging the linguistic approach to discourse is based on a simple question: shouldn't there be linguistic markers whose function is to scope over discourses rather than sentences? These markers give instructions about how to understand a discourse. Four linguistic phenomena stand out among all possible candidates: *anaphoric pronouns, verbal tenses, discourse connectives,* and *ellipsis*. These processes are known as *cohesion markers** because they contribute to discourse cohesion (Halliday and Hasan 1976).

Let us begin with the *ellipsis**, which is not restricted to language. In a Spanish TV series, a gangster holds up a nightclub. He demands that the owner's wife give him the combination for the safe. When she says she doesn't know it, he points a gun at her niece's head and threatens to shoot her at the count of five. When he reaches two he puts the bullet in the barrel. Change of scene: the gangster leaves the nightclub carrying a bag, and tells the driver to step on it. How can we explain this ellipsis? The end of the sequence with the safe is not shown; we jump to a scene that takes place a few minutes later outside the nightclub. How can we understand this new shot? What is in the bag? One hypothesis might be that the niece told the gangster she had called the police, causing him to rush out of

---

125 It is this property that makes the search for discourse structures hopeless. Apart from some stereotypical types of discourse, such as folktales (Propp 1968), the ways an author can successfully communicate his overall intention are unlimited, much like the way musical notes can be combined in multiple manners. See also the way popular melodies constantly change over time.
126 This corresponds to the situation described in chapter 3: little efforts, little effects.

the nightclub without the contents of the safe. However, this assumption doesn't make sense: why do we see the gangster leaving with a bag? If he hasn't emptied out the safe, he shouldn't be carrying a bag. Another assumption, the one that first springs to mind, is that the bag contains the contents of the safe. We have no evidence of this, but we can infer it. There is an ellipsis between the two scenes: a sequence of events that is not shown and therefore must be inferred. Why is this process used? Simply because an ellipsis speeds up the narrative. A film ellipsis is therefore the same as implicit content in language, which is defined as an *implicature**.

We will now discuss some cases of discourse ellipses. Discourse ellipses are not grammatical ellipses, or constructions that contain the repeated linguistic material in a sentence, as shown in (207a), which is the truncation of (207b):

(207) a. *John's big brother is very talkative, his little one much less so.*
 b. *John's big brother is very talkative, [John's] little [brother] [is] much less [talkative].*

The linguistic material that is underlined and in brackets [x] is not repeated, and constitutes a grammatical ellipsis. But, along with grammatical ellipses, there are also pragmatic ellipses, such as in (208), in which the elliptical material is inferable and is not required for comprehension:

(208) Mary: *Where are you?*
 Peter: *At the station.*
 [I am] at the station.

In the following examples, another type of ellipsis, discourse ellipses, involves non-explicit content. In (209), how is it possible to connect *hungry* and *the Michelin Guide*? And in (210), how can one link the cost of an *operation* and *Uncle Harry*? In both cases, discourse comprehension is accomplished through the reconstitution of the elliptical content (Schank and Abelson 1978):

(209) *Willa was hungry. She took out the Michelin Guide.*

(210) *John knew that his wife's operation would be very expensive. There was always Uncle Harry. . . He reached for the suburb phone book.*

In these examples, missing contents make sense of the discourse:

(211) The Michelin Guide contains a list of restaurants.
Someone who is hungry wants to eat.
A restaurant is a place to eat.
Using a restaurant guide is a way to find a restaurant to eat in.
Willa is planning to go to a restaurant she found in the Michelin Guide to ease her hunger.

(212) Expensive surgery is generally beyond one's personal budget.
Uncle Harry is rich.
John is going to phone Uncle Harry.
John wants to ask Uncle Harry for money to pay for his wife's operation.

What about other cohesion markers? At first glance, they would appear to play an important role in discourse. *Anaphoric pronouns* make it possible to not repeat the expression referring to an entity. Proper names, for instance, are generally not repeated. In (213), (a) is odd, whereas (b) is ordinary, and contains a pronoun:

(213) a. # *Fred is drunk. <u>Fred</u> drank schnaps.*
 b. *Fred is drunk. <u>He</u> drank schnaps.*

What about *tenses*? Verbal tenses enable us to locate events and states in time. Discourse interpretation changes if they are missing or are replaced with a neutral tense like the Present. Whereas the representation of time with the Simple Past and the Past Progressive differentiates between events and states, or what is foregrounded and what is backgrounded, the use of the Historical Present makes the story more lively but does not differentiate between events and states, as these two excerpts from the *incipit* of Michael Crichton's *Airframe* show. The first excerpt is the original, the second is the same text in the Present:[127]

---

[127] The French translation gives a better contrast between background and foreground because of the contrast between the Passé Simple (perfective) and the Imparfait (imperfective): *Emily Jansen <u>poussa</u>* [passé simple] *un soupir de soulagement. Le long vol <u>approchait</u>* [imparfait] *de son terme. Le soleil <u>filtrait</u>* [imparfait] *par les hublots de l'avion. Assise dans son giron, la petite Sarah <u>cligna</u>* [passé simple] *les yeux dans cette lumière inhabituelle tandis qu'elle <u>aspirait</u>* [imparfait] *bruyamment la fin de son biberon.*

(214) *Emily Jansen <u>sighed</u> in relief. The long flight <u>was nearing</u> an end. Morning sunlight <u>streamed</u> through the windows of the airplane. In her lap, little Sarah <u>squinted</u> in an unaccustomed brightness as she noisily <u>sucked</u> the last of her bottle.*

(215) *Emily Jansen <u>sighs</u> in relief. The long flight <u>is nearing</u> an end. Morning sunlight <u>streams</u> through the windows of the airplane. In her lap, little Sarah <u>squints</u> in an unaccustomed brightness as she noisily <u>sucks</u> the last of her bottle.*

When the Present is used instead of past tenses, all the information is at the same level and presents no contrast.

The third type of *cohesion marker** is the *discourse connective**, which is often called a pragmatic connective. At first glance its role in discourse comprehension appears obvious. Let us examine the following text fragment:

(216) *Nous le reconnaissons, nos collègues ont raison: nous n'aurions jamais dû écrire ce livre, nous aurions dû aborder tel ou tel sujet que nous ne mentionnons pas (il nous semble entièrement dénué d'intérêt), nous aurions dû. . . Nous avons un argument pour notre défense: nous espérons que cet ouvrage amusera, instruira, fera comprendre l'intérêt du sujet, plus généralement, pourquoi la recherche scientifique peut être un plaisir, une passion, comment on trouve autant l'aventure dans un fauteuil avec un livre que seul au milieu de l'Atlantique.*

[We realise that our colleagues are right: we never should have written this book, we should have talked about such and such topics that we didn't mention (they seem to us entirely without interest), we should have... We have one argument in our defence: we hope that this book will amuse, instruct, make the interest of the topic known, more generally why scientific research may be a pleasure, a passion, and of how one can find as much adventure in an armchair with a book as alone in the middle of the Atlantic Ocean.] (my translation)

This text can be understood, but it lacks binders, or grammatical morphemes that convey instructional rather than descriptive meaning. This is illustrated by reading the complete text of the above-mentioned fragment. Connectives and other pragmatic markers are underlined:

(217) <u>Alors</u>, <u>d'avance</u>, nous le reconnaissons, nos collègues ont raison: nous n'aurions jamais dû écrire ce livre, nous aurions dû aborder tel ou tel sujet que nous ne mentionnons <u>même</u> pas (<u>parce qu</u>'il nous semble entièrement dénué d'intérêt), nous aurions dû... <u>Mais</u> nous <u>n</u>'avons <u>qu</u>'un arguent pour notre défense: nous espérons que cet ouvrage amusera, instruira <u>et surtout</u> fera comprendre l'intérêt du sujet <u>et</u>, plus généralement, pourquoi la recherche scientifique peut être un plaisir et une passion <u>et</u> comment on trouve autant l'aventure dans un fauteuil avec un livre que seul au milieu de l'Atlantique. (Reboul and Moeschler 1998b: 9)

[<u>So</u>, <u>to begin with</u>, we realise that our colleagues are right: we never should have written this book, we should have talked about such and such topics we didn't <u>even</u> mention (<u>because</u> they seem to us entirely without interest), we should have... <u>But</u> we have <u>only</u> one argument in our defence: we hope that this book will amuse, instruct, <u>and above all</u> make the interest of the topic known <u>and</u>, more generally show why scientific research may be a pleasure, and a passion, <u>and</u> how one can find as much adventure in an armchair with a book as alone in the middle of the Atlantic Ocean.] (my translation)

Now the text can be fully understood, and also satisfies the obligations mentioned earlier: the reader is encouraged to understand that the authors wrote their book for his enjoyment, free from the obligations imposed by academia, which include exhaustivity in providing references and tackling questions from all possible angles – in other words, the same obligations that rule the book you are now reading.

That said, for a theory of cohesion markers to work, these markers must play a role in discourse. The function which is generally assigned to them is *coherence**. Coherence is the property of discourses that corresponds to grammaticality in sentences: in other words, coherence is to discourse what grammaticality is to sentences. With this analogy in mind, we can now talk about discourse rules in the same way we address grammatical rules for sentences.

But this line of reasoning is unfortunately cancelled out by the following phenomenon: the theory of cohesion markers predicts that a discourse without cohesion markers will be less coherent than a discourse that contains them, and that there can be no incoherent discourses that contain cohesion markers. But neither of these predictions is correct. Here are four cases to prove this point:

(a) coherent discourses with cohesion markers,
(b) coherent discourses without cohesion markers,
(c) incoherent discourses with cohesion markers, and
(d) incoherent discourses without cohesion markers.

The control criterion is the predicted characteristic and the attested characteristic, as examples (218)–(221) show:

(218) Coherent discourses with cohesion markers: predicted and attested
Mark was looking for a quiet place for his holidays. That is why he thought Bhutan. This country welcomes very few tourists.

(219) Coherent discourses without cohesion markers: not predicted but attested
Mark was looking for a quiet place for his holidays. Bhutan welcomes very few tourists.

(220) Incoherent discourses with cohesion markers: not predicted but attested
 # John bought a cow. In fact it is red like a squirrel. It lives in the forest and hibernates in winter. But it is very cold in this region.

(221) Incoherent discourses without cohesion markers: predicted but not attested
 # John bought a cow whose name is Roussette. Roussette is red like a squirrel. Squirrels live in the forest. Squirrels hibernate in winter. Winter is very cold in the region.

Two of these discourses are not coherent. One does not contain cohesion markers (221) and the other one does (220). We can therefore conclude that the presence of cohesion markers does not contribute much to discourse quality. But there is more: the coherent discourse without cohesion markers (219) seems more natural because the example that includes cohesion markers (218) is redundant: it seems more like a demonstrative discourse than an argumentative one. What conclusions can be drawn here? One possibility is that there is no causal relationship between the presence of cohesion markers and discourse coherence. This would mean that the equation "coherence:discourse = grammaticality:sentence" is false. We can conclude from this explanation that discourse is not governed by linguistic rules.

But how can we then explain our intuitions about discourses? Some discourses are extraordinarily well constructed, efficient, and interpretable, while others are not. In order to convince you of this fact, here is an excerpt from the speech Barack Obama gave on 8 January 2008, after winning the primary of the presidential election:

(222) *But in the unlikely story that is America, there has never been anything false about hope. For when we have faced down impossible odds; when we've been told that we're not ready, or that we shouldn't try, or that we can't,*

> *generations of Americans have responded with a simple creed that sums up the spirit of a people.*
> *Yes we can.*
> *It was a creed written into the founding documents that declared the destiny of a nation.*
> *Yes we can.*
> *It was whispered by slaves and abolitionists as they blazed a trail toward freedom through the darkest of nights.*
> *Yes we can.*
> *It was sung by immigrants as they struck out from distant shores and pioneers who pushed westward against an unforgiving wilderness.*
> *Yes we can.*
> *It was the call of workers who organized; women who reached for the ballot; a President who chose the moon as our new frontier; and a King who took us to the mountaintop and pointed the way to the Promised Land.*
> *Yes we can to justice and equality. Yes we can to opportunity and prosperity. Yes we can heal this nation. Yes we can repair this world. Yes we can.*

We will return to this speech later. For the moment, I will simply state that everything about it is perfect: its rhythm, the repetition of *Yes we can*, and above all the emotions that occur when reading it, and especially when hearing it.

5 Discourse relations as life buoys?

One way to salvage the approach of cohesion markers and the notion of coherence is to address coherence issue in terms of *discourse relation**: according to this definition, a discourse is a set of relationships between discourse units. Two questions now arise: Which ones are discourse units? And which are discourse relations?

The most popular approaches to discourse relations take a variety of forms, but they are only notational variants, as they were called in the 1970s, or alternative versions of the same scientific paradigm:[128] Rhetorical Structure Theory, Discourse Relation Theory, and Segmented Discourse Relation Theory.[129] From

---

128 Chomsky often used this argument to show that generative semantics and extended standard theory are notational variants. See Harris (1995) for a complete account of this sequence in the history of linguistics.
129 See respectively Mann and Thompson (1988) for RST; Kamp and Reyle (1993) for DRT; Asher (1993) and Asher and Lascarides (2003) for SDRT.

the standpoint of these approaches, discourse units are semantic in nature, and represent what utterances describe, that is, events and states. These concepts belong to our natural metaphysics. Here is how Nicholas Asher describes these entities (Asher 1993: 7–8): "Many linguists and philosophers have distinguished between states and events, or activities and accomplishments. Events have often been described as 'punctual' or as 'containing their initial and final endpoints', while states and activities have been described as 'open-ended' or 'not containing their initial and final, temporal endpoints'".

Discourse relations are therefore relationships that states and events described in sentences entertain with each other. But which is the set of discourse relations? They must have a certain generality in order to be applicable in a variety of settings. In SDRT, the set of discourse relations is limited to relationships between events and/or states such as NARRATION, EXPLANATION, ELABORATION, RESULT, and BACKGROUND:

(223) NARRATION: relation of temporal succession between two events
Max stood up. John greeted him.

(224) EXPLANATION: an event explains why the previous event happened
Max fell. John pushed him.

(225) ELABORATION: an event is a part of another event
The council built the bridge. The architect drew the plans.

(226) BACKGROUND: a state is the backdrop in which another event occurs
Max opened the door. The room was completely dark.

(227) RESULT: the described event causes an event or a state
Max turned the light off. The room was completely dark.

This approach yields rather impressive results on discourse structure. Let's take another look at the earlier excerpt from *Airframe* (Michael Crichton), which appears again in (228):

(228) (1) *Emily Jansen sighed in relief.* (2) *The long flight was nearing an end.* (3) *Morning sunlight streamed through the windows of the airplane.* (4) *In her lap,* (5) *little Sarah squinted in an unaccustomed brightness* (6) *as she noisily sucked the last of her bottle.*

Discourse relations between events and states can be described quite simply: the implied discourse relations, as seen in this excerpt, are BACKGROUND, ELABORATION, and NARRATION.

(229) (2) is the BACKGROUND of (1)
(3) is the BACKGROUND of (2)
(5) is the ELABORATION of (4)
(5) follows (1) via NARRATION
(6) is the BACKGROUND of (5)

The idea is that discourse relations are the ingredients of discourse on which its coherence is based. We might now wonder what determines the choice of one discourse relation over another. In the presentation above, the definition of discourse relations sets the conditions in which a specific discourse relation is licensed. For instance, the relation between (1) and (5) – NARRATION – is selected because (5) is not caused by (1) or by any other preceding events described in the text (RESULT). Nor is it an EXPLANATION, a BACKGROUND or an ELABORATION, which all are specific discourse relations.[130] The most appropriate discourse relation is therefore NARRATION, that is, the least specific one, shown in this abbreviated version of Crichton's text (230):

(230) *Emily Jansen sighed in relief. Little Sarah squinted in an unaccustomed brightness.*

One might ask whether discourse relations can be triggered by specific linguistic clues. Connectives, for instance, would be a fantastic way of triggering discourse relations. We could thus hypothesise that *because* is associated with EXPLANATION, *therefore* with RESULT, *when* with BACKGROUND, *then* with NARRATION, and so forth. However, two issues arise. First, if connectives trigger discourse relations, each connective should be associated with one specific discourse relation. But is it possible to explain the absence of correspondence between connectives in different languages? Every French speaker knows that *mais* does not have the same usages as *but*, and that *en effet* can be translated by *indeed* only in certain contexts.

This is true because there is no biunivocal correspondence between connectives in different languages. Sandrine Zufferey and Bruno Cartoni (2012) have shown that the translation of English connectives (*because, since, as*) into

---

[130] In SDRT, NARRATION is defined as a default discourse relation, i.e. the least specific one, which is triggered when no enriched meaning is available, such as CAUSE for EXPLANATION. See Lascarides and Asher (1993).

French (*parce, car, puisque*), as well as the converse translations, depend on three criteria: objective/new, subjective/new and subjective/given: the opposition objective/subjective depends on the nature of the description, and the state of the world (the speaker's perspective), whereas the new/given contrast is about the nature of the information conveyed, either new or old. Zufferey and Cartoni conclude that there is no biunivocal correspondence between *because* and *parce que*: *because* is translated by *parce que* under the objective/new criteria, which is also the case for *parce que* and its translation with *because*; but under the subjective/new criterion, *because* is translated with *car*, and *parce que* with *because*. The overlap is therefore only partial between *because* and *parce que*, as Table 3 shows:

Table 3: Non-correspondence between French and English causal connectives.

	objective/new	subjective/new	subjective/given
because	parce que	car	
since		car	puisque, étant donné que 'given that'
as	étant donné que 'given that', dans la mesure où 'insofar as'	car	puisque, étant donné que 'given that'
parce que	because	because	
car		because	since
puisque		since	since, as

This initial difficulty is aggravated by a second one: the absence of a biunivocal relationship between the connective and specific discourse relation. Since the research on discourse connectives began – it started for French with publications by Oswald Ducrot and his colleagues in the 1970s[131] – it has been observed that the meanings of connectives in use show contextual variation. According to these conditions, associating a single discourse relationship with a connective, that is, with its linguistically encoded meaning, proves impossible.

Let us consider the example of causal connectives, which have been described in many ways for French (Zufferey 2012; Moeschler 2011, and 2019; Degand and Fagard 2012), English (Sweetser 1990), Greek (Chrysovalantis 2012, 2014), and Dutch (Stukker, Sanders, and Verhagen 2009). A connective like *because* is semantically associated to a CAUSE relation, but its usages operate in different

---

131 Among others, Anscombre and Ducrot (1977), Groupe λ-l (1975), Ducrot et al. (1980).

ways from the relation of causality: *because* can be a causal relation between events, an explicative relation, or a justification. In the first case, known as *content* (Sweetser 1990), an event causes another event, but the relation adheres to the CONSEQUENCE-CAUSE order. In the explicative relation, also known as *epistemic* (Sweetser 1990), the connective introduces an argument that explains why the speaker reached a conclusion in the order CONCLUSION-ARGUMENT. Finally, in the third usage, known as *speech act* (Sweetser 1990), the connective introduces a reason that justifies the accomplishment of a speech act, such as a question (Sweetser 1990: 77):

(231) a. *John came back because he loves her.*
b. *John loves her, because he came back.*
c. *What are you doing tonight, because there's a good movie on.*

Is it possible that three different discourse relations are associated with the same connective: CAUSALITY (a), EXPLANATION (b), and JUSTIFICATION (c)? Things become even more complicated with the superposition of discourse relations for the same connective. *When*, for instance, which generally introduces a temporal relation (a), can also introduce a causal one (b):

(232) a. *It was raining when we left the theatre.*
b. *The shirts got wrinkled when Luke put them away in the closet.*

To conclude, it appears that the discourse relations approach is more complex than we first imagined, and that these relations raise more issues than they solve.

6 Discourse pragmatics

We now know that discourse is not governed by linguistic rules and that it is not organised by discourse relations. What does characterise a discourse, then? It must be possible to explain our intuitions about coherence, and to address for example the extreme difference between the Burgholzli patient's discourse and the story of the curate and the maid. Such an explanation must focus on how we understand discourses rather than on their formal properties.

This is the approach Anne Reboul and I adopt in *Pragmatique du discours* (Reboul and Moeschler 1998b, Moeschler 2010). Our central hypothesis is based on the principles that organise utterance comprehension and interpretation as seen through Relevance Theory. In Relevance Theory, speaker meaning is obtained through the recognition of two intentions: the speaker's informative intention (i), which is accessible only if the addressee recognises the speaker's communicative intention (ii). Since both intentions concern utterances, we call them *local*. Local informative intentions play a central role in the construction of the *global informative intention**, which supposes the recognition of the speaker's *global communicative intention**. The main point we must explain is how the addressee constructs a global informative intention. In discourse pragmatics, the global informative intention is constructed on the basis of the local informative intentions, which are associated with the comprehension of each utterance that makes up the text or discourse.

Now, the construction of a global intention does not require that every utterance be produced. Indeed, we have a cognitive capacity for anticipating events – this capacity is fundamental for perception, because it allow us to anticipate future events: you see a tram coming and infer that you must not cross the street, unless you want to risk your life. Our anticipatory ability is also activated in utterance comprehension: how many times have you finished your addressee's utterance? How many times have you guessed who the murderer was in an Agatha Christie novel? And how many times have you been fooled? In suspense movies, the bad guy is killed, but then comes back to life. Everyone remembers the famous steel mill scene in Terminator 2, when the nasty T-1000 is frozen by liquid nitrogen and breaks into a thousand pieces . . . only for them to thaw in the heat and come back together again.

In other words, the conclusions we draw are as strong, but never stronger than the weakest assumptions we entertain. This explains that the process of hypothesis formation and confirmation, which is the foundation for verbal communication comprehension, is highly risky: the conclusions we draw can be false and must be modified.

In some extreme cases, our knowledge of the world itself must be modified. But this knowledge is generally stronger than what our linguistic knowledge allows us to infer. Here is an excellent example, excerpted from the short story *The Problem of Summer Time* (*Le décret* 'the decree' in French) by Marcel Aymé, a French writer born in the early 20th century. In this short story, the narrator goes on a trip. When he returns, the decree that was enacted before his departure, which moved time forward seventeen years, from 1942 to 1959, seems to have suddenly been cancelled. The narrator gradually discovers that he is no longer in 1959, that he is seventeen years younger, and that he cannot return the bike he rented because the shop does not yet exist. The reader gradually discovers this conflict between two worlds through the narrator's thoughts about the decree, time, and parallel worlds. In order to make sense of the utterances he reads, the reader must take these elements of the narrative context into account, though they make no sense in the real world:

(233) *A moment earlier, I had met Jacques Sariette, fiancé to my daughter Marie-Thérèse. He was clutching a stick and hoop and his other hand held tightly to his mother. I stopped to talk to Madame Sariette who enlightened me on the progress of all her children, especially Jacques. No less anxious than her husband to work towards the moral improvement of France, this excellent lady told me that they intended the little boy for a position in the clergy. I told her that they were quite right.*[132]

Indeed, a fiancé cannot be a five-year old child or a curate. Jacques Sariette's description thus corresponds to the state of the world when he was a child, but the narrator knows that his daughter, because of the decree, is no longer a three-year old girl in 1959, but a twenty-year old young woman who is engaged to the young man Jacques Sariette, who has not become a curate. Without this information, the text would be contradictory. The charming thing about this short story is that we have to constantly modify our hypotheses about the world and the nature of time.

However, in most cases we can trust our hypotheses about the world and make assumptions that will later be confirmed. This is why Stendhal's anecdote seems so consistent to us: we make an anticipatory assumption that is then confirmed. Indeed, we rapidly assume that the curate is sleeping with the maid – *The curate wasn't old at all; the maid was pretty*. This assumption is confirmed a first time by *the gossip about them*, and at the end when the subterfuge is revealed and definitively confirmed – *Come on then, tell me where you've put the tongs I've been looking for everywhere since you left. The joke's gone on long enough*. Another thing that is confirmed is the young man's understanding that the maid is having an affair with the curate – *Her lover kissed her, teary-eyed, and left*.

Stendhal also and in a more general way gives the reader strong clues about what he is going to recount: *Dare I tell the anecdote related to me while I was sheltering from the heat in the shadow of a cemetery wall among the charming green alfalfa?* We still don't know that the subject is the clergy, but when the anecdote begins, the first word – *the curate* – allows us to make this assumption. We are then rewarded, in terms of relevance, by the conclusion we have made. If we didn't come to this conclusion, we can't understand why the young man cries when he leaves.

What is the function of a global assumption? In *Pragmatique du discours*, we answer the following: because we can build hypotheses at various points during

---

[132] Marcel Aymé. [1943] 2012. The Problem of Summer Time. In *The man who walked through walls*, 135. Padstow: Pushkin Press.

the processing of a text, we receive in return the impression of a coherent judgement. Seen from this perspective, the coherence of a discourse is merely the effect of the possibility of making global assumptions. Two principles guide us in our search for a global assumption: its accessibility and its complexity.

(234) a. The more accessible the global informative intention is, the greater the coherence effect is.
b. The more complex the global informative intention is, the greater the coherence effect is.

We have now an answer to the question of text and discourse coherence: coherence is the consequence of comprehension. This explains why our coherence judgements may vary, and that this variation is caused by our ability to access the global informative intention as well as the nature of its content. Global comprehension that results in a trivial conclusion will have a weak coherence effect, whereas, like in Stendhal's short story, when the author writes about a relationship between human beings, and more generally speaking about the clergy, the coherence effect will be as great as its global informative intention is complex.

However, in order to produce an overall picture of the relationship between language and discourse, two questions must be addressed: How can we explain that a discourse can affect the hearer's emotional state? And how can we explain that a discourse can affect his beliefs? In Relevance Theory, these two types of effects are traditionally known as *non-propositional** and *propositional**. Let us begin by examining non-propositional effects.

7 Non-propositional effects, emotion and adhesion

In a philosophical tradition that essentially spread through Cartesianism – or rather a popular version of Cartesianism[133]– reason and emotion are separated. Basing his conclusions on current knowledge about neuroscience, the neuropsychologist Antonio Damasio has shown, in his book on cognition and emotion, that this hypothesis is false (Damasio 1994).

In a similar way, but using other arguments, most of them archaeological, Steven Mithen (2007), a paleoanthropologist who specialises in Neanderthals,

---

[133] For a more sophisticated and up-to-date conception of Cartesianism, especially on the subject of Descartes and the emotions (or passions), see Schmitter (2016). See also Kambourchner (1995) for the traditional French perspective on Descartes and emotions.

hypothesised that this cousin of Homo sapiens used a communication system he called *Hmmmm* – for *holistic, manipulative, multi-modal, musical*, and *mimetic*. Mithen postulated that Neanderthal, whose anatomy contained a hyoid bone, which is necessary for the production of sounds, used a mode of communication that was closer to whistling than to speech. One advantage of whistling was that it could be heard from a greater distance: 150 meters as opposed to 50 meters for the human voice. According to Mithen, *Hmmmm* was a mode of action and thought that was both pre-linguistic and musical. The separation of language and music occurred approximately 200,000 years ago, when Homo sapiens appeared. Music then became specialised in emotional communication, retaining from *Hmmmm* its properties of being holistic (non-compositional) and manipulative. Language, on the other hand, became a system that specialised in transmitting information. Music, therefore, transmitted emotions, while language transmitted information.

This vision of language, which clearly separates information and emotion, can legitimately be questioned. Although we cannot contest the fact that music is a medium specialised in the transmission of emotion, we can ask whether language also has this faculty. The poetic usage of language is a good candidate. Language can not only produce pleasure during its processing; it can also arouse certain mental states that do not give rise to *propositional* representations*, or contents that correspond to propositions (sentence content) and that are evaluated as true or false. In the next chapter, we will return to discourse figures such as metaphor in order to show that certain usages of language aim at producing effects that are traditionally known as *poetic*: these effects are *non-propositional**.

Here are some simple examples of non-propositional representations: newspaper headlines sometimes try to evoke representations that go beyond the content of the article and, through non-ordinary usage of language, produce supplementary and non-propositional effects. Sports newspapers are good at this kind of linguistic performance. In France, the daily sports newspaper *L'Équipe* is well known for the linguistic quality of its headlines. For example, it titled Gaël Monfils' victory in the quarter-finals, at the Roland Garros tournament on 5 June 2008, *La gloire de Monfils* 'Montfils' glory', which referred to Marcel Pagnol's novel *La gloire de mon père* 'My father's glory'. The last name of the French tennis player Gaël Monfils, *Monfils*, is homophonic to *mon fils* 'my son', making the title *La gloire de Monfils* proximate to *La gloire de mon père*.[134] This direct allusion to French literature produces many non-propositional effects in the reader's mind,

---

[134] Frederick Newmeyer (personal communication) mentioned that the same tendency is true in sports newspapers in the United States.

provided that he is aware of the book *My father's glory* (see Moeschler 2009 for a detailed analysis).[135]

A related phenomenon with a more general scope is language usage in humour. What is the principal function of verbal humour? To yield a non-propositional effect that is manifested by laughter. A great number of theories on humour have been formulated, and the most famous is Freud's (Freud [1905] 1957). According to his theory, the function of humour is to release censors, resulting in laughter. A cognitive version of Freud's theory has been given by Marvin Minsky (1985): the main function of humour is to cross the barriers of rationality in order to calibrate them in a more accurate way. According to this definition laughter is the echo of crossing these barriers to rationality.

Sigmund Freud's corpus of *Witz* is ideal for illustrating Marvin Minsky's theory. Here is his best example, which plays with our abilities to acknowledge – or not to acknowledge – an intellectual scam:

(235) *A gentleman entered a pastry-cook's shop and ordered a cake; but he soon brought it back and asked for a glass of liqueur instead. He drank it and began to leave without having paid. The proprietor detained him. "You've not paid for the liqueur." "But I gave you the cake in exchange for it." "You didn't pay for that either." "But I hadn't eaten it".* (Freud [1905] 1957, from Minsky 1985: 175)

I am sure you at least smiled, or maybe even burst out laughing. Now read the story again. Who is right and who is wrong? The client or the proprietor? At first glance the client's argument – why pay for something that has not been consumed? – seems consistent; but the proprietor is also within his right when he says that what has been consumed must be paid for. Where is the scam? It is located in the exchange, which results in the non-payment by the client of what he has not consumed. Meanwhile, however, the client has consumed the product of the swap, so he is in the wrong. Rapid processing of the story makes it seem that the client is in the right, but this is not the case when time is taken to analyse the situation.

This is a typical situation that requires a second processing. Daniel Kahneman, a psychologist and winner of the Nobel Prize in Economics in 2002, is renowned for his theory on two modes of thought: the first system implies intuition, while the second implies reasoning (Kahneman 2011). The first system is fast,

---

135 The film *La gloire de mon père* (Yves Robert, 1990) was so successful that almost all French native speakers are familiar with Marcel Pagnol's literary works.

parallel, automatic, effortless, associative, slow-learning, and emotional, whereas the second system is slow, serial, controlled, effortful, rule-governed, flexible, and neutral. These two systems give rise to conceptual representations and temporal representations (which differentiate between past, present, future), and can be evoked through language (Mercier and Sperber 2017: 65). If we return to Freud's example, the first system, based on intuition, tells us that the client is right. But when the second system intervenes and reasoning occurs, the scam becomes obvious. The conflict between two different conclusions stemming from two cognitive systems that come into play one after the other is what causes laughter.

Emotions are thus an integral part of language comprehension. Separating reason and emotion is an artifice that is mainly advocated by a simplified version of rationalism. If the usage of our cognitive faculties implies the participation of the brain area devoted to the processing of emotions, then it is not surprising that some types of language usage, as well as certain situational contexts, are emotionally charged. Political speeches are good examples of this, especially when they accompany victories. I referred above to the speech Barack Obama gave on 8 January 2008. Another example of an emotionally charged speech is the one Martin Luther King gave on 28 August 1963 in Washington. Here is a well-known excerpt:

(236) *I say to you, my friends, and so even though we face the difficulties of today and tomorrow, I still have a dream. It is a dream deeply rotted in the American dream.*
I have a dream that one day this nation will rise up and live out the true meaning of its creed: "We hold the truths to be self-evident, that all men are created equal."
I have a dream that one day on the red hills of Georgia, the sons of former slaves and the sons of former slave owners will be able to sit down together at the table of brotherhood.
I have a dream that one day even the state of Mississippi, a state sweltering with the heat of injustice, sweltering with the heat of oppression, will be transformed into an oasis of freedom and justice.
I have a dream that my four little children will one day live in a nation where they will not be judged by the colour of their skin but by the content of their character.
I have a dream today!

The best-known part of the speech, as well as the one with the greatest emotional charge, is these two lines: "I have a dream that my four little children will one day live in a nation where they will not be judged by the colour of their skin but by the content of their character. I have a dream today!" How can we explain the strength of King's speech in general and this fragment in particular? At least two elements come into play.

First of all, the refrain *I have a dream* is important, because mentioning a dream allows us to imagine a world that does not yet exist, but which could: this type of reasoning is similar to counterfactual reasoning. It is in fact possible to change a section of King's speech into a counterfactual conditional construction (237):

(237) *If one day on the red hills of Georgia, the sons of former slaves and the sons of former slave owners could be able to sit down together at the table of brotherhood.*
If one day even the state of Mississippi, a state sweltering with the heat of injustice, sweltering with the heat of oppression, were transformed into an oasis of freedom and justice.
If my four little children would one day live in a nation where they would not be judged by the colour of their skin but by the content of their character.

This form has a major drawback, however: the consequent of the conditional is not said and is less efficient than the dream supposition: Martin Luther King should have explicitly stated in the consequent of these counterfactual sentences what a country without racial discrimination would be like.

The second element that strengthens King's speech is the reference to his children. He goes from an impersonal speech to one that implies the speaker himself, allowing every addressee, in Washington and elsewhere, to imagine him or herself as a parent whose children's lives are negatively affected by the colour of their skin.

These two elements give the speech its emotional content and yield many non-propositional effects. I will show in the next section why these non-propositional effects can play a role in persuasion; that is, in strengthening the arguments to which they refer.

8 Propositional effects, argumentation and persuasion

Barack Obama's and Martin Luther King's speeches have shown us the nature of some of their *non-propositional** effects. Now, the sole purpose of speeches such as these is not to stir the addressees' emotions; their main goal is to change their beliefs and their representations of the world. This is precisely what relevance theory predicts: "We see communication as a matter of enlarging mutual cognitive environments, not of duplicating thoughts" (Sperber and Wilson [1986] 1995: 193).

How can the mutual cognitive environment be enlarged? In traditional political speeches, whose goal is to remind the addressees of the principles and the main themes of a candidate's campaign, cognitive effects mainly strengthen old information. In Barack Obama's and Martin Luther King's speeches, however, the new element was the addition of new information. What was new for Barack Obama's electors was understanding that *yes we can* was a relevant proposition in their mutual cognitive environment: this proposition created new hope, and all the examples Obama gave of *yes we can* created a context of hope. In Martin Luther King's speech, the main cognitive effect was the proposition that the dream of a better world without racial discrimination could become a reality.

In both cases the repetition of *Yes we can* and *I have a dream* was fundamental in creating a mutual cognitive environment. Communication rather than rhetoric was brought into play in these two examples. What is known as an anaphora in classic rhetoric – the repetition of an expression, like *Blessed are the poor in spirit* in the Gospel of Matthew – is merely a way of increasing the strength of conviction in which these propositions are entertained. In Obama and King's examples, we understand why the production of propositional effects goes hand in hand with the emergence, spontaneous in this type of context (a political meeting, a demonstration for Afro-American civil rights), of non-propositional effects.[136]

How can we characterise these local and global effects in discourse? Do they all have equal weight? In Relevance Theory, the hypothesis is that *implicatures** – pragmatically implicated contents – can be cases of strong communication, in which case they fall under the speaker's responsibility; or weak communication, in which case they fall under the hearer's or reader's responsibility. We will examine cases of weak communication in Chapter 6, but we can already hypothesise that everything belonging to the category of poetic effects, or non-ordinary usages of language, is part of this category. However, the examples of repetition, as in *I have a dream*, *Yes we can*, or even *Moi Président* 'I President', are cases of strong communication. If they were not, their effects would have been undetermined, and it would have been difficult for those who gave the speeches to control them. This does not mean that their meaning is restricted to a single proposition. It means that, unlike what occurs when poetic effects are produced, the addressee is invited to draw a certain type of implicature and not others; for instance, "racial discrimination can be eradicated" and all the propositions this implies; "America can change" and all the propositions this implies (regarding justice, health, etc.); and "the government's previous actions will cease" and all that is implied.

---

[136] Another example is the well-known *Moi Président* 'I President' speech that François Holland gave during the debate leading up to the final of the French presidential election in 2012.

Where does the power of persuasion in these speeches come from? In their book on reason, Hugo Mercier and Dan Sperber (2017) argue for the thesis that the aim of verbal communication is persuasion, which can only be reached via argumentation, that is, by giving the reasons for such-and-such a conclusion. For Mercier and Sperber, the argumentative function of language explains the emergence of a rich code such as the linguistic code, whose usage in communication does not require the equivalence between encoding and decoding, but certain clues of informative and communicative intentions which lead the addressee to draw a certain conclusion.

According to Mercier and Sperber, the theory of argumentation is directly connected to one of the cognitive constraints on communication: the addressee must be epistemically vigilant, that is, he must be able to evaluate the relevance of the reasons to reach a certain conclusion. Epistemic vigilance, however, contrasts with a universal tendency known as the *myside bias**, which is the speaker's tendency to be lazy in terms of his own arguments, while giving more weight to them than to the arguments of others.[137]

It is possible to analyse this phenomenon in another way, along with the reasons why arguments must be given to draw a certain conclusion. In chapter 2 I mentioned Anne Reboul's claim (Reboul 2017a) that one way for the speaker to escape the addressee's epistemic vigilance is to let the addressee draw the implicature himself. One of the most important consequences of this escape is that the speaker cannot be accused of having a manipulative intention – of forcing the addressee to go in a certain direction or draw a certain conclusion. The argument, I repeat, is a simple one: implicatures are cancellable, which means that the speaker can always deny having meant such-and-such a thing.

Another element that questions Mercier and Sperber's position is that the theory of epistemic vigilance (Sperber et al. 2010) seems to contradict the predictions of Relevance Theory. In Relevance Theory, the communicative principle of relevance allows the addressee to presume that the speaker's utterance is optimally relevant. However, it also implies that the speaker must be strongly committed in order not to require undue processing efforts of his addressee: intentionally deceiving him is not in the speaker's or the addressee's best interest. But if the speaker is lazy, he is not highly vigilant about the quality of his arguments. This leads to a partial conflict between the myside bias and epistemic vigilance.

A way to escape this trap is to refer to – in addition to a procedure of comprehension* (238) – a procedure of production (239):

---

[137] I mentioned an initial application of this principle in my discussion of strategies of contradiction resolution in chapter 4 (see van der Henst et al. 2006).

(238) Relevance-theoretic comprehension procedure* (Wilson and Sperber 2004: 613)
   a. Follow a path of least effort in computing cognitive effects: Test interpretive hypothesis hypotheses (disambiguations, reference resolutions,[138] implicatures, etc.) in order of accessibility.
   b. Stop when your expectations of relevance are satisfied (or abandoned).

(239) Production procedure*
   a. Make the contextual assumptions necessary to utterance comprehension accessible.
   b. Make the comprehension effort minimal.
   c. Make the addressee's expectations of relevance satisfied.

Based on the above we can state that while the addressee must be epistemically vigilant, the speaker must be epistemically committed. We have all met people who are worthy of our trust, and others to whom we must exercise caution in terms of *their discourses*. It is therefore fundamental for a reader or an addressee to be able to distinguish between them; it is equally important for a speaker or writer to take her audience or readership into account in order to obtain the effects she wants.

9 Conclusion

What conclusions can be drawn from this chapter? Firstly, that discourse is neither a linguistic nor a pragmatic unit, but a sequence of non-arbitrary utterances (an utterance is a pragmatic unit). Secondly, that discourse is not governed by discourse rules, but organised by principles that manage verbal communication and pragmatic comprehension, that is, the construction of the speaker's global informative intention. Finally, that the positive cognitive effects which emerge in discourse comprehension are both non-propositional and propositional.

In chapter 6 the role of non-propositional effects in comprehension will be explored in terms of a specific type of discourse: literature.

---

138 For a pragmatic approach to reference, see Korta and Perry (2011).

Chapter 6
Ordinary and non-ordinary usages of language

This chapter will explore a specific usage of language, the one that is used in so-called *literary* texts. I will concentrate primarily on a single type of literary text, known as *narrative**, with certain detours into poetic usages of language.

But first of all I would like to remove an ambiguity by saying that I don't really know what literature is. An academic definition would state that literary texts as those that are examined in literary studies. This criterion is very restrictive. When one considers the wide range of novels published each year in the United Kingdom, France, Germany, Italy, and Spain, for instance, no one would question their literary character. Seen from an academic perspective, however, very few of them will become part of literature department libraries, and only a tiny portion of those will result in literary studies. We might imagine that an internationally recognised award like the Nobel Prize in Literature would result in a change of status for the author in question. Patrick Modiano, for instance, is mentioned more and more frequently in linguistic research on literature; his work is analysed, and he is considered to be a genuine French author worthy of academic interest.

The literary studies criterion is therefore not a good one. We cannot expect scholars to identify the criteria that make it possible to define literature, that is, to sort all so-called literary publications into two categories, those that qualify as literature and those that do not deserve this title.

Three other methods of defining literature remain. The first is to sidestep the question and to only examine works of fiction, a subset of the literary corpus. But this approach, which some literary critics have adopted,[139] is concerned more with philosophical issues, primarily ontological ones, than those linked to utterance comprehension.[140] The second method is to study literature's contribution to human cognition. Anne Reboul (2009), for instance, has studied the relationships between *fiction*, *narration*, and *rationality*, and particularly the relationships between fiction, moral education, and the critical mind. The third method is experimental and aims at identifying the difference between fiction and non-fiction, as well as the difference between literature and non-literature in fiction (Kidd and Castano 2013, Nazir and Reboul 2017).

I will adopt a fourth perspective in this chapter; it is my hope to expand the pragmatic approach to discourse in order to encompass issues that partially and

---
139 See for instance Schaeffer (1999), Jouve (2019), Pavel (2017).
140 For an exception see Searle (1979: chapter 3), and Reboul (1990), (1992) on Searle.

sometimes totally intersect with literary issues. The pragmatic approach is in fact not a new one; Umberto Eco's textual theory dating from the 1970s explicitly refers to pragmatics, as the preface of *Lector in fabula* shows:

> Quand, entre 1958 et 1962, j'écrivais *Opera aperta* (...), je voulais comprendre comment une œuvre d'art pouvait d'un côté postuler une libre intervention interprétative de la part de ses destinataires et de l'autre présenter des caractéristiques structurales descriptibles qui stimulaient et réglaient l'ordre de ses interprétations possibles. Comme je l'ai appris plus tard, *je faisais de la pragmatique du texte sans le savoir*. (...) J'abordais l'aspect de l'activité coopérative qui amène le destinataire à tirer du texte ce que le texte ne dit pas mais qu'il présuppose, promet, implique ou implicite (...). (Eco 1985: 5; italics are mine)

> [When, between 1958 and 1962, I was writing *Opera Aperta* (...), I wanted to understand how a work of art could on one hand postulate the free interpretative intervention of its addressees, and on the other hand present the structural descriptive characteristics that stimulated and governed the order of its possible interpretations. As I discovered later, *I was engaging in textual pragmatics without knowing it*. (...) I was approaching the aspect of cooperative activity which leads the addressee to draw from the text not what it says, but what it presupposes, promises, implies, or implicates (...)] (my translation)

Several decades later, typical pragmatic issues such as *free indirect discourse* and the status of *narration*, as well as other more traditional linguistics issues like *figures of speech* (metaphor, metonymy, and irony), have become customary topics of investigation in pragmatics. That said, institutional divisions have always kept these types of approach out of literary studies. In recent decades, however, some bridges have been built between linguistics and literature in terms of structural linguistics (Jakobson 1977) and generative grammar (Kuroda 1973, Banfield 1982, Ruwet 1982). The lastest bridge was built by a literary critic, Terence Cave, and a pragmaticist, Deirdre Wilson (Cave and Wilson 2018). The studies they include are certainly the most promising ones to have recently emerged, because they address traditional issues from the enlightening perspective of cognitive pragmatics.

In this chapter I will attempt to show how the tools of pragmatics, and particularly Relevance Theory, afford us a new look at old issues.

1 Ordinary and non-ordinary usages of language

During the first linguistics conference I attended, in May 1978 in Metz, France, the audience experienced an extraordinary event during the closing session. The session had been opened for questions for a couple of minutes when a young man asked for the microphone. The topic of the conference was the notion of aspect,[141] what was not very well known in traditional French grammar, because the verbal system in French and Romance languages is organised around verbal tenses rather than aspect, which is neither grammaticalized nor lexicalised, unlike Slavic languages, which differentiate between perfective and imperfective verbs in the lexicon.[142] One of the questions that is studied in a Romance language like French is whether the contrast between tenses like the Imparfait, corresponding to the English Past Progressive and Simple Past, and the Passé Simple (Simple Past in English) is aspectual – the Imparfait being imperfect, the Passé Simple perfective – or temporal – the Imparfait giving background information, and the Passé Simple foreground information (Weinrich 1973). The young man took the floor and said:

(240) *Your discussion is interesting, but you have forgotten to talk about one fundamental aspect: the aquatic aspect.*

The chairman elegantly managed to deflect the question, and the conference continued.

How can this incident be explained: was the young man playing a joke, did he have mental issues, or was he simply a poet? It is obvious that the intrusion of the expression *aquatic aspect* in a scholarly conference was highly inappropriate. But what is the difference between this occurrence and the incongruous images mentioned in Isodore Ducasse, Count of Lautréamont's famous sentence:

(241) *Beau [. . .] comme la rencontre fortuite sur une table de dissection d'une machine à coudre et d'un parapluie.* (Lautréamont, *Le chant du Maldoror*)
'Beautiful like the chance meeting on a dissection table of a sewing machine and an umbrella.'

There are at least two points in common between the young man's question and Lautréamont: they seem to appear out of nowhere and they encourage comprehension processes that stretch beyond the search for ordinary relevance. The main effect of *the aquatic aspect* was to call into question the relevance of the topic of the conference and the field it was exploring; in Lautréamont's sentence the search for relevance – what is the relationship between the three artefacts? – leads to interpreting it as a sexual encounter between a man and a woman.

---

141 For the proceedings of this conference, see David and Martin (1980).
142 See Moeschler et al. (1998) for the semantics and pragmatics of French tenses.

These examples illustrate non-ordinary usage of language. It is easy to understand why they are not ordinary: it is unexpected to talk about *the aquatic aspect* in an academic conference on grammatical aspect, and equally unusual to refer to an umbrella and a sewing machine as metaphors for sexual organs.

Alongside non-ordinary usages there are *ordinary* usages that stand out for their non-literal meanings. This is the case for metaphor, metonymy, irony, and zeugma. A metaphor* introduces a resemblance: one concept is understood in terms of another concept. An angel has certain properties such as protecting human beings, which are associated in (242) with a young woman; a pigsty is the dirty and disgusting place where pigs live, and comparing a teenager's room to a pigsty is a severe criticism and a request that the room be cleaned (243); a bulldozer is a piece of construction equipment that levels ground and removes obstacles: a human being's indestructibility and habit of flattening the opposition make the comparison possible (244):

(242) *Abi is an angel* = Abi is a person who cares about others.

(243) *Your room is a pigsty* = your room is dirty and must be cleaned.

(244) *Max is a bulldozer* = Max is a person who is not held back by any obstacle.

*Metonymy** is traditionally described as a correspondence relationship: the meal corresponds to the client, the author to his book, and the means to the result:

(245) *The ham omelette jumped into a taxi* = the client who ordered the ham omelette jumped into a taxi.

(246) *Agatha Christie is on the left hand shelf* = Agatha Christie's book is on the left hand shelf

(247) *Pelé's head was unstoppable* = the goal scored by Pelé with his head was unstoppable

*Irony** is not a non-ordinary usage of language, contrary to its traditional definition as a counter-truth. Even in the most extreme cases – where irony is manifestly not a case of counter-truth, like in (248) – nothing seems to diverge from linguistic rules:

(248) *Dans un restaurant de luxe, un client est attablé avec pour seule compagnie son chien, un petit teckel. Le patron vient faire la conversation et vante les qualités du restaurant: "Vous savez, monsieur, notre chef est l'ancien cuisinier du roi*

Farouk." – "Ah, bon?", dit seulement le client. Le patron, sans se décourager: "Et notre sommelier, c'est l'ancien sommelier de la cour d'Angleterre... Quant à notre pâtissier, nous avons recueilli celui de l'empereur Bao-Daï". Devant le mutisme du client, le patron change de conversation: "Vous avez là, monsieur, un bien joli teckel". À quoi le client répond: "Mon teckel, monsieur, c'est un ancien Saint-Bernard". (Ducrot 1984: 211–212)

[In an expensive restaurant, a client sits alone at a table with his dog, a small dachshund. The boss starts a conversation with the client and praises the restaurant's qualities: "You know, sir, our chef is King Farouk's former cook." – "Is that so?", the client says. Undiscouraged the boss continues: "And our wine steward is the former wine steward of the English court... As for our pastry chef, he used to work for Emperor Bao-Dai". Faced with the client's silence, the boss changes the topic of conversation: "Sir, you have a very pretty dachshund". The client answers: "My dachshund, Sir, is a former Saint Bernard".] (my translation)

The irony in this example stems from a simple analogy: *my X is the former X of Y*. This analogy makes sense with a cook or a wine steward, but not with dog breeds, hence the ironic effect.

And finally, zeugma* does not involve grammar, simply because zeugma contains syntactic parallelism but not semantic parallelism. (249) contains both syntactic and semantic parallelisms, whereas in (250) the parallelism is only syntactic:

(249) *Mary arrived with John, Sophia with Mark and Lucy with Peter.*

(250) *Mary arrived with John, Sophia with Mark and Lucy with a sad face.*

In the example of Lucy's sad face, one can indeed – and this is the reason for the zeugma's comic effect – wonder whether it was caused by the fact that Mary and Sophia arrived with male friends, or if John and Mark were not somehow involved in her sadness. In a nutshell, it can be stated that all figures of speech, including but not limited to metaphor, metonymy, irony, and zeugma, are not non-ordinary usages of language.

2 Figure of speech: The classic version

As we have just seen, figures of speech, as they are known in classic rhetoric, are not extraordinary usages of language. In his well-known 18th-century treatise, Du Marsais observed that there were more metaphors spoken in a single day in the Parisian Halles Market than in several days of scholarly assemblies (Du Marsais [1817] 2013: 1–2):

> En effet, je suis persuadé qu'il se fait plus de Figures un jour de marché à la Halle, qu'il ne s'en fait en plusieurs jours d'assemblées académiques. Ainsi, bien loin que les Figures s'éloignent du langage ordinaire des homes, ce seroit au contraire les façons de parler sans Figures qui s'en éloigneroient, s'il étoit possible de faire un discours où il n'y eût que des expressions non figurées.
>
> [Indeed, I am convinced that there are more Figures spoken in one day at the Halles Market than there are during several days of academic assemblies. Therefore, although these Figures are far removed from everyday language, it would be on the contrary unnatural to speak without such Figures, if it were indeed possible to make a speech that contained only non-figurative expressions.   (my translation)

This excerpt is quite extraordinary, because Du Marsais states exactly the opposite of the traditional version of rhetoric, which supposes that discourse figures are *deviations from a norm*. But what is the norm? The answer is simple: *the norm is literal meaning*.

But if this is the case then the comprehension of every figure must first transit through the stage of literal meaning. Literal meaning is assessed as inappropriate in a given context, and replaced with a non-literal one. In the case of metaphor – and this is also true of irony – literal meaning yields a false proposition. By saying *Abi is an angel* the speaker literally says something false, since Abi is a human being and angels are not human. Similarly, when she criticises her son who came home with a bad grade in math, a mother utters a proposition that is literally false:

(251)   *It's amazing how good you are in math.*

These approaches, which extend from classic rhetoric – see the two levels of language theory discussed in chapter 2 – to a majority of philosophical approaches to metaphor, like those of Grice (1975) and Searle (1979), are called *non-constructivist** by Ortony (1979). According to Grice's approach, metaphor and irony are the result of an ostensive violation of the first maxim of quality: "Do not say what you believe to be false" (Grice 1975: 46). The problem with this approach, as has been pointed out by Deirdre Wilson and Dan Sperber (1981: 161), is that it makes false predictions. To wit, the following utterances are neither cases of irony (252a) nor metaphor (252b), although they satisfy the definitions of these two figures:

(252) The speaker hands her addressee a £5 banknote:
   a. *This is not a £5 note.*
   b. *This is a 5 yen note.*

On the other hand, while Searle's (1979) theory is explicit, it has the disadvantage of operating only on frozen or dead metaphors and not on creative or vivid metaphors. Searle's analysis is based on three strategies of interpretation: (i) determine whether or not the hearer must look for a metaphorical interpretation; (ii) compute the value of the metaphorical meaning; (iii) determine this value among the range of all possible candidates. The first strategy aims at detecting whether speaker meaning does or does not correspond to sentence meaning. The second strategy determines the possible values of the paraphrase (PAR) *S is R* from the metaphor (MET) *S is P*. In other words it determines how *S* resembles *P* in order to determine *R*. Finally, the third strategy limits the possible values of *R*.

There are thus a certain number of *principles* that allow one to go from *S is P* to its paraphrase, *S is R*. These are (i) objects which are *P* are *R* by definition (253); (ii) objects which are *P* are *R* by accident (254); (iii) it is generally said that objects are *P* are *R*, even though this is false (255); and finally, (iv) objects which are *P* are not *R*, but for reasons due to one's culture or sensitivity, one associates objects which are *P* to properties of *R* (256) (Searle 1979: 107–108):

(253) (MET) *Sam is a giant.*
      (PAR) Sam is big (giants are big)

(254) (MET) *Sam is a pig.*
      (PAR) Sam is filthy, gluttonous, and sloppy, etc. (pigs are filthy, gluttonous, and sloppy, etc.)

(255) (MET) Richard *is a gorilla.*
      (PAR) Richard is mean, nasty, prone to violence, and so on (it is believed that gorillas are mean, nasty, prone to violence, when in fact they are shy, timid, and sensitive creatures)

(256) (MET) Sally *is a block of ice.*
      (PAR) Sally is unemotional (degrees of temperature are associated with emotions, coldness is associated with a lack of emotions)

As you might imagine, it is difficult to apply principles like these to vivid and creative metaphors such as (257) and (258):

(257) *La femme est l'avenir de l'homme.* (Aragon)
the woman is the future of the man
'Woman is man's future.'

(258) *No man is an island.* (John Donne)

There appears to be a problem with *non-constructionist** approaches; those approaches to metaphors whose comprehension depends on an initial decoding of its literal meaning (sentence meaning). An alternative approach is the *constructivist** one: according to this approach the comprehension process is independent of an initial and literal interpretation. How does this work?

First, constructivist approaches claim that creative metaphors cannot be paraphrased. How could Aragon's metaphor be paraphrased? Would its paraphrase be "without woman, humanity would not exist"? But couldn't it also be "women can improve men"? How can we determine the correct paraphrase? And isn't the *raison d'être* of a metaphor the fact that no paraphrase can convey it exactly, that there is no other way to express the speaker's thought?

Without giving precise answers to these questions, I can make two preliminary statements: first, that the cognitive function of metaphors is to express, in a non-literal way, complex contents which could not be exhausted in a literal translation. This makes it possible to distinguish between *metaphors* and *approximations*: in an *approximation**, the expressed proposition is literally false, but relevant. Unlike metaphor, its implicit meaning is easy to recover (Sperber and Wilson 1985–1986). An example of approximation follows: if a Japanese friend asks where I live I will answer *I live in Cluny*, a small medieval town in South Burgundy that is easy to identify for historical reasons. Since I actually live in a small village 10 km from Cluny, my utterance is literally false, but it is relevant. As we will shortly see, metaphors give rise to a range of weakly communicated implicatures, which explains why it is difficult and even impossible to paraphrase them. But before developing this issue, which is central to the comprehension of non-ordinary usages of language, I would like to discuss another approach to metaphor: the cognitive approach.

3 Metaphorical thought

The cognitive approach to figures of speech, in particular metaphor and metonymy, as presented in the research of the American linguist George Lakoff (UC

Berkeley),[143] is based on an approach to cognition, logic, and reason that differs from the Aristotelian tradition. Here is how George Lakoff presents these two types of approaches (Lakoff 1987: xi):

> On the traditional view, reason is abstract and disembodied. On the new view, reason has a bodily basis. The traditional view sees reason as literal, as primarily about propositions that can be objectively either true or false. The new view takes imaginative aspects of reason – metaphor, metonymy, and mental imagery – as central to reason, rather than as a peripheral and inconsequential adjunct to the literal.

Lakoff's approach is based on the notion of *category** – "most of our words and concepts designate categories" (Lakoff 1987: xiii) – and gives rise to *prototype theory**, which organises categories. The central idea of prototype theory (Rosch 1977, 1978) is simple. Rather than viewing categories, for instance the category BIRD, as a set of equal entities, defined by a truth-valuable membership criterion – an entity is or is not a bird – categories are organised around a particular member, representative and prototypical of the category. In western Europe the sparrow, a small urban bird, is a good candidate for the category BIRD. The concept of prototype emerged in response to apparently absurd questions such as "is a sparrow more a bird than a chicken?". According to the traditional *model of necessary and sufficient conditions**, chickens as well as sparrows are birds, and equally qualify as members of this category.

The question of which conditions define a category immediately arises: unlike sparrows, chickens do not fly, and if they are birds, then the property of FLYING cannot be a *necessary* condition. The property of having feathers is similar, because some birds, like kiwis, do not have feathers, but a thin, hair-like coat. In other words, for empirical reasons, very few conditions can be considered as necessary. Some of them, moreover, such as BEING OVIPAROUS, are shared by other species like reptiles and snakes. On the contrary, prototype theory and the new vision of categories have a cognitive basis. Indeed, it is fundamental to categorise entities into categories which have cognitive relevance – think for instance of the importance of plant categorisation for primitive cultures.

However, George Lakoff's new conception of reason is not entirely opposed to objectivism. His so-called *experiential realism* shares several properties with the realist approach, including: "(*a*) a commitment to the existence of the real world, (*b*) a recognition that reality places constraints on concepts, (*c*) a conception of truth that goes beyond mere internal coherence, and (*d*) a commitment to the existence of stable knowledge of the world" (Lakoff 1987: xv).

---

143 Lakoff and Johnson (1980), Lakoff (1987).

How can metaphors and metonymies be understood according to Lakoff's theory of categorisation and embodied cognition? These figures and others like them are *idealised cognitive models**. The organising principles of these models are as follows:

(i) The principle of structures of images schemas explaining the role of mental images in categorisation, in particular its role in sentences semantics (Langacker 1987, 1991);
(ii) the principle of metaphorical extensions, that is, the integration of metaphorical processes to categorisation (Gibbs and Steen 1999);
(iii) the principle of metonymic extensions, that is, the integration of metonymic processes to categorisation (Panther and Radden 1999).

The first principle gives a function to image schemas in sentential semantics. Imagine the following situation (Langacker 1991). You ask me to describe my kitchen and I tell you:

(259) *The lamp is above* the table.

What do you see? You imagine a lamp, certainly a prototypical one, although I didn't describe it; a table, and since I'm talking about a kitchen, it is certainly not an end table, and since I said nothing about its form, it is probably a rectangular one, like most tables, and since we are not in a weightless spaceship, you imagine a vertical relationship between the lamp and the table. The crucial point here, according to Ronald Langacker (1991), is that both the grammar and the semantics of languages are based on usage schemas. At the deepest level of natural languages cognition is not made up of abstract conceptual representations, but of image schemas whose motivation is mainly iconic: we visualise scenes described in language as images, complete with their spatial and temporal constraints – we know for example that a spatial relationship described by *over* is constant in time and space (see Lakoff 1987).[144]

The second principle stipulates that concepts are organised according to metaphorical schemas and structures. Lakoff distinguishes between two types of metaphorical schemas: orientational and ontological metaphors (Lakoff and Johnson 1980). *Orientational* metaphors use spatial axes and landmarks to conceptualise complex concepts like HAPPINESS, SADNESS, and TIME with assistance from spatial concepts:

---

[144] One of the main developments of cognitive grammar is the syntactic framework of the grammar of constructions. See among others Goldberg (2006).

(260) HAPPY IS up
I'm feeling up.

(261) SAD IS DOWN
He is really down these days.

(262) FORESEEABLE FUTURE EVENTS ARE UP (AND AHEAD)
What's coming up this week?
I'm afraid of what's up ahead of us.

The second type of metaphors, *ontological* metaphors, enable the conceptualisation of abstract concepts like TIME, LOVE, IDEAS, via concepts we have experienced such as MONEY, WAR, FOOD:

(263) TIME IS MONEY
I have invested too much time in this project.

(264) LOVE IS WAR
He is known for his many rapid conquests.

(265) IDEAS ARE FOOD
What he said left a bad taste in her mouth.

The function of metaphor is thus very different from the prediction of classic rhetoric: its main function is to express abstract and complex concepts via other concepts that we have experienced.

Lastly, the principle of metonymic extensions explains that an object can be designated via the description of another object to which, for pragmatic or cultural reasons, it is associated. For instance, it is possible to refer to a client in a restaurant with the meal he ordered (*the mushroom omelette*), to a book with its author (*Plato*), and to the institution with the people in charge (*the White House*), etc. This principle, which the French linguist Gilles Fauconnier (1985) has called the *identification principle**, explains what classic rhetoric pointlessly describes by distinguishing between *metonymy* and *synecdoche*. Metonymy is defined as a trope through correspondence, whereas synecdoche is defined as a trope through connection, a trope being "certains sens plus ou moins différens du sens primitif, qu'offrent, dans l'expression de la pensée, les mots appliqués à de nouvelles idées" [certain senses more or less different from the primitive sense, that offer, in the expression of thought, the words applied to new ideas] (Fontanier ([1930] 1968: 39).

According to cognitive semantics, examples (266)–(267) involve the same principle: the identification principle in mental spaces, which, through a description of an object a (*trigger**), may describe an object b (*target**) that is related to it via a pragmatic connector.¹⁴⁵ Classic rhetoric distinguishes among three cases: *sign* metonymy (*irons* for "slavery"), *place* metonymy (*Africa* for "African people") and *part* synecdoche (*sails* for "boats"):

(266) *In the 18th century, the slave traders engaged in their odious business and Africa was in irons.*

(267) *The sea was covered with sails.*

The theory of mental spaces* makes it possible to explain many facts about grammar that have appeared mysterious until now: for instance, that a pronoun can use the referent as a trigger (268) or a target (269), and can agree with it in terms of gender. When the pronoun refers to the target, a change in gender can occur, as in (269) (Fauconnier 1985: 5–6):

(268) Trigger
Plato is on the top shelf. You'll find that he is a very interesting author.

(269) Target
Plato is on the top shelf. It is bound in leather.

The relevant point is that only open connectors allow the reprise with both a trigger and a target. Less frequently used connectors, said to be closed, only allow the reprise with the target:

(270) Target
The mushroom omelette left without paying the bill. He jumped into a taxi.

(271) Trigger
The mushroom omelette left without paying the bill. It was inedible.

---

145 "*Identification (ID) Principle*: If two objects (in the most general sense), *a* and *b*, are linked by a pragmatic function F ($b = F(a)$), a description of *a*, d_a, may be used to identify its counterpart". (Fauconnier 1985: 3)

The pragmatic connector *meal-client* is less frequent that the connector *author-book*, what explains this strange grammatical behaviour.[146]

Thus far I have discussed two approaches to figures of speech: non-constructivist approaches, according to which access to non-literal meaning must transit through literal meaning, and constructivist approaches, which minimise and can even eliminate the difference between literal and figurative meaning. I will now examine a second constructivist approach, the pragmatic approach of Relevance Theory, and will show how figures of speech are interpreted from the standpoint of Relevance Theory. However, a motive is required in order to continue in this direction. This motive is mainly based on experimental research on metaphors, in particular that of Ray Gibbs (1994) and Sam Glucksberg (2001), who were the first to show that metaphor treatment does not take longer than the treatment of a literal utterance, and that access to metaphorical meaning does not transit through literal meaning.[147]

4 Weak implicatures and non-propositional effects

In the field of newspaper criticism about literature, drama, or cinema, there is a strong belief according to which the quality of an artwork, whatever it is, is proportional to its ambiguity. The more "open" an artwork is, that is, the more interpretations it yields, the better it is. Where does this idea come from? It is in fact a direct consequence of structuralism, which refuses to take into account the intentions of the author, and only considers an artwork's form.

This description is of course a caricature, but it is meaningful in terms of how we understand the function of language with respect to non-ordinary usages, in particular for literature and drama. Paradoxically, however, although the concept of communication is put forward, the idea that an artwork is detached from its author's intentions is certainly the most frequently asserted commonplace. What is more, a great number of writers subscribe to such claims themselves, and leave it up to the reader to give meaning to their writing.

A paradox occurred when an academic critic, at the peak moment of structuralism, affirmed exactly the opposite without suffering any consequences. In 1966 Tzvetan Todorov, a French structuralist literary critic, stated: "L'œuvre est en même temps un discours: il existe un narrateur qui relate l'histoire; et il y a en

---

[146] For a general description presentation of cognitive linguistics, see Evans and Green (2006).
[147] For a general presentation of experimental approaches to metaphors, see Noveck (2018: 159–171).

face de lui un lecteur qui la perçoit" [The work is at the same time a discourse: there is a narrator who relates the story; and there is opposite him a reader who perceives it] (Todorov 1966: 126). If this were the case, a literary work would therefore be an act of communication, even though the active principles of communication are not applicable to its comprehension.

This creates a real dilemma: if literary works are acts of communication, how can we make the assumption that they are essentially ambiguous? No communication acts seek to be ambiguous. Grice's maxim of manner stipulates "Be perspicuous", and the submaxim of manner states "Avoid ambiguity". Therefore, if a literary work is an act of communication, either it ostensively violates Grice's maxim or manner, or it is communication that differs from cooperative communication.

There are some cases of true ambiguity, mainly in pictorial artworks. Here are two examples: Wittgenstein's *duck-rabbit* (Figure 2), and Dali's *The Slave Market with the Disappearing Bust of Voltaire* (1940). In both cases the artist's intention was to represent ambiguous forms. With the duck-rabbit the viewer switches from one representation to another, but cannot see both at the same time. In Dali's painting, the same process occurs, but with a technique of concealment: first, one sees the two nuns, then Voltaire's portrait emerges. These cases are exceptional and are artistic games, as is anamorphosis.

Figure 2: Wittgenstein's duck-rabbit.[148]

Is it possible to apply this theory to pictorial works in general, and to fiction in particular? Might we consider that Giorgione's *The Tempest* is an ambiguous painting, for instance? Does it depict an approaching storm (inferable from the lightning in the clouds), or does it show the young shepherd's emotional

---

148 https://fr.wikipedia.org/wiki/Canard-lapin

storm as he looks at the young woman? *The Tempest* example is interesting because it shows that artworks such as these are not ambiguous: they may be indeterminate, because it is difficult to associate a precise and unique intention to their author. But their processing in the spectator's or the reader's mind triggers a wide range of indeterminate weak implicatures* which fall under his responsibility.

This is exactly what Relevance Theory predicts for the processing of tropes in general and of metaphors in particular: by using a frozen metaphor the speaker communicates a determinate range of strong implicatures that fall under her responsibility, whereas a creative metaphor gives rise to an indeterminate range of weakly communicated implicatures that fall under the audience's or reader's responsibility. Does the notion of weak implicature account for metaphors? In other words, how is a metaphor understood? And how can we explain the non-propositional effects of figures of speech?

Dan Sperber and Deirdre Wilson ([1986] 1995: 236) argue in favour of the hypothesis that a metaphor gives rise to "a wide array of contextual implications [implicatures]" (Sperber and Wilson [1986] 1995: 236). These implicatures can be either strong, as in the case of conventional metaphors, or weak, as in the case of rich and creative metaphors:

> In general, the wider the range of potential implicatures and the greater the hearer's responsibility for constructing them, the more poetic the effect, the more creative the metaphor. (...) In the richest and most successful cases, the hearer or reader can go beyond just exploring the immediate context and the entries for concepts involved in it, accessing a wide area of knowledge, adding metaphors of his own as interpretations of possible developments he is not ready to go into, and getting more and more very weak implicatures, with suggestions for still further processing. The result is a quite complex picture, for which the hearer has to take a large part of responsibility, but the discovery of which has been triggered by the writer. The surprise or beauty of a successful creative metaphor lies in this condensation, in the fact that a single expression which has itself been loosely used will determine a very wide range of acceptable weak implicatures.
> (Sperber and Wilson [1986] 1995: 236–237)

The important point is that the comprehension of creative metaphors, which trigger poetic effects, does not result in ambiguity, but rather in indeterminacy in meaning: several implicatures, even weak ones, enrich the comprehension of utterances and strengthen their relevance. For these reasons, pragmatic approaches do not retain the ambiguity thesis.

Now, what about another aspect of figures, their non-propositional effects, such as those produced by creative metaphors? For instance, how can we explain the effect of these two verses by Verlaine (*Romances sans parole*), in which the verb *pleurer* 'to cry' triggers a range of weak implicatures:

(272) *Il pleure dans mon cœur*
Comme il pleut sur la ville.

'It rains in my heart
As it rains on the town.'

And how can we explain the comic effect of its pastiche by the French poet Guillaume Apollinaire (*Poèmes retrouvés*)?

(273) *Il flotte dans mes bottes*
Comme il pleut sur cette ville.

'It pours in my boots
Like it rains on that town.'

In both cases, a feeling of sadness is implicated, but the cause of the sadness is very different: sadness caused by grief, a pain as strong as the rain (Verlaine), and sadness caused by the weather and the rain (Apollinaire).

In *Relevance*, Dan Sperber and Deirdre Wilson bind *style* and *implicature* in the following way: "A speaker aiming at optimal relevance will leave implicit everything her hearer can be trusted to supply with less efforts than would be needed to process an explicit prompt. The more information she leaves implicit, the greater the degree of mutual understanding she makes it manifest that she takes to exist between her and her hearer" (Sperber and Wilson [1986] 1995: 218). The new concept that emerges here is *mutual understanding*. The search for relevance is thus not simply what justifies, for a hearer or a reader, the launching of the comprehension process: the presumption of optimal relevance guarantees that he will not make undue processing efforts. The search for relevance also justifies acts of communication, or *mutual understanding*. I will observe the implications of this conclusion as well as the problems it produces later on. For now I will investigate how style can contribute to relevance.

Sperber and Wilson ([1986] 1995: 222) define the *poetic effect** as "the peculiar effect of an utterance which achieves most of its relevance through a wide array of weak implicatures". What is its function? According to these authors, "poetic effects create common impressions rather than common knowledge. Utterances with poetic effects can be used precisely to create this sense of apparently affective rather than cognitive mutuality" (Sperber and Wilson [1986] 1995: 224). The main goal of communication is therefore to create a *climate of mutuality*, or shared feelings. This goes beyond any informative goals of communication that are formulated in terms of the cognitive environment: "We want to suggest that the communicator's informative intention is better described as an intention *to* *modify directly not the thoughts but the cognitive environment of the audience*" (Sperber and Wilson [1986] 1995: 58, my emphasis).

In producing poetic – or non-propositional – effects, the speaker or author aims at creating a mutual cognitive environment that includes the sharing of mental states. Summoning up non-propositional effects is thus not an accidental effect: it is constitutive of every utterance and therefore of every discourse. The means used to produce these effects, at once propositional and non-propositional, and which determine the speaker's mental and emotional state, constitute what is commonly called *style**. At the end of this chapter I will observe an optimal use of style in representing the mental states of fictional characters rather than of the speaker.

Before developing this aspect of non-propositional effects in fiction, I would like to give another illustration of propositional effects. The example I will discuss is Chimène's famous line, which is spoken after Rodrigue's desperate monologue in Corneille's *Le Cid*:

(274) Rodrigue: *Au nom d'un père mort, ou de notre amitié,*
Punis-moi par vengeance, ou du moins par pitié.
Ton malheureux amant aura bien moins de peine
À mourir par ta main qu'à vivre avec ta haine.
Chimène: *Va, je ne te hais point.*

[Rodrigue: In the name of a dead father, or our amity,
Punish by vengeance, or at least by pity.
Your unfortunate lover finds here less pain,
Death at your hand, than life with your disdain.
Chimène: Go, I do not disdain you.][149]

What does Chimène mean by asserting *I do not disdain you*? Why did she not say directly to Rodrigue what she means: that she loves him. The alternative would have been for Chimène to say, *Go, I love you*. But by saying this she would not have allowed Rodrigue to do what he had to do: understand that Chimène loves him. Rodrigue thinks that she must hate him, since he has just killed her father, don Gomès. It is not possible in this context for Chimène to explicitly confess her love, especially because Rodrigue has just told her that he would prefer she kills him rather than disdain him. Nor is it possible for Chimène to deny she loves Rodri-

---

[149] Translated by A. S. Kline, The New York Public Library, Digital Collections, https://www.poetryintranslation.com/PITBR/French/LeCid.php, accessed 30 August 2018.

gue. How is it possible that by saying *I do not disdain you*, Chimène implicates "I love you"?

The classic explanation involves *litotes** (understatement): that which says less means more. A typical example is a driver confessing he *drank a little* when his breathalyzer test is positive: in this case a quantitative scale connects *a little* and *a lot*. But no semantic scale exists between *to love* and *to hate*. So how can we explain that we understand *not hating* as meaning *loving*? Here is the pragmatic answer (Horn 1989, Moeschler 2020b).

Contrary predicates*, which are traditionally called *antonyms**, can be represented in the logical square (Figure 3), which defines three logical relationships:

(i)   *contrariety**: contrary predicates cannot be true together, but can be false together;
(ii) *subcontrariety**: subcontrary predicates can be true but not false together;
(iii) *contradiction**: only one of contradictory predicates is true.

Whereas *to hate* and *to love* are *contrary* predicates, *not to love* and *not to hate* are subcontrary predicates, while *to hate* and *not to hate*, as well as *to love* and *not to love*, are contradictories.

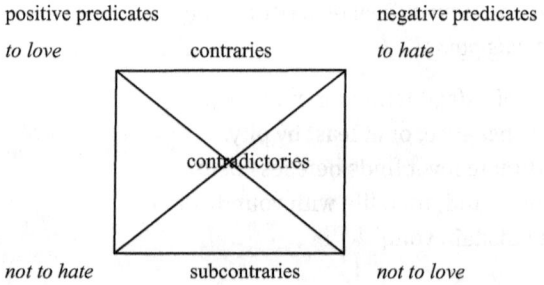

Figure 3: The logical square of antonyms.

The linguist Laurence Horn discovered a fundamental relationship between the negation of an antonym and its contrary: *the negated predicate conversationally implicates its contrary*. In other words, saying *I don't love you* is equal to saying, in a weak but implicit way, *I hate you*; and saying *I don't hate you* implicitly means *I love you*. This implicature is an *R*-implicature (*R* for Relation, or Relevance) according to Horn's classification of implicature (Horn 1984). These relevance implicatures – what Horn terms the *MaxContrary Effect** or the maximum contrary effect – are, however, fragile, because they are easily cancellable. In the above example, Chimène could have said:

(275) *Go, I do not* disdain *you, but I do not love you either.*

The crucial point is that Chimène gives the responsibility of understanding what she means to Rodrigue, which is a totally ordinary and relevant usage of implicatures.[150]

We have strongly affirmed the following propositions in this chapter: (i) figures of speech are ordinary usages of language; (ii) figures yield effects, some strong and others weak; (iii) some weakly communicated effects have no representation contents, but convey a speaker or author's mental state; and finally, (iv) implicit communication has the advantage of leaving the choice of drawing or not drawing the implicature up to the addressee or reader.

It is now time to explore a general issue which concerns the domain of fiction, and in particular a certain type of fiction known as *narration*: is it possible in such cases to speak of communication? If so, between which parties does it take place?

5 Narration and temporal order between events

The David Fincher film *The Curious Case of Benjamin Button*, 2009, starring Brad Pitt and Cate Blanchett, is based on a short story by F. Scott Fitzgerald. It starts in an interesting way, which is not part of Fitzgerald's original short story. A woman is at the hospital during her dying mother's last moments. The mother (Daisy) tells her daughter the following story before giving her a diary that contains Benjamin's tale. Born as an old man, Benjamin lived life backwards, and died as a newborn.

(276)   Daisy: *They built the train station* in *1918. My father was there the day it opened. He said they had a tuba band playing. They had the finest clockmaker in all the South to build that glorious clock. His name was Mr. Gateau. Mr. Cake. He was married to a Creole of Evangeline Parish and they had a son. Mr. Gateau was from birth absolutely blind. When their son was old enough, he joined the Army. And they prayed God would keep him out of harm's way. For months, he did nothing but work on that clock. One day, a letter came. And Mr. Gateau, done for the night, went up, alone, to bed. And their son came home. They buried him in the family plot where he would be with them when their time came. Mr. Cake worked on his clock*

---

150 There are exceptions to these relationships between antonyms. Some antonyms, positive as well as negative, do not display symmetric behaviour: *not nice* is generally understood as *nasty*, but *not nasty* does not implicate *nice*. For a development, see Moeschler (2020b).

> *labouring to finish. It was a morning to remember. Papa said there were people everywhere. Even Teddy Roosevelt came.* [People clapping]
>
> A man: *It's running backwards!*
> [Murmuring]
>
> Mr. Gateau: *I made it that way so that perhaps the boys we lost in the war might stand and come home again.* [Soldiers stand up on the battlefield and walk backwards] *Home to farm, work, have children.* [Teddy Roosevelt takes his hat off] *To live long, full lives. Perhaps my own son will come home again.* [Soldiers exit the train backwards and Mr. Gateau's son join his parents on the platform] *I'm sorry if I've offended anybody. I hope you enjoy my clock.*
>
> Daisy: *Mr. Cake was never seen again. Some say he died of a broken heart. Some say he went to sea.*

In the war scene that plays while Mr. Gateau speaks, events do not occur in chronological order but in antechronological order. What is odd about the scene? From the point of view of visual perception, our experience of the world never reverses temporal order: we see events as flowing in time, and the arrow of time points in one direction only.[151] A surprising fact is that left to right orientation is also true for *movement*, even when an image is static, like in a photograph, because this is the direction in which our eyes move when we read. A few years ago I suggested a photo of a five-year old archer for the cover of an issue of *Nouveaux cahiers de linguistique française*, the journal of the University of Geneva's Department of Linguistics. The direction of the movement in the original photo went from right to left. One of my colleagues requested that we switch the direction of the photo. The contrast between the two images clearly shows that when the arrow points to the right the image is more easily processed, while it is harder to process when the arrow points to the left (Figure 4).

How are the Benjamin Button example, the photo of the young archer, and language related? The interesting point is that, in language usage, one way of reporting events is known as *narrative*. The trivial definition of a narrative* states that it has a beginning, a middle, and an end. The crucial aspect is that an initial situation leads to a final situation, which generally contains the reasons why the narrative was told.

---

[151] For the physics of time, see Price (1996).

Figure 4: Movement orientations (original picture on the left, published photograph on the right).

This is particularly true of funny stories: the punchline of the story justifies its narration, apart from the fact that funny stories try to make us laugh and often trick the hearer. A funny story can be a simple pun or have a real narrative structure, as the following examples show:

(277) *Why did they bury Washington on a hill? Because he was dead.* (Raskin 1985: 248).

(278) Marguerite *Duras   n'   a   pas seulement écrit   que des*
 Marguerite Duras neg has neg only   written only some
 conneries. Elle en   a   aussi filmé.[152]
 crap   she   pro has also   filmed
 'Marguerite Duras has not only written crap. She's filmed some, too.'

(279) *An impoverished individual borrowed 25 florins from a prosperous acquaintance, with many asseverations of his necessitous circumstances. The very same day his benefactor met him again in a restaurant with a plate of salmon mayonnaise in front of him. The benefactor reproached him: "What?*

---

[152] Pierre Desproges, in *Hiroshima mon amour*. See https://www.youtube.com/watch?v=eRUjp-F9uUcg, accessed 28 November 2019.

> *You borrow money from me and then order yourself salmon mayonnaise? Is that what you've used my money for?" "I don't understand you", replied the object of the attack; "if I haven't any money I can't eat salmon mayonnaise, and if I have some money I mustn't eat salmon mayonnaise. Well, then, when am I to eat salmon mayonnaise?"*
>
> (Freud [1905] 1957: 34–35)

In these funny stories, the situation is described through a question (Washington), the subject of the joke (Marguerite Duras), and a problem of logic (Freud). These extreme examples demonstrate that a narrative is not defined by structure. Think about all the novels you have read. Is there a common narrative structure in novels like *Oliver Twist, The Catcher in the Rye, To Kill a Mockingbird*, etc.? It is immediately apparent that a common structure is not easy to find; at best, one can say that *events are temporally ordered* in a narrative*. Indeed, we understand what is described in a narrative because we can put events in order one after the other.[153] Here are two excellent examples, excerpted from works by Italian writers. The first is the beginning of *The Sunday Woman* by Carlo Fruttero and Franco Lucentini, and the second is the opening of *Il giorno della civetta* 'The Day of the Owl' by Leonardo Sciascia:[154]

(280) *That Tuesday in June on which he was murdered, Signor Garrone, the architect, looked at his watch many times. He had begun by opening his eyes in the pitch darkness of his bedroom, where the carefully sealed window did not allow a ray of light to penetrate. While his hand, clumsy with impatience, groped along the loop of wire, hunting for the switch, the architect was seized by an irrational fear: it was terribly late, the moment for his telephone call had already gone by.*[155]

(281) *L'autobus stava per partire, rombava sordo con improvvisi raschi e singulti. La piazza era silenziosa nel grigio dell'alba, sfilacce di nebbia ai campanili*

---

[153] There is an exception, which resembles a style exercise, in Martin Amis' novel *Times's Arrow* (1991). In this narrative everything happens backwards:

Anyway, I lay there, in a mood of quiet celebration, for however long it was, until the evil hour – and the orderlies. The golfing doctors I could handle, the nurse was an unqualified plus. But then came the orderlies, who dealt with me by means of electricity and air. There were three of them. They were unceremonious. They hurried into the room and bundled me into my clothes and stretchered me into the garden. That's right. Then with the jump leads, like two telephones (white – white-hot), they zapped my chest. Finally, before they went away, one of them kissed me. I think I know the name of this kiss. It is called the kiss of life. Then I must have blacked out.

[154] Leonardo Sciascia. 1993. *Il giorno della civetta*, 3. Milano: Adelphi Edizioni.
[155] Carlo Fruttero and Franco Lucentini. 1976. *The Sunday Woman*, 5. Glasgow: Collins.

della Matrice: solo il rombo dell'autobus e la di panelle, panelle calde panelle, implorante ed ironica. Il bigliettaio chiuse lo sportello, l'autobus si mosse con un rumore di sfasciume. L'ultima occhiata che il bigliettaio girò sulla piazza, colse l'uomo vestito di scuro che veniva correndo; il bigliettaio disse all'autista "un momento" e aprì lo sportello mentre l'autobus ancora si muoveva. Si sentirono due colpi squarciati: l'uomo vestito di scuro, che stava per saltare sul predellino, restò per un attimo sospeso, come tirato su per i capelli da una mano invisibile; gli cadde la cartella di mano e sulla cartella lentamente si afflosciò.[156]

[The bus was about to leave, growling with sudden scrapes and sobs. The square was silent in the grey of dawn, wisps of fog on the cathedral's bell towers: only the roar of the bus and the voice of the panelle merchant, panelle hot panelle, imploring and ironic. The conductor closed the door, the bus moved with a crashing noise. The conductor's last glance at the square caught the man dressed in dark clothing who was running; the conductor told the driver "just a moment" and opened the door while the bus was still moving. Two blows were heard: the darkly-dressed man, who was about to jump onto the step, remained suspended for a moment, as if an invisible hand were pulling him up by the hair; the briefcase fell from his hand and he slowly collapsed onto the briefcase.] (my translation)

These two opening scenes are traditional in the way they give information about events. In the beginning of *The Sunday Woman*, a flashback follows the first temporal landmark (*the day of Garrone's murder*); it is recounted in a series of Pluperfects. In the beginning of Sciascia's novel, the narrative context is given in the Italian Imperfetti, and the events that constitute the narrative frame are in Passato Remoto – the difference between these two tenses is generally neutralised in English, as the translation shows. However, in both cases, events follow one another in order.

This process is known as *temporal order** in the literature on verb tenses.[157] Temporal order has in fact only recently been defined. The first observations were made by the sociolinguist William Labov, who describes narrative as follows: "We define narrative as one method of recapitulating past experience by matching a verbal sequence of clauses to the sequence of events which (it is inferred) actually occurred" (Labov 1972b: 359–360). Labov's definition clearly includes both the

---

156 Leonardo Sciascia. 1993. *Il giorno della civetta*, 3. Milano: Adelphi Edizioni.
157 See Moeschler et al. (1998), Moeschler (2000) and (2019), Wilson and Sperber (2012: chapter 8).

order of events, a property of the described world, and the order of utterances in the discourse, a linguistic property. Labov gives the following example (Labov 1972b: 360):

(282) a. *The boy punched me*
b. *and I punched him*
c. *and the teacher came in*
d. *and stopped the fight.*

These four clauses describe events that follow each other in temporal order, providing an example of *chronological order*. Interestingly, however, Labov suggests another method of reporting events: temporal order inversion, which uses the Pluperfect, as shown in (283) (Labov 1972b: 360):

(283) a. *The teacher stopped the fight.*
b. *She had just come in.*
c. *I had punched this boy.*
d. *He had punched me.*

These two methods can be used together in the same narrative, but have different functions: temporal order is used to answer the question *what happens next?*, whereas reverse temporal order answers the question: *why did this event happen?* Temporal order, therefore, corresponds to what is known as the NARRATION discourse relation, whereas reverse temporal order corresponds to an EXPLANATION.

Here is a very simple example. You encounter the following sentence (284) in a text. It can call up two different questions: *what did John do next?* and *why did John go into a bar?* The following short discourses provide answers to these questions. Only the first one is a *narration** (285), however; the second (286) is an *explanation**:

(284) *John went into a bar.*

(285) *John went into a bar. I sat down in the back of the room.*

(286) *John went into a bar. He was looking for a quiet place to drown his sorrows.*

These examples show that two methods of representing real or fictitious events, the *narration* and the *explanation*, are at our disposal. In the next section we will examine another method that does not represent events, but gives access to the point of view from which they are represented.

6 The representation of speech and thought

The British writer Jonathan Coe was a guest on the French radio station *France Culture* on 24 October 2019[158] for the release of the French translation of his book *Middle England* (*Le Coeur de l'Angleterre*). The book's main topic is Brexit. Jonathan Coe answered a question about the writer's role in this way:

(287) *I am actually a very selfish writer. I write* for *myself. I write* to try to understand the world, to understand human nature, to better understand my country. And if in the process of doing that I tell a story that maybe helps to share something I discovered myself, that's great.

One of the best ways of understanding the world is to understand the thoughts and utterances of human beings. Literature, for many centuries, has allowed us to access the inner worlds of characters through so-called *free indirect discourse** (FID), which the linguist Ann Banfield (1982) calls *reported speech and thought*.

Ann Banfield is one of the first scholars who has attempted to use linguistic arguments to understand what literary fiction is. Her point of departure can be summarised in two strong theses. First, fiction, and particularly narration, is not communication; second, some sentences in literary fiction have no speaker. These are known as *unspeakable sentences*. These two claims, which are rejected by polyphonic approaches to semantics in linguistics (Ducrot 1984) as well as by narratology in literary studies (Genette 1980), are at the heart of the theses I have developed on language and communication in this book. It is now time to expand them further.

Narration is not communication: Banfield's argument is based on first-person narration. Semantically, the first-person pronoun *I* does not imply *you*. On the contrary, the second person-pronoun *you* implies *I*: a speaker must have said *you*, whereas a speaker can say *I* without the presence of an addressee. But as Banfield has pointed out, there are no second person narratives.[159] First person and third person narratives are, therefore, not acts of communication. This allows Banfield to raise the question of fiction in terms that differ from those of communication, and to focus instead on characters' thoughts and speeches, that is, on *free indirect discourse* (see below).

---

[158] *La Grande table*, Olivia Gesbert, 24 October 2019, https://www.franceculture.fr/emissions/la-grande-table-culture/jonathan-coe-il-y-a-des-conseillers-conjugaux-specialises-en-brexit-aujourdhui-en-grande-bretagne.
[159] See for instance Michel Butor's novel *La Modification* (Minuit, 1957), which is entirely written in the second person. It was translated into English as *Second Thoughts* (Faber and Faber, 1958).

To sum up, Ann Banfield distinguishes between three narrative types:
(i) Third person narratives without a narrator; that is, without a discourse entity who takes charge of narrative utterances and is distinct from the author, who is responsible for the production of the narrative.
(ii) First person narratives with a narrator, but no addressees and therefore no communication, like in the works of Proust.
(iii) A new category of narratives in which a first person addresses a second person – known as *skaz** (discourse in Russian) – as well as narratives containing dialect words, as if these expressions were in inverted commas.

Unspeakable sentences: Banfield's free indirect discourse analysis is based on the concepts of *self* or *subject of consciousness** and of *Expression**. By default, in communication the *subject of consciousness* – the perspective from which utterances and thoughts are represented – is associated with a first person. But in fiction, this perspective can be attributed to one of the characters described by a third person. In the example below, from *L'Éducation sentimentale* 'Sentimental Education' (Gustave Flaubert), the subject of consciousness is Frédéric, since the prediction cannot be attributed to the author (Flaubert). Since Frédéric will never become Madame Arnoux's lover, Flaubert would make contradictory statements in implying that Frederic will and will not become Madame Arnoux's lover.

(288) *Il [Frédéric] s'y montra gai. Mme Arnoux était maintenant près de sa mère, à Chartres. Mais il la retrouverait bientôt, et finirait pas être son amant.*[160]

[He [Frédéric] displayed the utmost gaiety on the occasion. Madame Arnoux was now with her mother at Chartres. But he would soon come across her again, and would end by being her lover.][161]

The sentences in FID are *Mme Arnoux était maintenant près de sa mère, à Chartres* 'Madame Arnoux was now with her mother at Chartres' and *Mais il la retrouverait bientôt, et finirait pas être son amant* 'But he would soon come across her again, and would end by being her lover'. Indeed, it is Frédéric who makes the prediction that he will come across her again, and the presence of *maintenant*

---
160 From Reboul (1992); Gustave Flaubert. 1965. *L'Éducation sentimentale*, 107. Paris: Gallimard.
161 Gustave Flaubert. 1904. *Sentimental Education*. New York: Walter Dumz.

'now', which is an *indexical** – a temporal expression interpreted relative to the speech point – can be explained only if it is interpreted at the moment when Frédéric thinks that Madame Arnoux is with her mother and that he will come across her soon. In direct and indirect discourse, this discourse would have been as follows:

(289) *"Madame Arnoux is now with her mother at Chartres. But I will soon come across her again, and will end by being her lover", thought Frédéric.*

(290) *Frédéric thought that Madame Arnoux was at that time with her mother at Chartres, but he would soon come across her again, and would end by being her lover.*

Indexicals are preserved in direct discourse, but the pronouns and tenses change; in indirect discourse, the indexical *now* becomes a non-indexical temporal expression (*at that time*), but the tenses and pronouns are not changed, as the following odd direct (291) and indirect (292) discourses show:

(291) # *"Madame Arnoux was now with her mother at Chartres. But he would soon come across her again, and would end by being her lover", thought Frédéric.*[162]

(292) # *Frédéric thought that Madame Arnoux is now with her mother at Chartres, but I will soon come across her again, and will end by being her lover.*[163]

In FID, the pronouns and tenses have not changed and are interpreted in the *context of utterance*, whereas indexicals are interpreted in the *context of thought*, in which the thinker is Frédéric.[164]

We may now wonder who is qualified to say that Frédéric has these thoughts and makes these predictions? For Banfield, there is only one subject of consciousness per *Expression**, that is, the syntactic category which cannot be embedded and does not describe the world, but expresses the attitudes, feelings, thoughts, and words of the subject of consciousness. Exclamations, for example, are a type

---

[162] This example is in FID but is confusing because of the quotation marks.
[163] One possible reading is that the indexicals *I* and *now* refer to the context of utterance rather than to the context of thought (Schlenker 2004).
[164] Context of utterance and context of thought are the two components of discourse context (Schlenker 2004).

of *Expression** that differs from ordinary sentences. In (293) (Banfield 1982: 38), the structure *NP + or + sentence* is not a common structure in English syntax; moreover, it does not describe anything, but expresses the speaker's annoyance. Expressions like these can appear only in direct discourse (294), and never occur in indirect discourse (295):[165]

(293)   John: *One more can of beer, or I'll leave.*

(294)   *John said: "One more can of beer, or I'll leave".*

(295)   * *John said that one more can of beer, or he'll leave.*

Banfield attributes to FID sentences a subject of consciousness that is different from the speaker. This explains why Flaubert neither says that Madame Arnoux is with her mother, nor predicts that Frédéric will come across her and end up being her lover. But if an FID sentence refers to a third person as a subject of consciousness, then it cannot have a speaker. FID sentences are therefore without speakers: they are *unspeakable* sentences.

This approach to fiction, narrative, and FID is very stimulating. It explains why we experience a feeling of proximity to characters through non-narrative sentences. But it also explains why there are personal pronouns and no proper names in FID. Indeed, in order to designate oneself, one uses first person pronouns rather than one's name. In FID a third person pronoun is the transposition of a first-person pronoun.

Banfield's approach has another advantage: it allows for a new approach to *style**, which according to Banfield's theory is the presence of subjectivity in an utterance. In other words, style is that which expresses the subjectivity of a subject of consciousness.

7 Causality in narration

I began this discussion about narratives by showing a property, temporal order, that was illustrated backwards through the example of soldiers who had fallen on the battlefield, sprang back up again, and returned to their parents on the railway

---

[165] One noteworthy exception in French literature is the novel *Cabinet-portrait*, by the Swiss writer Jean-Luc Benoziglio (Éditions du Seuil, 1980), in which Expressions are embedded in indirect discourse.

station platform. Again using the example of the film *The Strange Case of Benjamin Button*, I will now discuss another property of narration: *causality*. Events in a narrative form *causal chains**. We have all felt responsible for having indirectly caused an event, although we were not its direct cause: if we had done one thing differently, the course of events would have changed.

Causal links and counterfactuality can be defined as follows:

> On a pu décrire le lien causal entre A et B par une double contrefactuelle (positive et négative): Si un événement de type A s'était produit, un événement de type B se serait produit. Si un événement de type A ne s'était pas produit, un événement de type B ne se serait pas produit. (Reboul 2003: 45)

> [We have described the causal link between A and B with a double counterfactual (positive and negative): If an A type event had happened, a B type event would have happened. If an A type event had not happened, a B type event would have not happened.]

Counterfactuality, therefore, is the supposition that a fact, a state, or an event could be the case in the actual world, whereas it is not the case, because another fact, another state, or another event could also be the case – in that case, it is said to be true in another possible world. Counterfactual reasoning is typically given in answer to a question like: *What would happen if such and such a situation occurred?* Generally, counterfactual reasoning imagines that something that happened in the actual world did not occur. This type of reasoning can be illustrated with questions like the following:

(296) *What would World War II have been like if Hitler had been killed?*

(297) *What language would have been spoken in the USA if the Norman Kingdom had defeated the Kingdom of France in the Hundred Years War?*

(298) *What would my football career have been like if I had not crashed my car two days before the last match of the Swiss League B championship?*

There is a direct connection between counterfactuality and narration. A narration is a road made up of a network of events, each path between events has a story behind it, and the narration is one path among the set of all paths between events. Two examples of this definition of narration follow. The first case is illustrated by Benjamin's interior monologue at the hospital while he waits to visit Daisy, who has been run over by a cab. In his narration – this sequence is not in Fitzgerald's short story – Benjamin imagines what could have happened to prevent the accident of his childhood friend and future love Daisy.

(299) *Sometimes we're on a collision course, and we just don't know it. Whether it's by accident or by design, there's not a thing we can do about it. A woman in Paris was on her way to go shopping. But she had forgotten her coat, went back to get it. When she had gotten her coat, the phone had rung. So, she had stopped to answer it and talked for a couple of minutes. While the woman was on the phone, Daisy was rehearsing for a performance at the Paris Opera House. And while she was rehearsing, the woman, off the phone now, had gone outside to get a taxi. Now, a taxi driver had dropped off a fate earlier and had stopped to get a cup of coffee. And all the while, Daisy was rehearsing. And this cab driver, who dropped off the earlier fare and had stopped to get the cup of coffee, he picked up the lady who was going shopping and had missed getting the earlier cab. The taxi had to stop for a man crossing the street who had left for work five minutes later than he normally did because he forgot to set his alarm. While that man, late for work, was crossing the street, Daisy had finished rehearsing and was taking a shower. And while Daisy was showering, the taxi was waiting outside a boutique for the woman to pick up a package which hadn't been wrapped because the girl who was supposed to wrap it had broken up with her boyfriend the night before and forgot. When the package was wrapped, the woman, who was back in the cab, was blocked by a delivery truck. All the while, Daisy was getting dressed. The delivery truck pulled away and the taxi was able to move while Daisy, the last to be dressed, waited for one of her friends who had broken a shoelace. While the taxi was stopped, waiting for a traffic light, Daisy and her friend came out the back of the theatre.*

And if only one thing had happened differently, if that shoelace hadn't broken, or that delivery truck had moved moments earlier, or that package had been wrapped and ready because the girl hadn't broken up with her boyfriend, or that man had set his alarm and got up five minutes earlier, or that taxi hadn't stopped for a cup of coffee, or that woman had remembered her coat and got into an earlier cab, daisy and her friend would have crossed the street and the taxi would have driven by.

This excerpt shows that things could have been different. A narrative is thus a path among a tree diagram of possible paths. The second illustration of narration is given in Jorge Luis Borges' short story *The Garden of Forking Paths*, where all paths occur simultaneously, not in time, but within the space of a labyrinth:

(300) *The Garden of Forking Paths is an incomplete, but not false, image of the universe such as Ts'ui Pên conceived it. In contrast to Newton and Schopenhauer, your ancestor did not believe in an infinite series of times, in a growing, dizzying net of divergent, convergent and parallel times. This network of times which approached one another, forked, broke off, or were unaware of one another for centuries, embraces all possibilities of time. We do not exist in the majority of these times; in some you exist, and not I; in others I, and not you; in others, both of us. In the present one, which a favourable fate has granted me, you have arrived at my house; in another, while crossing the garden, you found me dead; in still another, I utter these same words, but I am a mistake, a ghost.*[166]

8 Conclusion

We can now state several conclusions. First, figures of speech are not extraordinary usages of language, but are part of ordinary usage. Second, creative metaphors do not mobilise comprehension mechanisms specific to figures of speech, but are general strategies used in utterance comprehension. Third, the more creative a metaphor is, the weaker are the implicatures that the hearer or reader is invited to draw, and the more the implicatures trigger non-propositional effects, that is, the search for emotive states experienced by the speaker or author. Fourth, a narrative told in the third- or first-person is not communication, and is characterised by temporal order between events. Fifth, a manner that allows for the representation of characters' mental states in a narration is known as free indirect discourse. Unlike discourse and indirect discourse, free indirect discourse is not reported speech, but a linguistic strategy that enables a third person's speech and thought to be represented. And finally, narration is made possible not only by the temporal order between states and events, but especially by causal links: a story is just one possible route among an infinite possible network of links between events, whose only exhaustive possible representations are spatial and not temporal, as shown in Borges' short story.

We have, in these three last chapters, taken the measure of the complexity of language usage in terms of its social, discursive, and literary dimensions. Are there further territories to be explored? I would now like to sketch out what I feel could be a new direction for pragmatics.

---

[166] Jorge Luis Borges. 1998. *The Garden of Forking Paths*, 14–15. London. Penguin Books.

Chapter 7 will introduce the concept of superpragmatics, which is a type of pragmatics that goes far beyond speaker meaning description and explanation. Superpragmatics plays an important role in the comprehension of social and political phenomena. I will also develop concepts like presupposition and implicature, which are two central concepts in pragmatics. I will end the next chapter with a discussion of the contrast between the slogans *I am Charlie* and *I am not Charlie*, which emerged after the attacks in January 2015 on the satirical French magazine *Charlie Hebdo*.

Chapter 7
Superpragmatics

A new direction in research on language and language usage has been emerging for about a decade. This convergent idea has been approached from a variety of directions, and goes beyond the domain of investigation of the disciplines in question while using their methods. Super Linguistics, as it has been termed by Philippe Schlenker, uses the tools of formal linguistics (syntax and semantics) to study singing (Berwick et al. 2011), dance (Patel-Grosz et al. 2019), music (Schlenker 2017), and sign language (Schlenker 2013), as well as animal communication (Schlenker et al. 2016). Super Linguistics' goal is not to demonstrate the validity of formal methods, but to understand human cognition activities that are linked to systems close to or analogous to language.

An exciting recent movie, *Arrival* by Denis Villeneuve (2016), tells the story of a young linguist, Louise Banks, played by Amy Adams. Louise is a specialist in ancient languages as well as language typology, and is asked by the US army to decipher an alien system of communication. The linguist succeeds in making sense of circles resembling ink spots projected against a window and to understand, using linguistic methods, what the messages of her interlocutors' – whom the army dubs Abbott and Costello – mean. This task, carried out by a linguist, presents a strong contrast to the role of the phonetics professor Henry Higgins (played by Rex Harrison) in George Cukor's 1964 film *My Fair Lady*. Here Eliza Doolittle (played by Audrey Hepburn), a beautiful young flower girl who speaks Cockney, the popular variety of London English, is taught Received Pronunciation by Higgins.

The example of *Arrival* is sociologically interesting, because it is the first time that the science of language has been the main topic of a movie, and especially because the ability to comprehend a communication system that is alien to human linguistic systems and the varieties of human writing was given not to a computer or to artificial intelligence, but to a human being, in this case a female linguistics professor.

2001: A Space Odyssey, by Stanley Kubrick (1968), is another example of a film in which language plays an important role. What happens here is different, though: first of all HAL, the onboard computer, verbally communicates with the two astronauts, David Bowan and Frank Pool, who pilot the spacecraft on its flight to Europa, one of Jupiter's moons. HAL is going to be shut down after making decisions that had lethal consequences for the crew, which is in artificial hibernation, and especially for Frank, who dies in space. David decides to shut HAL down in one of the most striking scenes of the movie: HAL, following David's suggestion, begins to sing *Daisy Bell*, and as David shuts down HAL's processors

https://doi.org/10.1515/9783110723380-010

its dying voice gradually becomes slower and deeper. HAL's "death" is shown by its loss of language. It is especially important to note that HAL is a computer that has passed the Turing test, the test that all scientists believe can determine whether a machine has true intelligence and can think. Here is the description of HAL :[167]

> Whether Hal could actually think was a question which had been settled by the British mathematician Alan Turing back in the 1940s. Turing had pointed out that, if one could carry out a prolonged conversation with a machine – whether by typewriter or microphone was immaterial – without being able to distinguish between its replies and those that a man might give, then the machine was thinking, by any sensible definition of the word. Hal could pass the Turing test with ease.

In other words,

> Selon ce test, on pourra dire qu'une machine pense le jour où elle pourra soutenir une conversation prolongée sans sujet préétabli, de telle façon qu'on puisse prendre ses réponses pour celles d'un être humain. (Reboul and Moeschler 1998b: 11)
>
> [According to this test, one can say that a machine can think when it is able to carry on an extended a conversation without a preestablished topic, so that one can take its answers for those of a human being.]

Although computers of today have beaten human beings in chess and Go, no artificial intelligence system has yet passed the Turing test.

Which current domains are concerned by the Super approach? I will restrict my discussion to the domain of pragmatics, which I call *superpragmatics**. I will demonstrate the challenge of going beyond meaning in order to understand verbal communication, and how two central concepts of pragmatics, presupposition* and implicature*,[168] are fundamental for understanding the issues of our society and its crises. I will show why the Super approach in pragmatics is not currently used in media commentary and analysis. Finally, I will suggest how the superpragmatics approach can contribute to understanding the meaning of the slogans that were used after the attacks against Charlie Hebdo in January 2015.

1 Beyond meaning

The superpragmatics approach implies understanding verbal communication beyond the recognition of speaker meaning. Formal analysis has shown that the

---

[167] Arthur C. Clarke. 1968. 2001: A space odyssey, 50. London: Hutchinson.
[168] On presupposition and implicature, see Moeschler (2018b).

implicature approach to speaker meaning does not solve the issue of what is communicated by an utterance.

Demonstrating this is slightly off-putting, but the results are quite pleasing. I will present the light version here.[169] In chapter 3 I mentioned the example of *Cheese or dessert*. The implicature is "you cannot have both cheese and dessert", that is, NOT[CHEESE AND DESSERT]. But this implicature means [NOT-CHEESE OR NOT-DESSERT],[170] and, as the disjunction *or* can be understood as a conjunction – it is possible that both disjuncts are true – we can imagine a situation in which both NOT-CHEESE (you cannot have cheese) and NOT-DESSERT (you cannot have a dessert) are true together. Thus, a restaurateur could decide that *Cheese or dessert* means *neither cheese nor dessert*, and offer neither of the two choices to his clients. Table 4 explains this prediction:

Table 4: The unpredictable meaning of *not-and*.

p	q	p or$_{inclusive}$ q	p and q	not (p and q)	not-p	not-q	not-p or$_{inclusive}$ not-q
1	1	1	1	0	0	0	0
1	0	1	0	1	0	1	1
0	1	1	0	1	1	0	1
0	0	0	0	1	1	1	1

Fortunately, restaurateurs are not logicians; on the contrary, they have common sense and know that if a menu advertises *Cheese or dessert* the restaurant must be ready to serve both. If a client chose cheese when there was no cheese or dessert when there was no dessert, this would be problematic for everyone, and no professional restaurateur would proceed in this way.

How then can we explain that the restaurateur is committed, and that the client understands that he can have only one choice and not both? A logically valid solution consists of conjoining both the logical or inclusive meaning of *or* and its scalar implicature – the negation of the conjunction or NOT[CHEESE AND DESSERT].[171] The conjunction of these two propositions cancels out the situation in which there is neither cheese nor dessert. This new meaning corresponds to the exclusive meaning of *or*, in which only one of the disjuncts can be true because

---

169 For a complete demonstration, see Moeschler (2017).
170 This is an application of the de Morgan law: *not [p and q]* ≡ *not-p or not-q*.
171 For a description of scalar implicatures and its issues, see Gazdar (1979), Horn (1989), Levinson (2000), Geurts (2010), Chierchia (2013). For a synthesis, see Zufferey, Moeschler, and Reboul (2019: chapter 5).

the other is false: this is exactly what is predicted by pragmatic meaning. Table 5 clarifies this analysis:

Table 5: Pragmatic meaning of *or*.

p	q	p or$_{inclusive}$ q	p and q	not (p and q)	(p or q) and not (p and q)	p or$_{exclusive}$ q
1	1	1	1	0	0	0
1	0	1	0	1	1	1
0	1	1	0	1	1	1
0	0	0	0	1	0	0

In other words, there is more in speaker meaning than the speaker's implicature. Moreover, in the Gricean approach, what is *said* plus what is *implicated* is equivalent to what is *communicated** (or *conveyed* in Grice's terms). In order to understand speaker meaning, therefore, one should take into account both what is *explicitly said* and what is *implicitly meant*.

However, this approach contradicts the Relevance Theory comprehension strategy, according to which the addressee must follow the path of least effort in his search of relevance, as well as accessing explicit and implicit contents in order of accessibility. Thus the most important consequence of the example *Cheese or dessert* is that at least two meaning computations must be drawn: access to the linguistic or logical meaning and to its implicature.

A generalisation of the above could be stated in this way: speaker meaning is made up of a set of linguistic and pragmatic meanings. It is like a *mille-feuille* pastry: in a mille-feuille there are many layers, and eating one implies ingesting all the layers at the same time rather than separately. The meanings in an utterance are similarly multiple and stratified. We can therefore assume that meaning is structured – organised in layers of varying significance – depending on the context (Moeschler 2019).

Two questions now arise. First, which are the layers of meaning, and what are they like? Second, how can these different meanings emerge and be differentiated from each other? The second question will be addressed in the next two sections. For now, let us answer the first one.

What are the layers of meaning that play a role in utterance comprehension? We have already examined some of them: conversational and conventional implicatures, presuppositions, and entailments. We can now add explicit pragmatic content, known as *explicature** in Relevance Theory. An explicature is thus the explicit pragmatic content that corresponds to the proposition expressed by the utterance. A higher order explicature, on the other hand, corresponds to the illocutionary force, or the action value of the utterance.

Understanding an utterance therefore amounts to accessing different types of content, which vary in *accessibility* and *strength*. The assumption is that semantic contents such as entailments and presuppositions are stronger than pragmatic ones, whereas pragmatic contents are more accessible than semantic ones, because the latter are covert, or invisible in the communication process. These observations are shown in the following scales (from Moeschler 2019: 41):

(301) Strength scale
Entailment > conventional implicature > presupposition > explicature > conversational implicature.

(302) Accessibility scale
Explicature > conversational implicature > conventional implicature > presupposition > entailment.

The main characteristic of an utterance, therefore, is that it displays a difference between *accessibility* and *strength*. The comprehension of an utterance is a modulation function between what is *explicitly* and *implicitly* communicated (*accessibility*), and what is *strongly* or *weakly* communicated (*strength*). I will elaborate on two types of content, a semantic meaning (*presupposition*) on one hand, and a pragmatic meaning (*implicature*) on the other. I will end with an interesting example that goes beyond semantic and pragmatic contents.

2 The role of presupposition in communication

What are *presuppositions** used for? They have traditionally been analysed in terms of discourse as invariable information that ensures *discourse cohesion* (Ducrot 1972). According to the Super approach, presuppositions define the *conversational common ground**, or a set of non-disputable propositions (Stalnaker 1977, 1999). The main point as regards presupposition is the following: a well-known manipulative strategy in conversation and in any other type of discourse is to insidiously introduce information that is presented as shared, accepted as true, non-disputable and old, when in fact is not shared, not accepted, disputable, and new.

The difficulty for addressees and readers is not only to detect false presuppositions, but above all to correct them. I have already mentioned the case of the police questioning, and the same is also true in more basic syntactic constructions including all *wh*- questions: questions that contain interrogative pronouns such as *who, what, when, where*, etc., and that trigger presuppositions:

(303) <u>Who</u> *called?*
PRESUPPOSITION: <u>someone</u> called

(304) <u>When</u> *are you coming back?*
PRESUPPOSITION: you are coming back <u>someday</u>

(305) <u>What</u> *have you done?*
PRESUPPOSITION: you have done <u>something</u>

(306) <u>Where</u> *have you hidden your wife's body?*
PRESUPPOSITION: you have hidden your wife's wife <u>somewhere</u>

In these examples the presupposition can be denied with negative words like *nobody, never,* and *nothing,* which correspond to negative universals. However, in other linguistic contexts containing *definite descriptions,* which presuppose the existence of an entity, or with *factive verbs,* which presuppose the truth of the subordinate clause, the only possible strategy is to negate the presupposition by using a *metalinguistic negation*;* a negation which not only negates the explicit content of the sentence, but also scopes over its presupposition (Moeschler 2018c, 2019).

(307) Jacques: *I just met the king of France. He's cool.*
Anne: *Look Jacques, you didn't meet the king of France: there is no king of France.*

(308) Jacques: *I had a call with Abi: she regrets having failed her exams.*
Anne: *Look Jacques, she doesn't regret having failed her exams, because she passed them.*

These examples show that in order for the conversation to progress smoothly, presuppositions must be shared: presupposition mutuality and sharing are thus crucial for communication. Here again we are far from the code model: the question here is one of information and context*, that is, of the *common ground* of a conversation.

3 The role of implicature in communication

The role of implicature in communication has been addressed several times in this book: the fact of implicitly communicating speaker meaning – the speaker's informative intention – makes a detour around the addressee's epistemic vigilance, because the responsibility of meaning ascription falls to him and speaker meaning is not imposed.

That said, I will now investigate the role played by implicatures in communication, and particularly in political communication. The increase in the infantilisation of the public is reinforced by the injunctions directed at politicians to "be didactic", which supposes that if intentions are not explained slowly, repeatedly, and explicitly, the good people will not understand their message.

Until proven otherwise, however, people who vote are no longer children, but adults; they do not suffer from mind-blindness or any other cognitive impairment, and they do not vote irrationally, like they would choose a lottery number: the commentary of most political scientists on elections refers after all to "voters' wisdom". What might the role of implicatures in communication be? Do implicatures correspond to covert meaning, implying "decoding" or even deciphering? I would answer no, but this is exactly how the media approaches communication. The ideology of the media maintains that, as information becomes increasingly complex, coupled with the way social networks and the GAFA scramble meaning, information must be "prioritized" and "deciphered". Websites like *Les Décodeurs*, 'the code-breakers' of the French newspaper *Le Monde*, are good examples of this trend.

The media's conception of information and communication is erroneous, and I would like to show why. In fact the media uses the same ideology that presides over classic rhetoric, the two levels of language theory (chapter 2). According to journalists who provide commentary on political news, *what a politician says* and *what he does not say* must be *decrypted*. Knowledge about the political environment, history, and context makes the media and journalists willing and able to "contextualize" politicians' statements.

What can be said about this approach? First, that contextualization is certainly a relevant feature, because it allows incorrect interpretations to be avoided. Though everyone agrees on this point, the main characteristic of what are known in French as *petites phrases* 'sound bites' is precisely the fact that they are in fact *decontextualized*.[172] One of the key issues in commentary on politicians'

---

[172] The expression *petites phrases* 'sound bites' has been used since a famous speech was given by the French Prime Minister Raymond Barre, just after the terrorist attack on the Rue Copernic, Paris, 3 October 1980: "cet attentat odieux qui voulait frapper les Israélites qui se rendaient à la synagogue et qui a frappé des Français innocents qui traversaient la rue Copernic" ['this odious attack which aimed at targeting Jews going to the synagogue and hit innocent French people who were crossing the Rue Copernic']. This phrase is well-known because of its implicit meaning: Jews are not innocent people. See https://www.ina.fr/video/I09082508, accessed on 27 December 2020.

speeches, therefore, is how and why their utterances are decontextualized and their context altered.

Here is an example in which context was *modified*. On 23 January 2012, during the French presidential campaign, the online news website Slate.fr[173] published an article entitled *Les politiques doivent-ils se méfier des journalistes? Ces derniers déforment-ils vraiment les propos des hommes politiques aussi souvent que ces derniers l'affirment?* [Must politicians beware of journalists? Do the latter misrepresent politicians' words as often as the former claim?] This article discusses the words of the President of the National Assembly, Bernard Accoyer, as reported by the AFP (French Press Agency):

(309) Bernard Accoyer
Si nous ratons ce rendez-vous de la responsabilité et du courage, les conséquences économiques et sociales pourraient être comparables à celles provoquées par une guerre.
'If we miss this opportunity to be responsible and courageous, the economic and social consequences could be similar to those provoked by war.'

(310) AFP
Si la gauche passe, des "conséquences comparables à une guerre".
'If the left gets in, "consequences comparable to a war".'

How can we explain this change in linguistic context? Without going into detail, the two utterances have totally different implicatures. Bernard Accoyer's implicature is simple:

(311) Accoyer's implicature
If the majority loses the presidential election, the economic and social consequences could be as serious as those of war.

On the other hand, the AFP's implicature deals with the threats of a victory on the left:

(312) AFP's implicature
The victory of the left would have consequences similar to the consequences of war.

---

[173] Article available online: http://www.slate.fr/story/48857/mode-emploi-sortir-phrase-politique-contexte, accessed on 21 December 2019.

What are the differences? My analysis is that the differences lie in two shortcuts made by the press agency.

First is a shortcut in the *antecedent of the conditional*. Accoyer identifies the presidential election as an opportunity to be responsible and courageous, and insists on the moral weight of the voters' choice. On the other hand, the AFP text jumps from the antecedent of the original discourse (313a) to the AFP's shortened one (313b):

(313) a. *Si nous ratons ce rendez-vous de la responsabilité et du courage.*
'If we miss this opportunity to be responsible and courageous.'
b. *Si la gauche passe.*
'If the left gets in.'

Second, there is also a change in the consequent of the conditional when Accoyer's utterance (314a) is compared to the AFP's (314b): the most significant change is the omission of the epistemic modal verb *pouvoir* 'be able to' used in the conditional, *pourrait* 'could'.

(314) a. *Les conséquences économiques et sociales pourraient être comparables à celles provoquées par une guerre.*
'The economic and social consequences could be similar to those of war.'
b. *Des "conséquences comparables à une guerre".*
'"Consequences similar to war".'

These changes have consequences for the comprehension of these utterances, apart from the fact that they are shortcuts, which give rise to truncated interpretations. In a nutshell, a chain of inferences, including *implicatures* and *entailment*, arises. Here are the respective chains of inferences for the antecedents:

(315) Accoyer's inferences
a. *Si nous ratons ce rendez-vous de la responsabilité et du courage* IMPLICATES "si la majorité perd".
b. "Si la majorité perd" ENTAILS "si l'opposition gagne".
c. "Si l'opposition gagne" ENTAILS "si la gauche gagne".
d. "Si la gauche gagne" ENTAILS "si la gauche passe".

a. *If we miss this opportunity to be responsible and courageous* IMPLICATES "if the majority loses".
b. "If the majority loses" ENTAILS "if the opposition wins".
c. "If the opposition wins" ENTAILS "if the left wins".
d. "If the left wins" ENTAILS "if the left gets in".

As mentioned above, the difference between Accoyer's words and the AFP report implies four inferential steps: *implicature + entailment + entailment + entailment*. The consequence of these inferential steps is going from a weak interpretation of the antecedent (implicature) to strong ones (entailments).[174] What the AFP has done, therefore, is not to report words, but to interpret them based on four inferential steps.

The truncation of the consequent of Accoyer's conditional also has strong effects:

(316) Bernard Accoyer
Les conséquences économiques et sociales pourraient être comparables à celles provoquées par une guerre IMPLICATES "*les conséquences d'une victoire de la gauche seraient catastrophiques*".
'The economic and social consequences could be similar to those provoked by war IMPLICATES "the consequences of a victory on the left would be catastrophic".'

(317) AFP
Des "conséquences comparables à une guerre" ENTAILS "*des conséquences catastrophiques*".
'"Consequences comparable to war" ENTAILS "catastrophic consequences".'

The consequences of these changes are not only changes in words, however; they are changes in the nature of the contents, because *implicatures* are cancellable contents while *entailments* are not. In short, while Bernard Accoyer's utterance gives rise to an implicature, the change made by the AFP is the result of three indefeasible entailments for its antecedent, and its consequent yields an entailment rather than an implicature. It is obvious that the journalists did not do their job of reporting a speech here. Their report is not about an utterance; it is an interpretation of an utterance. Moreover, strength and accessibility scales allow the following conclusions to be drawn:

(i) the AFP's reformulation leads to an interpretation that is stronger than its source, because entailments are stronger than implicatures;
(ii) the accessibility scale shows that the AFP's reformulation highlights a weak accessible content (entailment) instead of a highly accessible one (implicature).

How can these changes be explained? A simple reason stems directly from the word journalists use to describe their job: *decipherment*.

---

174 See the strength scale in (301).

4 Anti-decipherment, for epistemic vigilance

In philology, *decipherment* means "the discovery of the meaning of texts written in ancient or obscure languages or scripts".[175] The *decipherment metaphor* is as follows: a politician's or a government's utterance is encrypted; because encryption implies a code or a key that enables decrypting, the work of journalists and the media is to reconstitute its covert meaning.

An encrypted meaning is not inferable, inferred, or implicated. On the contrary, it is covert, invisible, and can only be understood by using a decryption key. The meaning of the decipherment metaphor is as follows:

(318) The decipherment metaphor
As a journalist, I possess a decryption key, and I can access the covert meaning of the encrypted message. But you, the reader, listener, or television viewer, don't have this key. You therefore need an interface between the source (the political discourse) and the destination (its meaning). As a journalist and an expert, I am able to give you this key for decryption.

Journalists therefore provide the interface between politicians and their speeches on one hand, and what they mean on the other. In other words, journalists and the media are vital go-betweens in the political world, because they translate it for the rest of us. Behind the term decipherment is a self-proclaimed justification for the necessity of mediators like journalists, especially at a moment in the history of information when newspapers are threatened by social networks and the fact that certain Internet users are self-proclaimed journalists.

Moving away from this context, which partially explains why and how the media world has dramatically changed, I will try to explain what is implied by the asymmetrical relationship between those who hold information and its meaning and the general public. The idea is simple: in the same way that "pedagogical" politicians infantilize citizens, journalists who are adept at the theory of decipherment treat their readers, listeners, and viewers as uncultured people lacking in knowledge and the ability to reason. This division of labor is, for listeners, readers, and viewers, a far cry from the statements that have been made about communication in this book regarding the necessity of creating a community of ideas, knowledge, feelings, and emotions.

---

175 https://en.wikipedia.org/wiki/Decipherment, page accessed on 8 January 2020. In French, the word used in such journalistic contexts is *décryptage* 'decryption', meaning "to retrieve the original text from a digit message without having the key of encryption". https://fr.wikipedia.org/wiki/D%C3%A9cryptage, page accessed on 8 January 2020.

At this stage the situation is rather dark. However, I would like to shine some light on an alternative to the media's ideology about information and communication. This light comes from the superpragmatics approach. In order to illustrate this approach, I will discuss two slogans that appeared on the Internet after the attack on the French magazine Charlie Hebdo in January 2015 in Paris. I chose this example because, as far as I know, the media has never called the meaning of these slogans into question.

5 To be or not to be Charlie

Shortly after the terrorist attacks on Charlie Hebdo on 7 January 2015 in Paris, the message *Je suis Charlie* 'I am Charlie' appeared on Internet and in the streets of Paris. A few hours later, the message *Je ne suis pas Charlie* 'I am not Charlie' began to spread on the Internet. It imitated the message *Je suis Charlie*, but the negative words (*ne, pas*) were in red.

Figure 5: Internet slogans about Charlie Hebdo (January 2015) from https://fr.wikipedia.org/wiki/Je_suis_Charlie and https://www.facebook.com/Je-ne-suis-pas-charlie-336794493182638/?ref=ts&fref=ts.

The second message was endorsed by young French people who did not support *Charlie Hebdo* because of his position on Islam – see *Charlie Hebdo's* publication of cartoons of Muhammad on 8 February 2006. In the following section, I do not wish to call into question the reasons for this counter-message, but to explore its meaning. I will show that what was called into play was the metalinguistic usage of the negation used in *Je ne suis pas Charlie* 'I am not Charlie'.

Before understanding what *Je ne suis pas Charlie* 'I am not Charlie' means, we should consider what *Je suis Charlie* 'I am Charlie' means. An initial answer could be that this positive utterance weakly implicates certain propositions:

(319)   *Je suis Charlie* 'I am Charlie' IMPLICATES
       a. "I am in solidarity with Charlie".
       b. "I am in mourning for Charlie".

c. "I am devastated by this attack".
d. "I condemn terrorism."
e. "Freedom of expression is the most important value of the republic".
f. "Violence will not overcome intelligence and thought".
etc.

All these meanings are weak implicatures. They are various and numerous, and their sheer number can explain why so many Internet users posted *Je suis Charlie* 'I am Charlie'.[176] What can be said about the contradictory proposition, *Je ne suis pas Charlie* 'I am not Charlie'? We can put forward three hypotheses about its meaning.

Hypothesis 1: The meaning of *Je ne suis pas Charlie* is the opposite meaning of *Je suis Charlie*, and thus communicates its opposite implicatures, as shown in (320):

(320) *Je ne suis pas Charlie* 'I am not Charlie' IMPLICATES
   a. "I am not in solidarity with Charlie".
   b. "I am not in mourning for Charlie".
   c. "I am not devastated by this attack".
   d. "I do not condemn terrorism".
   e. "Freedom of expression is not the most important value of the republic".
   f. "Violence will overcome intelligence and thought".
   etc.

This hypothesis immediately encounters a difficulty: the implicatures of a negative utterance are not the opposite implicatures of its positive correspondent. I will demonstrate this claim through the following explanation. In saying the positive utterance (321), I implicate that my daughter is no more than beautiful, because of Grice's maxim of quantity – I am supposed to give the strongest information, and if she were more than beautiful, I should have said so:

(321) *My daughter is beautiful* IMPLICATES "my daughter is no more than beautiful".

However, if I produce the negative utterance (322), this does not mean that it is false that my daughter is no more than beautiful. What is meant with a corrective clause is that she is either *ordinary* (323) or *ugly* (324). In any case, what is entailed is that she is *less* than beautiful:

---

[176] The message *Je suis Charlie* was also beamed from the top of a large building in Berlin.

(322) *My daughter is not beautiful*
ENTAILS "my daughter is less than beautiful"

(323) *My daughter is not beautiful but ordinary-looking*
ENTAILS "my daughter is ordinary-looking"

(324) *My daughter is not beautiful but ugly*
ENTAILS "my daughter is ugly"

There is, however, an exception to this ordinary and descriptive* meaning of negation: the metalinguistic* usage of negation, given in (325). In this case, and only in this case, the implicature of the positive counterpart is under the scope of negation, and the corrective clause entails the positive one:

(325) *My daughter is not beautiful, but very beautiful*
IMPLICaTES "it is not the case that my daughter is no more than beautiful"
ENTAILS "my daughter is beautiful"

So, the first hypothesis must be rejected: *Je ne suis pas Charlie* expresses a refusal.[177]

Hypothesis 2: Je ne suis pas Charlie 'I am not Charlie' means the refusal to belong to the community that asserts *Je suis Charlie* 'I am Charlie'. However, this hypothesis has a strong implication: the polarisation of society into two antagonistic groups, those who are for and those who are against *Charlie Hebdo*. This type of polarisation is never what a society wishes for, especially in the context of terrorist attacks, because it would imply a division in society. This hypothesis must therefore be abandoned as well.

Apart from this sociological argument, a solely linguistic analysis of the descriptive meaning of the negative sentence can be given: the descriptive meaning of *Je ne suis pas Charlie* 'I am not Charlie' would simply be the negation of a state of affairs, one that describes the individual who posts the message as a member of the Charlie community:

---

[177] There is an exception to this conclusion, which is the case with logical words such as scalar quantifiers. *Some* implicates *not all*, and *not all* implicates *some* (Horn 2004). But in our example, *beautiful* does not belong to the same scale as *ugly* (they are contraries or antonyms) – see Figure 3. In the Charlie case, *Charlie* is not a scalar predicate.

(326) *Je ne suis pas Charlie*
'I am not Charlie'
MEANS "it is not the case that the individual posting the message is a member of the Charlie community"

Hypothesis 3: *Je ne suis pas Charlie* 'I am not Charlie' is the metalinguistic negation of *Je suis Charlie* 'I am Charlie'. What is the meaning of metalinguistic negation? In studies on metalinguistic negation (Horn 1985; Moeschler 2018c), a negative utterance *not-p* with a metalinguistic negation means "I cannot affirm *p*", and not "it is false that *p*"; in other words the ordinary or descriptive meaning of negation. The meaning of *Je ne suis pas Charlie* 'I am not Charlie', therefore, would be the meaning given in (327):

(327) *Je ne suis pas Charlie*
'I am not Charlie'
MEANS "I cannot affirm *I am Charlie*, I refuse to say *I am Charlie*"

In this reading, in other words, the negative assertion *Je ne suis pas Charlie* is a refusal to make an assertion, and not a denial of a state of affairs like the interpretation given in (326). This makes sense, because it is consistent to understand the negative message about Charlie as signaling an attitude or a position rather than asserting something.

But there is a caveat which must be specified for this reading: metalinguistic negation is generally followed by a *corrective clause* that is introduced by the connective *but*, or by an *explicative clause* that is introduced by *because* or *since* (Moeschler 2013). In the case of *Je ne suis pas Charlie* 'I am not Charlie', what is expected in a metalinguistic reading of negation is the reason why the speaker cannot say *Je suis Charlie* 'I am Charlie'. In other words, if a negative sentence is interpreted metalinguistically, an explanation should be forthcoming.[178]

Now, the absence of a justification has an important effect: it makes the negative utterance underspecified, or undetermined, because the reason of the refusal to affirm *Je suis Charlie* 'I am Charlie' cannot be reconstructed.

---

178 The absence of a corrective clause introduced by *but* or a justification clause introduced by *because* or *since* is rare. This occurs only in cases of formal metalinguistic use of negation, in which negation scopes over the form of an utterance rather than its meaning, such as an implicature or a presupposition (Carston 1996):

A: *We saw two mongeese at the zoo.*
B: *No, come on, you DIDN'T seEe two mongeese.*

How can we explain this absence of justification? It is clear that the style of the message, a slogan, as well as the type of media used to communicate it, explain why the slogan is not followed by a *because* clause. However, what might such a justification be? If we had to do the same thing for *Je suis Charlie* 'I am Charlie', we would obtain the weak implicatures which constitute its meaning.

(328)   *I am Charlie because*
      a. *I am in solidarity with Charlie.*
      b. *I am in mourning for Charlie.*
      c. *I am devastated by this attack.*
      d. *I condemn terrorism.*
      e. *Freedom of expression is the most important value of the republic.*
      f. *Violence will not overcome intelligence and thought.*
      etc.

What can we say about *Je ne suis pas Charlie* 'I am not Charlie'? A strong interpretation is to say that people who endorse this utterance by publicly displaying it refuse to say *Je suis Charlie* 'I am Charlie' and refuse to give the reason why. A weaker interpretation would be that this utterance is tenable only with difficulty, because its implicatures, even the weak ones, are undetermined: they cannot be the opposite propositions of *Je suis Charlie* 'I am Charlie'. No one would in fact imagine that *Je ne suis pas Charlie* 'I am not Charlie' means the reverse implicatures of *Je suis Charlie* 'I am Charlie':

(329)   *I cannot say I am Charlie because*
      a. *I am not in solidarity with Charlie.*
      b. *I am not in mourning for Charlie.*
      c. *I am not devastated by this attack.*
      d. *I do not condemn terrorism.*
      e. *Freedom of expression is not the most important value of the republic.*
      f. *Violence will overcome intelligence and thought.*
      etc.

We understand why: the implicatures in (329) are in fact not weak, but strong, and above all, their content is both inacceptable and shocking. Not giving the reason for *Je ne suis pas Charlie* 'I am not Charlie' can therefore be explained in a simpler way: the reasons are not given because they are inacceptable in a world of democracy, freedom, equality, and fraternity.[179]

6 Conclusion

You might feel that what I have presented in this chapter is splitting hairs and making distinctions without differences, in short, using scholarly jargon. The examples I have discussed, however, show that this is not the case. In the Accoyer example, the shortcuts made by journalists were neither innocent nor simply formal details: on the contrary, they evidenced the change from a *weak* interpretation to a *strong* one, and from a highly accessible interpretation to a weakly accessible one. The changes in these dimensions should have been immediately obvious to every media professional. This was not the case, however, which points out the insensitivity of the media to linguistic and pragmatic issues.

I have called into question journalists' lack of sensitivity in differentiating between complexity of meaning and communication. In our ordinary lives we often wonder what a speaker means, especially when he or she is not part of our lives. We must ask these questions, because the issues are often important. The simple query, therefore, is why this concern is not central to questions asked by information and communication professionals? I have no answers to this question, but I believe that one conclusion can be asserted: *the goals of media professionals' acts of communications are not the same as those of ordinary acts of communication.* The increasing distrust of the media and journalists is certainly one of the most depressing facts of the early 21st century. Thorough consideration of language and the implications of its usage by the media in general and journalists in particular is cruelly lacking today.

---

179 The motto of France is *Liberté, égalité, fraternité* ('liberty, equality, fraternity').

Conclusion: What we do and still do not know about language

Syntheses are always difficult to formulate, and I have no wish to return to ground I have already covered in this book. I simply hope that its general messages are clear: languages and its usages are defined by general principles, and linguistic variation and social usages of language show that behind variation there are general principles, or a common linguistic DNA.

1 What we know: From syntax to pragmatics, the interface issue

We know many things about language and languages and their different subfields, which stretch from phonology to syntax. The most interesting point about recent language research, however, does not stem from a particular domain that contrasts with others – traditional approaches reinforce subfields and their institutional and scientific legitimacy, as in phonology as opposed to morphology and syntax, and semantics as opposed to pragmatics. No, the striking thing about the new approaches is that they proceed in terms of *interface**. In other words, the complexity of phenomena related to language is so great that no one discipline can single-handedly explain even its best-defined objects.

I will give two examples that demonstrate the importance of interfaces today, and that show above all how these questions can be addressed. I do not claim to resolve them, because it is a well-known fact that questions are more important than answers in research.

The first example explores the difference between two kinds of negation: descriptive and metalinguistic negation.[180] The issue is to determine what triggers, in the context of a negative utterance, the ordinary interpretation of a negative utterance that can be paraphrased by "it is false that p", and the metalinguistic interpretation that corresponds to "I cannot say p".

Imagine that the speaker says (330). You probably think the interpretation of this utterance is unambiguous, and that it corresponds to the reading shown in the corrective clause (331). But things can change, and your interlocutor may say (332) in response to your assertion in (333):

---

180 On metalinguistic negation, see Horn (1985), (1989), Carston (1996), (2002), Moeschler (2018c), (2019), (2020b), and also Martins (2020).

https://doi.org/10.1515/9783110723380-011

(330) *It is not raining.*

(331) *It is not raining; the sun has appeared.*

(332) *It is not raining; it's raining cats and dogs.*

(333) *It is raining.*

(331) and (332) have different entailments:

(334) *The sun has appeared*
ENTAILS "it is not raining"

(335) *It's raining cats and dogs*
ENTAILS "it is raining"

Which clues allow one to choose between the descriptive reading and the metalinguistic one? The easy answer is to say that it depends on the context. But is there something in an utterance that allows us to anticipate one reading rather than the other? The answer is *prosody*.[181] A metalinguistic reading would insist on *raining*, since the word choice is inappropriate: for the speaker, *raining* is insufficient to qualify what is happening, because what is falling from the sky is "cats and dogs".

The addressee therefore has good reason to anticipate a metalinguistic reading.[182] It is only when metalinguistic usages of negation are used in humor, whose aim is to trick the addressee, that the speaker leads his audience along the path of a descriptive reading, only to show him that the path is not descriptive but metalinguistic, as in Pierre Desproges' well-known example about Marguerite Duras (336):

(336) Marguerite *Duras   n'   a   pas   seulement écrit   que   des*
      Marguerite Duras   neg   has neg   only   written only some
      conneries. Elle en   a   aussi filmé.
      crap   she   pro has also   filmed
      'Marguerite Duras has not just written crap. She has filmed some, too.'

---

181 See Wichmann, Dehé, and Barth-Weingarten (2009) on the prosody-pragmatics interface.
182 For experimental results, see Blochowiak and Grisot (2018).

We can therefore state that in specific settings such as humour, negation requires a two-step procedural interpretation.[183]

The second example is the issue of the *semantics-pragmatics interface**; that is, the thin and permeable borders between encoded meanings and those which must be inferred. To understand this, simply look at a map (Figure 6) of the canton of Vaud (Switzerland), whose territory contains four enclaves, or territories, of two other cantons, those of Fribourg and Geneva. The enclaves are the result of these communities' complex history.

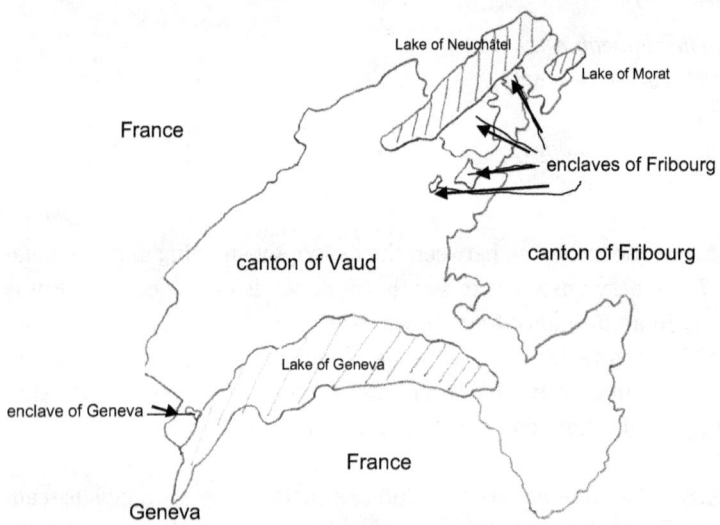

Figure 6: The enclaves in the canton of Vaud, Switzerland (drawing by the author).

The relationship between what is *encoded* (semantics) and what is *inferred* (pragmatics) is similar: there are pragmatic enclaves in semantics and semantic enclaves in pragmatics. In Figure 7, I use six criteria to distinguish between two semantic meanings (entailment and presupposition) and three pragmatic meanings (explicature, conventional and conversational implicatures).[184] The remarkable thing about this figure is the sinuous nature of its borders. The territories of semantics and pragmatics are, therefore, complex, and are similar to the borders of the Swiss cantons represented in Figure 7.

---

183 In Moeschler (2019), I argue that this results in the scope of negation, which leads to the following procedural meaning: narrow scope for descriptive negation, wide scope for metalinguistic negation.
184 For a development, see Moeschler (2019: chapter 1).

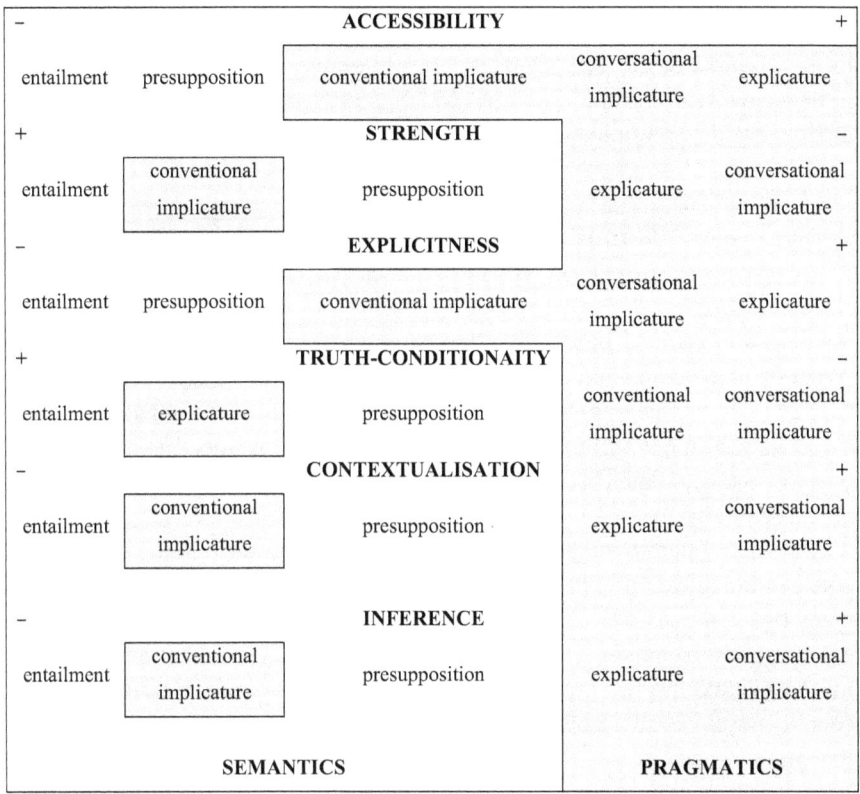

Figure 7: The sinuous semantics-pragmatics border.

As Figure 7 shows, conventional implicature is a pragmatic meaning that behaves like an enclave in the semantics territory in terms of strength, contextualization, and inference, but which moves from pragmatics territory into semantics for the accessibility and explicitness features. On the other hand, presupposition, which is a semantic meaning as regards accessibility and explicitness, intrudes into pragmatics territory in terms of strength, truth-conditionality, contextualization, and inference. Hence it is not surprising that according to Potts' classification of semantic and pragmatic meaning (Potts 2005: 23), conventional implicatures as well as conventional presuppositions and at-issue entailment are defined as entailments, unlike context dependent meanings such as conversational implicatures and conversationally-triggered presuppositions (pragmatic presuppositions in Stalnaker 1977).

What can be gathered from these two examples? First, that the interface issue is central; and second, that language complexity, especially for semantic meaning and pragmatic meaning, stems both from the spoken nature of language – shown in the example of the prosody-pragmatics interface – and from the complexity of the semantics-pragmatics border, which is caused by the difference between language and communication.

2 What we still do not know: Emotion, origin of language, machine translation, and man-machine communication

It would be presumptuous to state that language science is complete. It is still in progress, in development, and much is yet unknown. As we observed earlier, no machine has ever passed the Turing test, and thankfully we do not yet spend our evenings chatting with Siri, Google or Alexa. Several perspectives about topics that will become trends in linguistic and pragmatic research over the next decade are listed below.

Emotion: Cognitive scientists' and pragmaticists' interest in the relationship between language and emotion is now a given. However, as I have mentioned many times, the main thrust of this research is not the part of language in which emotions intervene, but the interaction between several cognitive systems: narrow syntax, the sensorimotor and conceptual-intentional interfaces, and the cognitive systems that govern emotions. How these systems interact and why they are dissociated are crucial questions. One might imagine that only neuroscience can provide answers, but that would be too narrow a vision, because emotions are closely related to our comprehension of situations. Why do we feel anxious when waiting for our luggage at the airport and our suitcase is delayed? Why are we sure, when standing on a railway platform, that our train will be late, especially if we have a connection to make? Why do these situations cause sweating and other changes in our physical state? These questions are central to us as human beings, and have begun to be addressed by the sciences of emotion (Sander and Scherrer 2009).

A recent and promising topic in computational linguistics is *sentiment analysis*, or the detection of the emotional attitudes of Internet contributors. Are contributions positively or negatively oriented? Are they for or against such and such a proposition? Empirical methods, or the treatment of significant amounts of digital corpora, allow us to obtain results that are unavailable to traditional qualitative analyses of corpora (Cambria et al. 2017). The relationship between language and emotion is also central to this domain.

Origin of language: As we have observed, there are no linguistic fossils. But today our knowledge about the origins of language is constantly expanding, particularly due to growing understanding of how non-human primates communicate, and also because answers about language origins cannot be given without comprehending how language has contributed to communication. The history of language evolution is the history of the close and complex entanglement between one system, language, which is optimal as regards its computations but imperfect in terms of its representational and communicational abilities, and cognitive development, which has strengthened cooperation, altruism, and mutuality. In this book I have defended the pragmatic perspective on the origin of language, which is one proposal among others. This scenario is of course not accepted by all formalist and functionalist linguistic theories, but it does have the advantage of stating that pragmatic issues are decisive in obtaining the most plausible scenario about the evolution of language. It is not surprising that pragmatics is now in the limelight. In his plenary lecture at the 19th International Congress of Linguists (Geneva, July 2013), for example, Tecumseh Fitch (2013) stated that a major challenge is focusing on the pragmatics of animal communication systems in order to better understand the evolution of human language. What we have become as a speaking species is largely the result of complex interactions between cognition, the usage of language, and the development of societies.

Machine translation: Everyone has observed the spectacular progress that has taken place in machine translation systems, the most well-known of which is Google Translate. Some years ago, in 2003, a Google machine translation from German to French of a text about Lech Walesa resulted in the following paragraph. The underlined expressions are incorrectly translated or not translated at all:

(337)   *Le Lech Walesa compte parmi les chiffres de symbole de la lutte contre le communisme. Il fonde en 1980, le syndicat « Solidanosc » qui commence les Demokratisierungsbewegung en Pologne socialiste et dix ans son chef est. Quand en 1980 des élections libres en Pologne ont lieu, il va avec la confédération syndicale en tant que gagnant des élections.*

[The Lech Walesa counts among the numerals of symbols of the battle against the communism. He founds in 1980, the union "Solidanosc" which starts the Demokratisierungsbewegung in Poland socialist and ten years its chief is. When in 1980 elections free in Poland take place, he goes with the confederation labor as a winner of the elections.]

It is clear that machine translation has made enormous strides over the last two decades. This is demonstrated by regular use of machine translations applications like Google Translate for texts in many languages. The following Google Translate translation of a German text,[185] for example, is comprehensible:

(338) *The Swiss Confederation grants Swiss Government Excellence Scholarships every year. These government grants promote international exchange and research cooperation between Switzerland and over 180 countries. The Federal Scholarship Commission for Foreign Students (ESKAS) selects and awards them. The Swiss Government Excellence Scholarships are aimed at young foreign researchers who have completed a master's or doctoral degree and to foreign artists who have completed a bachelor's degree.*

As a comparison, (339) gives the official English translation of the original German version. Underlined expressions point out the differences between this version and the Google Translate version:

(339) *Each year the Swiss Confederation awards Government Excellence Scholarships to promote international exchange and research cooperation between Switzerland and over 180 other countries. Recipients are selected by the awarding body, the Federal Commission for Scholarships for Foreign Students (FCS). The Swiss Government Excellence Scholarships are aimed at young researchers from abroad who have completed a master's degree or PhD and at foreign artists holding a bachelor's degree.*

The differences are slight and merely formal. In other words, compared to the translation about Lech Walesa in 2003, Google Translate is now able to provide accurate transmutation as regards meaning, at least for simple administrative texts.

What is still missing in machine translation? The answer to this question implies information that goes beyond general understanding. It concerns fine-grained issues such as the translation of connectives and verbal tenses, or phenomena that deal with the semantics-pragmatics interface. As far tenses as concerned, Cristina Grisot and Thomas Meyer (2014) have succeeded in imple-

---

[185] "Die Schweizerische Eidgenossenschaft gewährt jährlich Bundes-Exzellenz-Stipendien. Diese Regierungs-Stipendien fördern den internationalen Austausch und die Forschungs-Zusammenarbeit der Schweiz mit über 180 Ländern. Auswahl und Vergabe erfolgen durch die Eidgenössische Stipendienkommission für ausländische Studierende (ESKAS).

Die Bundes-Exzellenz-Stipendien richten sich an junge ausländische Forschende mit abgeschlossenem Master- oder Doktorats-Studium und an ausländische Kunstschaffende mit abgeschlossenem Bachelor-Studium". https://www.sbfi.admin.ch/sbfi/de/home/bildung/stipendien/eskas.html, accessed on 9 November 2020.

menting pragmatic features into machine translation systems. To give an example of what they have accomplished, the implementation of the pragmatic feature [+Narrative] (Grisot and Moeschler 2014, Grisot 2018) for the translation of past tenses – Simple Past in English, and Passé Simple, Imparfait, Passé Composé, and Présent in French – has significantly increased the accuracy of translations of verbal tenses from English to French, as well as the accuracy of translations of the lexicon. We can therefore state that it is primarily the integration of pragmatic information into grammars that will lead to substantial progress in machine translation.

Human-machine communication: Computational linguistics in the 1990s developed around the human-machine dialogue issue. The idea was to simulate a dialogue via a computer in the spoken or written mode – for instance booking a train or plane ticket, nights in a hotel, and so on. Most research relied on the Wizard of Oz strategy – a human agent was hidden behind a computer and used very precise protocol to gather data that would show how a machine should behave towards a human agent. Alas, this research suddenly stopped when new techniques emerged at all levels of language analysis. These involved clustering syllables and words, which led to an infinity of messages created from a limited stock of data. This technique replaced traditional text-to-speech analysis, a technique that companies employ to announce train departures and arrivals, using stochastic algorithms for automatic translation that employ machine learning techniques. Briefly stated, traditional techniques of linguistic analysis have been replaced with computational techniques that use a great deal of data, and with machine learning methods. The world of computation has progressively suspended research based on linguistic analysis (phonological, morphological, syntactic, and semantic), and replaced it with statistical methods. These methods have clearly been successful in certain areas, but no statistical method can succeed without explicit knowledge of the properties of natural language that are related to language usage. The fundamental question for human-machine communication is how results stemming from pragmatics, such as the calculation of implicatures and presuppositions, can be incorporated into complex computational models. Though these challenges are enormous, they are largely ignored by computational scientists and researchers in artificial intelligence.[186] But it is these questions and their answers that may one day allow a machine to pass the Turing test.

---

186 According to a report on artificial intelligence (2018) commissioned by French President Macron from Cédric Villani, a former winner of the Fields Medal (2010), language is not a central topic for AI, and is only mentioned as a domain that is investigated through AI techniques. For a critical analysis of artificial intelligence, see Dessalles (2019).

3 A conclusion for the book

How shall I conclude this book? I could state there is a wide-ranging future for the study, research, use, valorisation, and application of knowledge about language and its usage. But the Charlie Hebdo example enables me to draw a much more sweeping conclusion: I chose this example because it shows that, for everyone, the complexity of today's social and political issues is such that it involves not only language experts, but also scholars in general and the wider public.

We must all take responsibility in tracking down and refuting sophisms and fake news, because we are the most intellectually equipped to do so. This implies that we must get our information from scientific articles and books, since scientific publications provide the most reliable information. We must also fight against restrictions in primary, secondary, and higher education, because not doing so would be lethal for our societies. We must mentor and educate more graduate students, because a world with more PhD students can only but a better world. And finally, we must take interest in others, because they are human beings like we are: human beings equipped with language.

Afterword

The time during which I wrote the French version of this book (May 2018 to January 2020) was a quiet period in comparison to what has happened since February 2020 due to the pandemic. No one, myself included, could have imagined how our daily lives, our verbal interactions, our work at workplaces and at home, could have changed so quickly. The sudden increase in Internet interactions, via Zoom for Web Seminars or Skype for private chats, has given language an even more important role than before: things that formerly seemed like limitations in certain contexts have become an essential social and emotional link to others.

During my preparation of the English version of this book in the autumn of 2020, the world was hanging on the outcome of the 2020 American presidential election. Before the results were in, I imagined adding a section on Trump's discourse manipulation. The outcome of the election has given me hope that the time of fake news and post-truth is behind us, and that a new era of truthfulness, sincerity, and honesty in speech will arise,[187] although there is no real reason for such optimism, mainly because the result of an election cannot change the beliefs of more than seventy million voters.

However, there is still good reason for hope. First, more than seventy-eight million Americans made the choice of reason. None of them believe the earth is flat, that there is an Illuminati plot, or that the 2020 American presidential election results were the result of massive fraud. In other words, they are all aware that brain manipulation begins with language manipulation.

The present moment is a time for experts on language to be on the *qui vive*. In 1947, after World War II, an eminent German philologist, Viktor Klemperer, published *LTI* (*Lingua Tertii Imperi: Notizbuch eines Philologen*), which was the first attempt to precisely describe the changes in how language was used during the German Third Reich, including the systematic use of certain words based on *Volk*, such as *Volkfest, Vorksgenosse,* and *volkfremd*.[188] Renewed interest in language science on this topic can be seen in many quarters. Examples include the recent book by Sally McConnell-Ginet (2020) on the relationship between language and power, as well as books by philosophers and semanticists on fascism (Stanley 2018), politics (Beaver and Stanley, to be published soon), the decline of democ-

---

[187] See McIntyre (2018) on post-truth, Bacharan (2019) on Trump's tweets and fake news, and Changeux (2009) on the biological basis of truth.
[188] See Hazan (2006) for a similar, though more journalistic than academic, description of the new French political language (LQR, for *Lingua Quintae Republicae* 'the language of the fifth republic').

racy (Simone 2015), and the relationship between language and truth (Moeschler 2021). This is all good news. It means that scholars trained in sophisticated linguistic analysis are now disseminating their scientific knowledge to a large audience – all the above-mentioned authors are scholars in one field of language science or another.

But this is also a challenging time. In a recent workshop, a PhD student presented his research project on politicians' interviews, and specifically on journalists' questions, a very appealing topic. The student addressed interesting and clever issues, but pragmatics' main concepts, such as presuppositions (*what is the background of a question?*) and implicatures (*what does a question implicate?*) were not included. It is crucial for our fields and disciplines not only to continue our research and especially to address new issues and questions, based on robust theoretical foundations.

My ambition with this book is, however, more limited: my only hope is that some of the ideas about our communication and language environment presented here will help create a better understanding of what we are. Thank you for having read my book.

Glossary

Adaptation modification of a feature by natural selection.

Ad hoc concept concept which is inferred in a specific context, and which results in concept narrowing or broadening.

Agent thematic role (semantic function) of the argument, denoting the entity which accomplishes the action described by the verb.

Ambiguity property of a word or a sentence that has more than one meaning.

Anaphoric pronoun third-person pronoun whose reference depends on a coreference relation with its antecedent.

Antonyms contrary predicates.

Aposemantism property of some species to signal information, for instance "I am not edible".

Approximation literally false utterance, producing relevant implicatures.

Autonomy of meaning assumption according to which meaning is located in words.

Batesian mimicry property of some species to imitate other species to communicate a message ("I am not edible").

Biolinguistics theory of language based on the assumption that the faculty of language is recorded into genetic material.

Broadening operation on an ad hoc concept whose goal is to modify the logical entry of a concept.

Category set of entities organised around a prototype.

Causal chain string of events causally related in a narrative.

Code model system of communication based on the sharing of a common code, and the transmission of signals from a source (communicator) to a recipient (addressee).

Code switching alternation between two languages by a speaker in a bilingual conversation.

Cognitive principle of relevance principle explaining the tendency for human cognition to be geared to maximize relevance.

Coherence discourse consistency ensuring its well-formedness and its interpretation.

Cohesion discourse consistency that is linguistically signalled by a cohesion marker.

Cohesion marker linguistic marker indicating discourse cohesion.

Communicated (conveyed) what is said + what is implicated.

Communication system allowing for a transfer of information from a source to a destination.

Communicative intention mental state that indicates a desire to communicate something.

Communicative principle of relevance principle that presumes the optimal relevance of the speaker's utterance.

Competence the set of knowledge a speaker has about her language.

Compositionality property of semantics to compute sentence meaning from its parts (predicates and arguments) to its whole (proposition).

Comprehension procedure (Relevance) cognitive heuristics that invites the addressee to seek the path of least effort in his search for relevance.

Concept word of the language of thought, with logical, encyclopaedic, and lexical entries.

Conditional relevance principle stating that in an adjacent pair of turns, the first part of the pair creates the expectation and the relevance of the second part.

Conduit metaphor frozen metaphorical system representing verbal communication as a train journey.

Connective operator whose arguments are propositions, such as negation, conjunction, disjunction, and conditional.

Constructivist approach theory of metaphor according to which the interpretation of a metaphor is not understood through its literal meaning.

Context set of contextual assumptions allowing a contextual implication to be drawn.

Contextual assumption assumption belonging to the cognitive environment necessary for drawing a contextual implication.

Contextual dependency assumption according to which meaning depends on context.

Contradiction logical relationship between a universal and a particular, one positive and the other negative.

Contrariety logical relationship between contraries which are forbidden to be true at the same time.

Conversation analysis domain of linguistics and micro-sociology that studies verbal interactions.

Conversational common ground set of mutually shared propositions in a conversation.

Conversational implicature implicit conveyed meaning obtained via a maxim of conversation.

Cooperation way of behaving in communication. See Cooperative principle.

Cooperative principle principle that requires the participants in a conversation to follow the direction of the exchange in which they are engaged.

Creole pidgin that has become a mother tongue, consisting of a syntax, a morphology, and a considerable lexicon.

Cue permanent markings, like those of a butterfly, that communicate a threatening message to predators.

Denotation descriptive relationship between a word and the world.

Derivation set of syntactic operations beginning with an abstract representation and resulting in a spoken sentence.

Descriptive negation truth-conditional negation, whose meaning is the contradictory proposition of the positive sentence.

Dialect variety of a standard language.

Diglossia plurilingual situation characterised by the presence of a standard language and a vernacular language.

Discourse sequence of non-arbitrary utterances.

Discourse analysis field of linguistics that defines discourse as a linguistic unit.

Discourse competence speaker knowledge about discourse structure, which is the foundation of discourse coherence.

Discourse connective non-logical connective with a procedural meaning.

Discourse relation semantic connection between states or events described in discourse (Narration, Explanation, Result, etc.).

Echolocation system of sonar communication used by large marine mammals and bats.

Ellipsis sequence of events or utterances that is not made explicit in discourse (pragmatics); suppression of the redundant linguistic material in a sentence and in dialogue (syntax).

Ethnomethods methods used by participants in a conversation to solve issues in verbal interaction.

Exaptation use of a feature of human cognition different from the function it developed through evolution.

Explanation reverse temporal order.

Explicature explicit intended content that is pragmatically inferred.

Expression grammatical category expressing the subjectivity of a subject of consciousness.

External language social and national dimension of language.

Face positive social value acquired through the actions of the speaker/hearer.

Face-work set of processes allowing face to be preserved.

Factive property of a proposition or a message to be true.

Faculty of language the human mind/brain faculty specific to language.

Faculty of language in the broad sense sensorimotor and conceptual-intentional interfaces.

Faculty of language in the narrow sense property of the linguistic system reduced to recursion.

Focus new information in a sentence, generally located in the final position.

Forclusive negative word located at the end of the clause.

Free indirect discourse representation of speech or thought attributed to a subject of consciousness and described in the third person.

FTA (face-threatening act) speech act that potentially threatens the addressee's face.

Garden-path sentence sentence whose grammatical parsing leads to a dead end.

Global communicative intention indication of the intentional character of the speaker's or author's discourse.

Global informative intention intentionally communicated content through discourse.

Grammatical category set of linguistic constituents that share grammatical and morphological properties (verb, noun, adjective, etc.).

Grammatical function syntactic relationship of a nominal phrase to the verb (subject, direct object, indirect object).

Grammaticalisation linguistic change from a lexical to a grammatical category.

Homo neanderthalis Hominidae who emerged on earth 400,000 years ago and who disappeared 40,000 years ago, probably because of Homo sapiens. They lived in northern Europe.

Homo sapiens Hominidae who emerged on earth about 300,000 years ago.

Homology property of a feature inherited from a common ancestor.

Hopi Amerindian language spoken in Arizona.

HOT higher-order thought, defined with four possible levels of embedding of mental states (beliefs, desires, and intentions).

Idealized cognitive models cognitive models that organize lexical semantics, such the structure of image schemas, as well as metaphorical and metonymic extensions.

Identification principle (in mental spaces) reference relationship from the description of a trigger-entity to the description of target-entity, via a pragmatic connector.

Idiom polylectal expression with non-compositional meaning.

Illocutionary force action value of a speech act (request, promise, order, etc.).

Implicature implicit content of an utterance, which corresponds to the speaker's intention.

Indexical deictic expression that refers to one parameter of the utterance context (speaker, speech time, or place).

Inference deduction based on premises leading to a conclusion.

Inferential model system of communication based on the contextualisation of transmitted signals and the deduction of a contextual implication.

Inflexion grammatical agreement markers such as gender, number, tense, and mode.

Information modification of a cognitive system's state.

Informative intention content of what is communicated through an utterance; speaker meaning.

Inslekampx Shalishan language spoken in western Canada.

Intentional system see HOT.

Interface locus of cognitive systems interaction.

Internal language linguistic knowledge of a particular speaker.

Intonation melodic dimension of language.

Irony figure of thought expressed in an utterance that echoes an utterance or thought that is distant from the speaker.

Jargon sub-language used by a well-defined set of speakers (experts, professionals, teenagers, etc.).

Language of thought (mentalese) system of thought composition whose words are concepts.

Language system of information representation defined by a phonology, a syntax, and a semantics.

Langue (Saussure) system of linguistic signs shared by a linguistic community.

Lexicon repertory of lexical units that define a natural language.

Linguistic code system that enables the matching of messages and signals as well as their transmission from a source to a recipient.

Linguistic competence set of knowledge that a speaker has of her language.

Linguistic determinism strong version of linguistic relativism, according to which language determines the speaker's representation of the world.

Linguistic relativism linguistic theory according to which language determines the nature of concepts.

Litotes saying less to mean more.

MaxContrary Effect Relevance-implicature from a negated antonym to its positive contrary.

Merge syntactic operation responsible for the grouping of syntactic units.

Metalinguistic negation non-descriptive and non-truth-conditional use of negation that signifies "I cannot affirm the positive corresponding utterance".

Metaphor figure of speech according to which the communicated meaning is an implicature resulting in the violation of the first quality maxim (Grice), an extreme case of specification (Relevance), or the explanation of a complex concept by another concept the speaker has experienced (Lakoff).

Metonymy figure of speech defined by a relationship of correspondence between two entities (container-content, means-result, etc.).

Morphology domain of linguistics that studies word structure.

Move syntactic operation responsible for the movement of syntactic constituents.

Mutual cognitive environment set of mutually manifest facts for a speaker and her audience.

Myside bias cognitive bias that gives more weight to the speaker's own beliefs than to those of her addressee or of others.

Narration ordered sequence of events in discourse.

Narrative discourse in which events are temporally ordered.

Narrowing operation of ad hoc concept construction that aims at the reduction of its encyclopaedic entry.

Natural meaning information implied by a fact, which is factive and not under the voluntary control of the communicator.

Necessary and sufficient conditions model cognitive model that defines categories from a set of necessary and sufficient conditions that are satisfied by all category members.

Negative face personal territory of a speaker/hearer.

Non-constructivist approach theory of metaphor based on literal meaning as a first interpretation.

Non-natural meaning information obtained through the recognition of the communicator's communicative intention.

Non-propositional effect modification of the addressee's or reader's emotional state triggered by his understanding of an utterance.

Non-truth-conditional meaning meaning of an implicature that can be cancelled without contradiction.

Ostension act of showing one's communicative intention.

Ostensive-inferential communication mode of communication that implies the communicator's communicative and informative intentions.

Parole (Saussure) individual usage of langue.

Performance implementation of linguistic competence in verbal communication.

Phoneme minimal speech unit without meaning, but which produces a change of meaning by commutation.

Phonology domain of linguistics that studies the system of sounds specific to languages.

Pidgin contact language, characterised by the absence of syntax and morphology, and with a limited lexicon.

Pirahã language spoken in Amazonia.

Poetic effect effect triggered by weak implicatures.

Politeness social rules designed to limit conflict and aggression.

Polysemy property of a lexical unit of having several meanings that are generally connected to one another.

Positive cognitive effect relevant information that results in the addition of new information or the modification of old information.

Positive face self-image of the speaker/hearer

Poverty of the stimuli argument given in the biolinguistics approach to language acquisition, based on the gap between a child's linguistic environment and her linguistic knowledge.

Pragmatics study of the usage of language in communication.

Preference organisation sequence of two turns in which the second turn corresponds to the speaker's expectations.

Premise proposition from which a conclusion can be drawn through inference.

Presumption of optimal relevance presumption that the speaker's utterance is worth being processed.

Presupposition proposition that resists negation and that belongs to the common ground.

Production procedure speaker's heuristics, which facilitate the treatment of her utterances by an addressee.

Proposition sentence in the language of thought with a truth-conditional content.

Propositional effect propositional explicit or implicit content inferred in utterance comprehension.

Propositional representation representational content of a proposition that results in a true or false evaluation.

Protolanguage modern language without its syntax.

Prototype central element of a category, which defines its prototypical properties.

Prototype theory theory of categorisation based on the notion of prototype.

Quantifier logical operator in natural language whose content is a relationship between sets of individuals (some, all, none).

Recursion property of grammatical constituents to be embedded in themselves. For instance, a relative clause is embedded in a matrix sentence.

Reductionism scientific method that aims at determining, via successive reductions, the minimal units of analysis.

Relevance balance between cognitive effects and cognitive efforts in utterance comprehension.

Remedial interchange interchange that allows a potential offense to be remedied through an indirect speech act (an indirect request, for instance).

Romansh Romance language spoken in the canton of Graubünden (eastern Switzerland), consisting of five varieties. It is one of the four Switzerland's national languages.

Semantics-pragmatics interface locus of the exchange between semantic (linguistically encoded) and pragmatic (contextually inferred) information.

Semantics domain of linguistics that studies linguistic meaning.

Sign (Hauser) non-permanent trace left by animals.

Sign (Saussure) unit of langue composed of a signifiant or acoustic image, and a signifié or concept.

Signal (Hauser) alarm call in some ape species.

Signifiant part of a sign that corresponds to its acoustic image.

Signifié part of a sign that corresponds to its concept.

Skaz narrative that includes a reference to a second person.

Speaker meaning what the speaker's utterance means.

Standard language language variety imposed as the reference (official) language (administration, education, and written language) in multilingual or monolingual contexts.

Style (Banfield) expression of subjectivity in an utterance.

Style (Relevance) propositional and non-propositional effects that describe the speaker's mental or emotional state.

Subcontrariety logical relationship between subcontraries that are forbidden to be false at the same time.

Subject of consciousness (self) entity (a speaker or a fictional character) to which indexical and subjective expressions are attributed.

Superpragmatics pragmatic approach that extends beyond speaker meaning.

Supportive interchange interchange that occurs in supportive rituals such as greetings.

Swahili Bantu language spoken in Austral Africa; it is the lingua franca in the region of the great lakes (East Africa).

Syntax domain of linguistics that studies sentence structure.

Target second argument of a pragmatic connector (theory of mental spaces).

Temporal order relation of temporal succession between events that are parallel to utterance order in discourse.

Thematic role semantic function such as Agent, Patient, Experiencer, Instrument, etc.

Theory of Mental Spaces semantic theory that connects entities belonging to connected mental spaces that are grammatically constrained.

Theory of Mind cognitive faculty that attributes to others the same mental states as one's own.

Trigger first argument of a pragmatic connector (theory of mental spaces).

Universal Grammar set of universal principles and parameters that define natural languages.

Utterance sentence used in context.

Variationist sociolinguistics domain of linguistics that investigates linguistic variation.

Vernacular language non-standard variety of a language in a multilingual context, often discredited sociologically and culturally.

Weak implicature weakly communicated implicature under the responsibility of the addressee.

Yupno language spoken in Papua New Guinea.

Zeugma figure of speech defined by a syntactic but without semantic parallelism.

References

Akmajian, Adrian, Richard A. Demers & Robert M. Harnish. 1980. *Linguistics: An introduction to language and communication*, 4th edn. Cambridge, MA: The MIT Press.
Anderson, Stephen R. 2004. *Doctor Dolittle's delusion: Animals and the uniqueness of human language*. New Haven: Yale University Press.
Anderson, Stephen R. 2012. *Languages: A very short introduction*. Oxford: Oxford University Press.
Anderson, Stephen R. 2016. Romansh (Rumantsch). In Adam Ledgeway & Martin Maiden (eds.), *The Oxford guide to the Romance languages*, 169–184. Oxford: Oxford University Press.
Anderson, Stephen R. 2017. The place of human language in the animal world. In Joanna Blochowiak, Cristina Grisot, Stephanie Durrlemann & Christopher Laenzlinger (eds.), *Formal models in the study of language: Applications in interdisciplinary contexts*, 339–351. Cham: Springer.
Andor, Jozsef. 2004. The master and his performance: An interview with Noam Chomsky. *Intercultural Pragmatics* 1 (1). 93–111.
Anscombre, Jean-Claude & Oswald Ducrot. 1977. Deux *mais* en français? *Lingua* 43. 23–40.
Arbib, Michael A. (ed.). 2013. *Language, music, and the brain. A mysterious relationship*. Cambridge, MA: The MIT Press.
Asher, Nicolas. 1993. *Reference to abstract objects in discourse*. Dordrecht: Kluwer.
Asher, Nicholas & Alex Lascarides. 2005. *Logics of conversation*. Cambridge: Cambridge University Press.
Atkin, Albert. 2013. Peirce's theory of signs. In Edward N. Zalta (ed.), *The Stanford encyclopedia of philosophy*. https://plato.stanford.edu/archives/sum2013/entries/peirce-semiotics/.
Atkinson, J. Maxwell & Paul Drew. 1979. *Order in court: The organisation of verbal interaction in judicial setting*. London: Macmillan.
Austin, John L. 1962. *How to do things with words*. Cambridge, MA: Harvard University Press.
Austin, Peter K. & Julia Sallabank. 2012. *Cambridge handbook of endangered languages*. Cambridge: Cambridge University Press.
Avanzi, Mathieu. 2017. *Atlas du français de nos régions*. Paris: Armand Colin.
Bach, Emmon. 1989. *Informal lectures on formal semantics*. New York: State University of New York Press.
Bacharan, Nicole. 2019. *Le monde selon Trump: Tweets, mensonges, provocations, stratagèmes, pourquoi ça marche?* Paris: Tallandier.
Banfield, Ann. 1982. *Unspeakable sentences: Narration and representation in the language of fiction*. London: Routledge & Kegan Paul.
Banerjee, Abhijit V. & Esther Duflo. 2019. *Good economics for hard times: Better answers to our biggest problems*. London: Penguin Books.
Bargiela-Chiappini, Francesca. 2003. Face and politeness: new (insights) for old (concepts). *Journal of Pragmatics* 35 (10–11). 1453–1469.
Baron-Cohen, Simon. 1995. *Mindblindness: An essay on autism and theory of mind*. Cambridge, MA: The MIT Press.
Barthes, Roland. 1970. L'ancienne rhétorique. *Communications* 16. 172–223.
Beaver, David & Jason Stanley. To appear. *Hustle: The politics of language*. Princeton: Princeton University Press.
Bentolila, Alain. 2007. *Urgence école*. Paris: Odile Jacob.

Berlin, Brent & Paul Kay. 1969. *Basic color terms*. Los Angeles: University of California Press.
Bernstein, Basil. 1966. Elaborated and restricted codes: an outline. *Sociological Inquiry* 36. 254–261.
Berwick, Robert C., Kazuo Okanoya, Gabriel J. L. Beckers & Johan J. Bolhuis. 2011. Songs to syntax: the linguistics of birdsong. *Trends in Cognitive Sciences* 15. 113–121.
Berwick, Robert C. & Noam Chomsky. 2016. *Why only us? Language and evolution*. Cambridge, MA: The MIT Press.
Bickerton, Derek. 1990. *Language and species*. Chicago: University of Chicago Press.
Bickerton, Derek. 2009. *Adam's tongue*. New York: Farar, Strauss & Giroux.
Bidese, Ermenegildo & Anne Reboul (eds.). 2019–2020. *Evolutionary Linguistic Theory*. Vol. 1–2. Amsterdam: John Benjamins.
Bilmes, Jack. 2014. Preference and the conversation analytic endeavor. *Journal of Pragmatics* 64. 52–71.
Bleuler, Eugen. 1987 [1913]. Dementia Praecox or the group of schizophrenias. In John Cutting & Michael Shepherd (eds.), *The clinical routes of the schizophrenia concept*. Cambridge: Cambridge University Press.
Blochowiak, Joanna & Cristina Grisot. 2018. The pragmatics of descriptive and metalinguistic negation: experimental data from French. *Glossa: A Journal of General Linguistics* 3 (1), 50. 1–23.
Bloom, Paul. 2000. *How children acquire the meaning of words*. Cambridge, MA: The MIT Press.
Boeckx, Cedric. 2006. *Linguistic minimalism: Origins, concepts, methods and aims*. Oxford: Oxford University Press.
Boeckx, Cedric. 2011. *The Oxford handbook of linguistic minimalism*. Oxford: Oxford University Press.
Bonnefon, Jean-François, Aidan Feeney & Gaëlle Villejoubert. 2009. When some is actually all: Scalar inference in face-threatening contexts. *Cognition* 112. 249–258.
Boyer, Pascal. 2001. *Religions explained: The evolutionary origin of religious thought*. New York: Basic Book.
Brown, Penelope & Stephen C. Levinson. 1978. Universals in language use: Politeness phenomena. In Esther N. Goody (ed.), *Question and politeness: Strategies in social interaction*, 56–289. Cambridge: Cambridge University Press.
Brown, Penelope & Stephen C. Levinson. 1987. *Politeness: Some universals in language use*. Cambridge: Cambridge University Press.
Cambria, Erik, Dipankar Das, Sivaji Bandyopadhyaya & Antonio Feraro (eds.). 2017. *A practical guide to sentiment analysis*. Cham: Springer.
Cann, Ronnie, Ruth Kempson & Eleni Gregoromichelaki. 2009. *Semantics: An introduction to meaning in language*. Cambridge: Cambridge University Press.
Carston, Robyn. 1996. Metalinguistic negation and echoic use. *Journal of Pragmatics* 15. 309–330.
Cavalli-Sforza, Luca. 2000. *Genes, people, and languages*. New York: North Point Press.
Cave, Terence & Deirdre Wilson (eds.). 2018. *Reading beyond the code: Literature and Relevance Theory*. Oxford: Oxford University Press.
Certeau, Michel de, Dominique Julia & Jacques Revel. 1975. *Une politique de la langue: La Révolution française et les patois*. Paris: Gallimard.
Chalmers, David J. 1996. *The conscious mind: In search of a fundamental theory*. Oxford: Oxford University Press.

Changeux, Jean-Pierre. 2009. *The physiology of truth: Neuroscience and human knowledge.* Cambridge, MA: Harvard University Press.
Chapman, Siobhan & Billy Clark (eds.). *Pragmatics and literature.* Amsterdam: John Benjamins.
Chierchia, Gennaro. 2013. *Logic in grammar: Polarity, free choice, and intervention.* Oxford: Oxford University Press.
Chierchia, Gennaro & Sally McConnell-Ginet. 1990. *Meaning and grammar: An introduction to semantics.* Cambridge, MA: The MIT Press.
Chomsky, Noam. 1957. *Syntactic structures.* The Hagen: Mouton.
Chomsky, Noam. 1965. *Aspects of the theory of syntax.* Cambridge, MA: The MIT Press.
Chomsky, Noam. 1986. *Knowledge of language: Its nature, origin, and use.* New York: Praeger.
Chomsky, Noam. 1995. *The minimalist program.* Cambridge, MA: The MIT Press.
Chomsky, Noam. 2016. *What kind of creatures are we?* New York: Columbia University Press.
Christiansen, Morten H. & Simon Kirby (eds.). 2003. *Language evolution.* Oxford: Oxford University Press.
Chrysovalantis, Bartzokas. 2012. *Causality and connectives: From Grice to relevance.* Amsterdam: John Benjamins.
Chrysovalantis, Bartzokas. 2014. Linguistic constraints on causal content: The case of Modern Greek markers. *Journal of Pragmatics* 60. 160–174.
Clark, Herbert. 1996. *Using language.* Cambridge: Cambridge University Press.
Comrie, Bernard. 1976. *Aspect: An introduction to the study of verbal aspect and related problems.* Cambridge: Cambridge University Press.
Cova, Florian. 2011. *Qu'en pensez-vous? Une introduction à la philosophie expérimentale.* Paris: Editions Germina.
Crystal, David (ed.). 2003. *The Cambridge encyclopedia of the English language*, 2nd edn. Cambridge: Cambridge University Press.
Crystal, David (ed.). 2010. *The Cambridge encyclopedia of language*, 3rd edn. Cambridge: Cambridge University Press.
Culpeper, Jonathan. 2011. *Impoliteness: Using language to cause offense.* Cambridge: Cambridge University Press.
Damasio, Antonio R. 1994. *Descartes's error: Emotion, reason, and the human brain.* New York: Avon Books.
David, Jean & Robert Martin (eds.). 1980. *La notion d'aspect.* Paris: Klincksieck.
Degand, Liesbeth & Benjamin Fagard. 2012. Competing connectives in the causal domain: French *car* and *parce que*. *Journal of Pragmatics* 34 (2). 154–168.
Dennett, Daniel. 1983. Intentional systems in cognitive ethology: The 'Panglosian' paradigm defended'. *Behavioral and Brain Science* 6. 343–355.
Dennett, Daniel. 1987. *The intentional stance.* Cambridge, MA: The MIT Press.
Déprez, Viviane & France Martineau. 2003. Micro-parametric variation and negative concord. In Julie Auger, J. Clancy Clements & Barbara Vance (eds.), *Contemporary approaches to Romance linguistics*, 139–158. Amsterdam: John Benjamins.
Dessalles, Jean-Louis. 2009. *Why we talk: The evolutionary origin of language.* Oxford: Oxford University Press.
Dessalles, Jean-Louis. 2019. *Des intelligences TRÈS artificielles.* Paris: Odile Jacob.
de Beaugrande, Robert & Wolfgang Dressler. 1981. *Introduction to text linguistics.* London: Longman.
de Waal, Frans. 2002. *Pacemaking among primates.* Cambridge, MA: Harvard University Press.

de Waal, Frans. 2007. *Chimpanzee politics: Power and sex among apes*. Baltimore: The John Hopkins University Press.
Di Sciullo, Anna Maria & Cedric Boeckx (eds.). 2011. *The biolinguistic entreprise: New perspectives on the evolution and nature of human language faculty*. Oxford: Oxford University Press.
Diamond, Jared. 1997. *Guns, germs, and steel: The fates of human societies*. New York: W. W. Norton.
Diamond, Jared. 2005. *Collapse: How societies choose to fail or to succeed*. London: Penguin Books.
Diamond, Jared. 2012. *What can we learn from traditional societies?* New York: Viking Press.
Diamond, Jared. 2019. *Upheaval: Turning points for nations in crisis*. New York: Little, Brown and Company.
Dowty, David R., Robert E. Wall & Stanley Peters. 1981. *Introduction to Montague semantics*. Dordrecht: Reidel.
Ducrot, Oswald. 1972. *Dire et ne pas dire: Principes de sémantique linguistique*. Paris: Hermann.
Ducrot, Oswald et al. 1980. *Les mots du discours*. Paris: Minuit.
Ducrot, Oswald. 1984. *Le dire et le dit*. Paris: Minuit.
Du Marsais, César Chesneau. 2013 [1817]. *Des tropes ou des différents sens dans lesquels on peut prendre un même mot*. Paris: Hachette Livre BNF.
Eco, Umberto. 1976. *A theory of semiotics*. Bloomington: Indiana University Press.
Eco, Umberto. 1985. *Lector in fabula: Le rôle du lecteur ou la coopération interprétative dans les textes narratifs*. Paris: Grasset.
Eco, Umberto. 1989. *The open work*. Cambridge, MA: Harvard University Press.
Edelman, Gerald M. 1992. *Bright air, brilliant fire: On the matter of mind*. New York: Basic Book.
Eelen, Gino. 2001. *A critique of politeness theories*. London: Routledge.
Encrevé, Pierre. 1988. *La liaison avec et sans enchaînement*. Paris: Seuil
Emmory, Karen. 2013. The neurobiology of language perspectives from sign language. In Stephen R. Anderson, Jacques Moeschler & Fabienne Reboul. *The language-cognition interface*, 157–178. Geneva: Droz.
Evans, Nicholas & Stephen C. Levinson. 2009. The myth of language universals: Language diversity and its importance for cognitive science. *Behavioral and Brain Science* 32. 429–492.
Evans, Vyvyan & Melanie Green. 2006. *Cognitive linguistics: An introduction*. Edinburgh: Edinburgh University Press.
Fairclough, Norman. 2010. *Critical discourse analysis: The critical analysis of language*. London: Routledge.
Fauconnier, Gilles. 1985. *Mental spaces: Aspects of meaning construction in natural language*. Cambridge, MA: The MIT Press.
Feeney, Aidan and Jean-François Bonnefon. 2012. Politeness and honesty contribute additively to the interpretation of scalar expressions. *Journal of Language and Social Psychology* 32 (2). 181–190.
Fitch, W. Tecumseh. 2010. *The evolution of language*. Cambridge: Cambridge University Press.
Fitch, W. Tecumseh. 2013. The biology and evolution of language: A comparative approach. In Stephen R. Anderson, Jacques Moeschler & Fabienne Reboul (eds.), *The language-cognition interface*, 59–81. Geneva: Droz.
Fodor, Janet Dean & Carrie Crowther. 2002. Understanding stimulus poverty arguments. *The Linguistic review* 19. 105–145.

Fontanier, Pierre. 1968 [1830]. *Les figures du discours*. Paris: Flammarion.
Fradin, Bernard. 2003. *Nouvelles approches en morphologie*. Paris: Presses Universitaires de France.
Frauenfelder, Ulrich H. & Hélène Delage. 2013. Modularity and domain specificity in language and cognition. In Stephen R. Anderson, Jacques Moeschler & Fabienne Reboul (eds.), *The language-cognition interface*, 375–394. Geneva: Droz.
Frege, Gottlob. 1892. Über Sinn und Bedeutung. *Zeitschrift für Philosophie und Philosophische Kritik*. 100. 25–50.
Frege, Gottlob. 1948 [1892]. Sense and reference. *The Philosophical Review* 57 (3). 209–230.
Freud, Sigmund. 1957 [1905]. *Jokes and their relations to the unconscious*. London: Hogarth Press.
Frith, Christopher D. 2015. *The cognitive neuropsychology of schizophrenia*. London: Psychology Press.
Frith, Uta. 1989. *Autism: Explaining the enigma*. Oxford: Basil Blackwell.
Gadet, Françoise (ed.). 2017. *Les parlers jeunes dans l'Île de France multiculturelle*. Paris: Ophrys.
Garfinkel, Harold. 2002. *Ethnomethodology's Program*. Lanham: Rowman and Littlefield.
Gazdar, Gerald. 1979. *Pragmatics: Implicature, presupposition, and logical form*. New York: Academic Press.
Genette, Gérard. 1980. *Narrative discourse: An essay in method*. Ithaca: Cornell University Press.
Gervain, Judit, Janet F. Werker, Alexis Black & Maria N. Geffen. 2016. The neural correlates of processing scale-invariant environmental sounds at birth. *NeuroImage* 133. 144–150.
Geurts, Bart. 2010. *Quantity implicatures*. Cambridge: Cambridge University Press.
Gibbs, Raymond W. 1994. *Poetics of the mind: Figurative thought, language and understanding*. Cambridge: Cambridge University Press.
Gibbs, Raymond W. & Gerard Steen (eds.). 1999. *Metaphor in cognitive linguistics: Selected papers from the fifth international cognitive linguistics conference (Amsterdam, July 1997)*. Amsterdam: John Benjamins.
Giraud Mamessier, Anne-Lise & David Poeppel. 2012. Speech perception from a neurophysiological perspective. In David Poeppel, Tobias Overath, Arthur N. Popper & Richard R. Fay (eds.), *The human auditory cortex*, 225–260. Cham: Springer.
Glucksberg, Sam. 2001. *Understanding figurative language: From metaphors to idioms*. Oxford: Oxford University Press.
Goffman, Ervin. 1971. *Relations in public: Microstudies of the public order*. London: Penguin Books.
Goffman, Ervin. 1972. *Interaction ritual: Essays on face-to-face behavior*. London: Penguin Books.
Goldberg, Adele E. 2006. *Constructions at work: The nature of generalization in language*. Oxford: Oxford University Press.
Goody, Esther N. (ed.). 1978. *Question and politeness: Strategies in social interaction*. Cambridge: Cambridge University Press.
Gordon, Raymond G. (ed.). 2005. *Ethnologue: Languages of the world*, 15th edn. Dallas: Summer Institute of Linguistics.
Greenberg, Joseph H. 1963. Some universals of grammar with particular reference to the order of meaningful elements. In Joseph H. Greenberg (ed.), *Universals of Language*, 40–70. Cambridge, MA: The MIT Press.

Greenberg, Joseph H. 2005. *Genetic linguistics: Essays on theory and method*. Oxford: Oxford University Press.

Grice, H. Paul. 1975. Logic and conversation. In Peter Cole & Jerry L. Morgan (eds.), *Syntax and semantics 3: Speech acts*, 40–58. New York: Academic Press.

Grice, H. Paul. 1989. *Studies in the way of words*. Cambridge, MA: Harvard University Press.

Grisot, Cristina. 2018. *Cohesion, coherence and temporal reference from an experimental corpus pragmatics perspective*. Cham: Springer.

Grisot, Cristina & Thomas Meyer. 2014. Cross-linguistic manual and automatic annotation for a pragmatic feature of verb tense. *Proceedings of LREC, May 2014*. Reykjavik: University of Reykjavik.

Grisot, Cristina & Jacques Moeschler. 2014. How do empirical methods interact with theoretical pragmatics? The conceptual and procedural contents of the English Simple Past and its translation into French. In Jesus Romero-Trillo (ed.), *Yearbook of corpus linguistics and pragmatics 2014: New empirical and theoretical paradigms*, 7–33. Cham: Springer

Groupe λ-l. 1975. Car, parce que, puisque. Revue Romane 10. 248–280.

Gumperz, John J. & Dell Hymes (eds.). 1972. *Directions in sociolinguistics: The ethnography of communication*, 346–380. New York: Holt, Rinehart & Winston.

Gumperz, John J. 1982. *Discourse strategies*. Cambridge: Cambridge University Press.

Haegeman, Liliane. 1994. *Introduction to government and binding theory*, 2nd edn. Oxford: Basil Blackwell.

Hale, Bob & Crispin Wright (eds.). 1997. *A companion to the philosophy of language*. Oxford: Basil Blackwell.

Halliday, Michael A. K. & Ruqaiya Hasan. 1976. *Cohesion in English*. London: Longman.

Harari, Yuval Noah. 2014. *Sapiens: A brief history of humankind*. London: Penguin Random House.

Harari, Yuval Noah. 2016. *Homo Deus: A brief history of tomorrow*. London: Penguin Random House.

Harari, Yuval Noah. 2018. *21 lessons for the 21st century*. London: Vintage.

Harris, Randy A. 1995. *The linguistics wars*. Oxford: Oxford University Press.

Hauser, Marc. 1996. *The evolution of communication*. Cambridge, MA: The MIT Press.

Hauser, Marc, Noam Chomsky & William T. Fitch. 2002. The faculty of language: What is it, who has it, and how did it evolve? *Science* 298. 1569–1579.

Hazan, Éric. 2006. *LQR: Lingua Quintae Republicae, la propagande du quotidien*. Paris: Raisons D'Agir Éditions.

Heim, Irene & Angelika Kratzer. 1998. *Semantics in generative grammar*. Oxford: Basil Blackwell.

Heritage, John & Max Atkinson. 1984. *Structures of social action: Studies in conversation analysis*. Cambridge: Cambridge University Press.

Holquist, Michael. 2002. *Dialogism: Bakhtine and his world*, 2nd edn. London: Routledge.

Horn, Laurence R. 1984. Toward a new taxonomy for pragmatic inference. In Deborah Schiffrin (ed.), *Form and use in context: Linguistic applications* (GURT'84), 11–42. Washington: Georgetown University Press.

Horn, Laurence R. 1985. Metalinguistic negation and pragmatic ambiguity. *Language* 61 (1). 121–174.

Horn, Laurence R. 1989. *A natural history of negation*. Chicago: The University of Chicago Press.

Horn, Laurence R. 2004. Implicature. In Laurence R. Horn & Gregory Ward (eds.), *The handbook of pragmatics*, 3–28. Oxford: Basil Blackwell.

Hornstein, Norbert, Jairo Nunes & Kleanthes K. Grohmann. 2005. *Understanding minimalism*. Cambridge: Cambridge University Press.
Hurford, James R. 2007. *The origin of grammar: Language in the light of evolution*. Oxford: Oxford University Press.
Hurford, James R. 2012. *The origin of meaning: Language in the light of evolution*. Oxford: Oxford University Press.
Jackendoff, Ray. 1983. *Semantics and cognition*. Cambridge, MA: The MIT Press.
Jackendoff, Ray. 1996. *Languages of the mind: Essays on mental representations*. Cambridge, MA: The MIT Press.
Jackendoff, Ray. 2002. *Foundations of language: Brain, meaning, grammar, evolution*. Oxford: Oxford University Press.
Jackendoff, Ray. 2012. *A user's guide to thought and meaning*. Oxford: Oxford University Press.
Jacob, Pierre. 2004. *L'intentionnalité: Problèmes de philosophie de l'esprit*. Paris: Odile Jacob.
Jakobson, Roman. 1977. *Huit questions de poétique*. Paris: Points Seuil.
Jespersen, Otto. 1917. *Negation in English and in other languages*. Copenhagen: A. F. Høst.
Jouve, Vincent. 2019. *Pouvoirs de la fiction. Pourquoi aime-t-on les histoires?* Paris: Armand Colin.
Kahneman, Daniel. 2011. *Thinking, fast and slow*. New York: Farrar, Straus & Giroux.
Kambouchner, Denis. 1995. *L'homme des passions: Commentaires sur Descartes*. Paris: Albin Michel.
Kaminski, Juliane, Josep Call & Julia Fischer. 2004. Word learning in a domestic dog: Evidence for "Fast Mapping". *Science* 304 (5677). 1682–1683.
Kamp, Hans & Uwe Reyle. 1993. *From logic to discourse: Introduction to modeltheoretic semantics of natural language, formal logic and discourse representation theory*. Cham: Springer.
Keenan, Eleonor. 1976. The universality of conversational postulates. *Language and Society* 5. 67–79.
Kidd, David C. & Emanuele Castano. 2013. Reading literary fiction improves Theory of Mind. *Science* 342 (6156). 377–380.
Klemperer, Viktor. 1947. *LTI. Lingua Tertii Imperii: Notizbuch eines Philologen*. Leipzig: Reclam Verlag.
Klemperer, Viktor. 2000. *The Language of the Third Reich: LTI. Lingua Tertii Imperii: A Philologist's Notebook*. London: The Athlone Press.
Knecht, Pierre. 1995. La Suisse romande. In Robert Schläpfer (ed.), *La Suisse aux quatre langues*, 125–169. Genève: Éditions Zoé.
Korta, Kepa & John Perry. 2011. *Critical pragmatics: An inquiry into reference and communication*. Cambridge: Cambridge University Press.
Kuroda, Sige-Yuki. 1973. Where epistemology, grammar and style meet – a case study from Japanese. In Stephen R. Anderson & Paul Kiparsky (eds.), *Festschrift for Morris Halle*, 377–391. New York: Holt, Rinehart and Winston.
Labov, William. 1972a. *Sociolinguistic patterns*. Philadelphia: University of Pennsylvania Press.
Labov, William. 1972b. *Language in the inner city: Studies in Black English Vernacular*. Philadelphia: University of Pennsylvania Press.
Lakoff, George. 1987. *Women, fire and dangerous things: What categories reveal about the mind*. Chicago: The University of Chicago Press.
Lakoff, George & Mark Johnson. 1980. *Metaphors we live by*. Chicago: The University of Chicago Press.

Lakoff, Robin. 1973. The logic of politeness: or minding your *p*'s and *q*'s. *Proceedings of the Ninth Regional Meeting of the Chicago Linguistic Society*. 292–305.
Langacker, Ronald. 1987. *Foundations of cognitive grammar, tome I*. Stanford: Stanford University Press.
Langacker, Ronald. 1991. *Concept, image, and symbol: The cognitive basis of grammar*. Berlin: Mouton de Gruyter.
Larson, Richard & Gabriel Segal. 1995. *Knowledge and meaning: An introduction to semantic theory*. Cambridge, MA: The MIT Press.
Lascarides, Alex & Nicholas Asher. 1993. Temporal interpretation, discourse relations and commonsense entailment. *Linguistics and Philosophy* 16 (5). 437–493.
Leech, Geoffrey N. 1980. Language and tact. In *Explorations in semantics and pragmatics*, 79–117. Amsterdam: John Benjamins.
Leeman-Bouix, Danielle. 1994. *Les fautes de français existent-elles?* Paris: Seuil.
Lepore, Ernest & Barry C. Smith (eds.). 2006. *The Oxford handbook of philosophy of language*. Oxford: Oxford University Press.
Lestel, Dominique. 1995. *Paroles de singes: L'impossible dialogue homme-primates*. Paris: Éditions de la Découverte.
Levinson, Stephen C. 1983. *Pragmatics*. Cambridge: Cambridge University Press.
Levinson, Stephen C. 2000. *Presumptive meanings: The theory of generalized conversational implicature*. Cambridge, MA: The MIT Press.
Levinson, Stephen C. 2003. *Space in language and cognition: Explorations in cognitive diversity*. Cambridge: Cambridge University Press.
Linguistic Politeness Research Group (eds.). 2011. *Discursive approaches to politeness*. Berlin: Mouton de Gruyter (MSP).
Longobardi, Giuseppe. 2001. Formal syntax, diachronic minimalism, and etymology: the history of French *chez*. *Linguistic Inquiry* 32 (2). 275–302.
Mann, William C. & Sandra A. Thompson. 1988. Rhetorical Structure Theory: Toward a functional theory of text organization. *Text* 8. 243–281.
Martineau, France & Raymond Mougeon. 2003. A sociolinguistic study of the origin of *ne* deletion in European and Quebec French. *Language* 79 (1). 118–152.
Martins, Ana Maria. 2020. Metalinguistic negation. In Viviane Déprez & M. Teresa Espinal (eds.), *The Oxford handbook of negation*, 349–368. Oxford: Oxford University Press.
Mazzarella, Diana. 2015. Politeness, relevance and scalar inferences. *Journal of Pragmatics* 79. 93–106.
McConnell-Ginet, Sally. 2020. *Words matter: Language and power*. Cambridge: Cambridge University Press.
McIntyre, Lee. 2018. *Post-truth*. Cambridge, MA: The MIT Press.
Meillet, Antoine. 1912. L'évolution des formes grammaticales. *Scientia* 6 (12). 130–158.
Mercier, Hugo. 2020. *Not born yesterday: The science of who we trust and what we believe*. Princeton: Princeton University Press.
Mercier, Hugo & Dan Sperber. 2017. *The enigma of reason: A new theory of human understanding*. London: Allen Lane.
Minsky, Marvin. 1985. Jokes and the logic of cognitive unconscious. In Lucia Vaina & Jaakko Hintikka (eds.), *Cognitive constraints on communication: Representations and processes*, 175–200. Dordrecht: Reidel.
Mithen, Steven. 2007. *The singing Neandertals: The origins of music, language, mind and body*. Cambridge, MA: Harvard University Press.

Moeschler, Jacques. 1991. Aspects linguistiques et pragmatiques de la métaphore: anomalie sémantique, implicitation conversationnelle et système métaphorique. *TRANEL* 17. 51–74.
Moeschler, Jacques. 1994. Structure et interprétabilité des textes argumentatifs. *Pratiques* 84. 93–111.
Moeschler, Jacques. 2000. Representing events in language and discourse. In Martine Coene, Walter De Mulder, Patrick Dendale & Yves D'Hust (eds.), *Tiaiani augusti vestigia pressa sequamur: Studia lingusitica in honorem Liliane Tasmowski*, 461–479. Padova: Unipress.
Moeschler, Jacques. 2004. Intercultural pragmatics: A cognitive approach. *Intercultural Pragmatics* 1 (1). 49–70.
Moeschler, Jacques. 2007. The role of explicature in communication and in intercultural communication. In Istvan Kecskes & Laurence R. Horn L. (eds.), *Explorations in pragmatics: Linguistic, cognitive and intercultural aspects*, 73–94. Berlin: Mouton de Gruyter (MSP).
Moeschler, Jacques. 2009. Pragmatics, propositional and non-propositional effects: Can a theory of utterance interpretation account for emotions in verbal communication? *Social Science Information* 48 (3). 447–463.
Moeschler, Jacques. 2010. Is pragmatics of discourse possible? In Alessandro Capone (ed.), *Perspectives on language use and pragmatics: A volume in memory of Sorian Stati*, 217–238. München: Lincom.
Moeschler, Jacques. 2011. Causal, inferential and temporal connectives: Why *parce que* is the only causal connective in French. In Sylvie Hancil (ed.), *Marqueurs discursifs et subjectivité*, 97–114. Rouen: Presses Universitaires de Rouen et du Havre.
Moeschler, Jacques. 2013. How 'logical' are logical words? Negation and its descriptive vs. metalinguistic uses. In Maite Taboada & M. Radoslava Trnavac (eds.), *Nonveridicality and evaluation: Theoretical, computational and corpus approaches*, 76–110. Leiden: Brill.
Moeschler, Jacques. 2017. How speaker meaning, explicature and implicature work together. In Rachel Giora & Michael Haugh (eds.), *Doing pragmatics interculturally: Cognitive, philosophical and sociopragmatic perspectives*, 215–232. Berlin: Mouton de Gruyter.
Moeschler, Jacques. 2018a. What is the contribution of connectives to discourse meaning? The With or Without Issue (WWI). In Steve Oswald, Jérôme Jacquin & Thierry Herman (eds.). *Argumentation and language: Linguistic, cognitive and discursive explorations*, 131–149. Cham: Springer.
Moeschler, Jacques. 2018b. Conventional implicatures and presupposition. In Frank Liedtke & Astrid Tuchen (eds.). *Handbuch Pragmatik*, 198–206. Stuttgart: Metzler.
Moeschler, Jacques. 2018c. A set of semantic and pragmatic criteria for descriptive vs. metalinguistic negation. *Glossa: A Journal of General Linguistics* 3 (1), 58. 1–30.
Moeschler, Jacques. 2019. *Non-lexical pragmatics: Time, causality and logical words*. Berlin: Mouton de Gruyter (MSP).
Moeschler, Jacques. 2020a. *Pourquoi le langage? Des Inuits à Google*. Paris: Armand Colin.
Moeschler, Jacques. 2020b. Negative predicates: Incorporated negation. In Viviane Déprez & M. Teresa Espinal (eds.), *The Oxford handbook of negation*, 26–46. Oxford: Oxford University Press.
Moeschler, Jacques. 2021. *Why truth matters? Where relevance meets truthfulness*. Ms.
Moeschler, Jacques, Jacques Jayez, Monika Kozlowska, Jean-Marc Luscher, Louis de Saussure & Bertrand Sthioul. 1998. *Le temps des événements: Pragmatique de la référence temporelle*. Paris: Kimé.

Mosegaard Hansen, Maj-Britt. 2018. The expression of clause negation: From Latin to early French. In Anne Carlier & Céline Guillot (eds.), *Latin tardif/français ancien: Continuités et ruptures*, 269–298. Berlin: Mouton de Gruyter.

Musolino, Julien. 2015. *The soul fallacy: What science shows we gain from letting go of our soul beliefs*. New York: Prometheus Books.

Nazir, Tatjana A. & Anne Reboul. 2017. Cognition incarnée et fiction. In Catherine Courtet, Mireille Besson, Françoise Lavocat & Alain Viala (eds.), *Violence et passion: Rencontres Recherche et Création du Festival d'Avignon*, 65–75. Paris: CNRS Éditions.

Newmeyer, Frederick J. 2005. *Possible and probable languages*. Oxford: Oxford University Press.

Noveck, Ira. 2018. *Experimental pragmatics: The making of a cognitive science*. Cambridge: Cambridge University Press.

Núñez, Rafael, Kensy Cooperrider, D. Doan & Jürg Wassmann. 2012. Contours of time: Topographic construals of past, present, and future in the Yupno valley of Papua New Guinea. *Cognition* 124. 25–35.

Ogden, Charles K. & Ivor Richard. 1989 [1923]. *The meaning of meaning: A study of the influence of language upon thought and the science of symbolism*. Brace: Houghton Mifflin Harcourt.

Origgi, Gloria. 2015. *La réputation: Qui dit quoi de qui?* Paris: Presses Universitaires de France.

Ortony, Andrew (ed.). 1979. *Metaphor and thought*. Cambridge: Cambridge University Press.

Panther, Klaus-Uwe & Günter Radden (eds.). 1999. *Metonymy in language and thought*. Amsterdam: John Benjamins.

Patel-Grosz, Pritty, Patrick G. Grosz, Tejawinee Kelkar & Alexander R. Jensenius. 2019. Coreference and disjoint reference in the semantics of narrative dance. *Proceedings of Sinn und Bedeutung* 22 (2). 199–216.

Patterson, Francine. 1978. Conversation with a gorilla. *The National Geographic* 154 (4). https://www.nationalgeographic.com/magazine/1978/10/conversations-with-koko-the-gorilla/.

Pavel, Thomas. 2017. La vérité de fiction. In Catherine Courtet, Mireille Besson, Françoise Lavocat & Alain Viala (eds.), *Violence et passion: Rencontres Recherche et Création du Festival d'Avignon*, 55–63. Paris: CNRS Éditions.

Peirce, Charles S. 1931–1935. *Collected papers*, vol. 1–6. Cambridge, MA: Harvard University Press.

Peirce, Charles S. 1998. *The Essential Peirce*, vol. 2. Bloomington: Indiana University Press.

Pfaff, Donald W. 2014. *The altruistic brain*. Oxford: Oxford University Press.

Piketty, Thomas. 2014. *Capital in the twenty-first century*. Cambridge, MA: The Belnap Press.

Pinker, Steven. 1995. *The language instinct*. New York: HarperPerennial.

Pinker, Steven. 1997. *How the mind works*. New York: Norton.

Pinker, Steven. 2002. *The blank slate: The modern denial of human nature*. London: Penguin Books.

Pinker, Steven. 2007. The evolutionary social psychology of off-record indirect speech acts. *Intercultural pragmatics* 4 (4). 437–461.

Pinker, Steven. 2013. *Language, cognition, and human nature: Selected articles*. Oxford: Oxford University Press.

Pinker, Steven. 2018. *Enlightenment now: The case for reason, science, humanism, and progress*. New York: Viking.

Pinker, Steven & Ray Jackendoff. 2005. The faculty of language: What's special about it? *Cognition* 95 (2). 201–236.

Pollock, Jean-Yves. 1997. *Langage et cognition: Introduction au programme minimaliste de la grammaire générative*. Paris: Presses Universitaires de France.
Pomerantz, Anita. 1984. Agreeing and disagreeing with assessments: Some features of preferred/dispreferred turn shapes. In John Heritage & Max Atkinson, *Structures of social action: Studies in conversation analysis*, 57–101. Cambridge: Cambridge University Press.
Pomerantz, Anita & John Heritage. 2012. Preference. In Jack Sidnell & Tanya Stivers (eds.), *The handbook of conversation analysis*, 210–228. Oxford: Basil Blackwell.
Potts, Christopher. 2005. *The logic of conventional implicatures*. Oxford: Oxford University Press.
Price, Huw. 1996. *Time's arrow and the Archimedes' point*. Oxford: Oxford University Press.
Propp, Vladimir. 1968. *Morphology of folktale*. Austin: University of Texas Press.
Pullum, Geoffrey K. 1991. *The great Eskimo vocabulary hoax and other irreverent essays on the study of language*. Chicago: The University of Chicago Press.
Quirk, Randolph, Sidney Greenbaum, Geoffrey Leech & Jan Svartvik. 1985. *Comprehensive grammar of the English language*. Pearson: Longman.
Radford, Andrew. 1981. *Transformational syntax: A student's guide to Chomsky's Extended Standard Theory*. Cambridge: Cambridge University Press.
Raskin, Victor. 1985. *Semantic mechanism of humor*. Dordrecht: Reidel.
Reboul, Anne. 1990. The logical status of fictional discourse: What Searle's speaker can't say to his hearer. In Armin Burkhardt (ed.), *Speech-acts, meaning and intention*, 336–363. Berlin: Mouton de Gruyter.
Reboul, Anne. 1992. *Rhétorique et stylistique de la fiction*. Nancy: Presses Universitaires de Nancy.
Reboul, Anne. 2003. Causalité, force dynamique et ramifications temporelles. *Cahiers de linguistique française* 25. 43–69.
Reboul, Anne. 2007. *Langage et cognition humaine*. Grenoble: Presses Universitaires de Grenoble.
Reboul, Anne. 2009. La fiction, la narration et le développement de la rationalité. *Nouveaux cahiers de linguistique française* 29. 83–113.
Reboul, Anne. 2013. The social evolution of language and the necessity of implicit communication. In Stephen R. Anderson, Jacques Moeschler & Fabienne Reboul (eds.), *The language-cognition interface*, 253–273. Geneva: Droz.
Reboul, Anne. 2017a. *Cognition and communication in the evolution of language*. Oxford: Oxford University Press.
Reboul, Anne. 2017b. A pragmatic and philosophical examination of Everett's claims about Pirahã. In Joanna Blochowiak, Cristina Grisot, Stephanie Durrlemann & Christopher Laenzlinger (eds.), *Formal models in the study of language: Applications in interdisciplinary contexts*, 83–96. Cham: Springer.
Reboul, Anne, Denis Delfitto & Gaetano Fiorin. 2016. The semantic properties of free indirect discourse. *Annual Review of Linguistics* 2. 255–271.
Reboul, Anne & Jacques Moeschler. 1997. Reductionism and contextualization in pragmatics and discourse analysis. *Linguistische Berichte Sonderheft* 8. 283–295.
Reboul, Anne & Jacques Moeschler. 1998a. *Pragmatique du discours: De l'interprétation de l'énoncé à l'interprétation du discours*. Paris: Armand Colin.
Reboul, Anne & Jacques Moeschler. 1998b. *La pragmatique aujourd'hui: Une nouvelle science de la communication*. Paris: Points Seuil.

Reddy, Michael. 1979. The conduit metaphor: A case of frame conflict in our language about language. In Andrew Ortony (ed.), *Metaphor and thought*, 284–324. Cambridge: Cambridge University Press.

Reinheimer, Sanda & Liliane Tasmowski. 1997. *Pratique des langues romanes: Espagnol, français, italien, portugais, roumain*. Paris: L'Harmattan.

Renfrew, Colin. 1987. *Archeology and language: The puzzle of Indo-European origins*. London: Jonathan Cape.

Rey, Alain. 2007. *L'amour du français*. Paris: Denoël.

Rey, Alain (ed.). 1998. *Dictionnaire historique de la langue française*. Paris: Éditions Dictionnaires Le Robert.

Rizzi, Luigi. 2013. Theoretical and comparative syntax: Some current issues. In Stephen R. Anderson, Jacques Moeschler & Fabienne Reboul, *The language-cognition interface*, 307–331. Geneva: Droz.

Roberts, Ian. 2017. *The wonder of language: Or how to make noises and influence people*. Cambridge: Cambridge University Press.

Rosch, Eleonor. 1977. Classification of real-world objects: Origins and representation in cognition. In Philip N. Johnson-Laird & Peter C. Wason (eds.), *Thinking: Reading in cognitive science*, 212–232. Cambridge: Cambridge University Press.

Rosch, Eleonor. 1978. Principles of categorization. In Eleonor Rosch & Barbara B. Lloyd (eds.), *Cognition and categorization*, 27–48. Hillsdale: Laurence Erlbaum.

Ruhlen, Merith. 1994. *The origin of language: Tracing the evolution of the mother tongue*. Hoboken: Wiley & Sons.

Ruwet, Nicolas. 1982. Parallelisms and deviations in poetry. In Tzvetan Todorov (ed.), *French literary theory today*, 92–124. Cambridge: Cambridge University Press.

Sacks, Harvey, Emanuel A. Schegloff & Gail Jefferson. 1974. A simplest systematics for the organization of turn-taking in conversation. *Language* 50 (4). 696–735.

Sander, David & Klaus R. Scherrer (eds.). 2009. *The Oxford companion to emotion and the affective sciences*. Oxford: Oxford University Press.

Sapir, Edward. 1912. Language and environment. *American anthropologist* 14 (2). 226–242.

Sapir, Edward. 1931. Dialect. *Encyclopedia of the social sciences* 5. 123–126.

Saussure, Ferdinand de. 1968 [1916]. *Cours de linguistique générale*. Paris: Payot.

Saussure, Ferdinand de. 1977. *Course in general linguistics*. Glasgow: Fontana/Collins.

Schaeffer, Jean-Marie. 1999. *Pourquoi la fiction?* Paris: Seuil.

Schank, Roger C. & Robert P. Abelson. 1978. Scripts, plans and knowledge. In Philip N. Johnson-Laird & Peter C. Wason (eds.), *Thinking: Reading in cognitive science*, 421–432. Cambridge: Cambridge University Press.

Schegloff, Emanuel. 1972. Sequencing in conversational openings. In John J. Gumperz & Dell Hymes (eds.), *Directions in sociolinguistics: The ethnography of communication*, 346–380. New York: Holt, Rinehart & Winston.

Scherrer, Yves. 2012. *Generating Swiss German sentences from Standard German: A multi-dialectal approach*. University of Geneva: PhD thesis.

Schlenker, Philippe. 2004. Context of thought and context of utterance: A note on free indirect discourse and the historical present. *Mind & Language* 19 (3). 279–304.

Schlenker, Philippe. 2013. Anaphora: Insights from sign language (summary). In Stephen R. Anderson, Jacques Moeschler & Fabienne Reboul, *The language-cognition interface*, 83–107. Geneva: Droz.

Schlenker, Philippe. 2017. Outline of music semantics. *Music Perception: An Interdisciplinary Journal* 35. 3–37.
Schlenker, Philippe, Emmanuel Chemla, Anne Schel, James Fuller, Jean-Pierre Gautier, Jeremy Kuhn, Dunja Veselinovic, Kate Arnold, Cristiane Cäsar, Sumir Keenan, Alban Lemasson, Karim Ouattara, Robin Ryder & Klaus Zuberbühler. 2016. Formal monkey linguistics. *Theoretical Linguistics* 42. 1–90.
Schmitter, Amy M. 2016. Descartes on the emotions. *Stanford encyclopedia of philosophy: Supplement to the 17th and 18th century. Theories of emotion*s. Stanford: Center for the Study of Language and Information. https://plato.stanford.edu/entries/emotions-17th18th/LD2Descartes.htm.
Scott, Kate, Billy Clark & Robyn Carston (eds.). 2019. *Relevance, pragmatics and interpretation*. Cambridge: Cambridge University Press.
Scott-Phillips, Thom. 2015. *Speaking our minds: Why human communication is different, and how language evolved to make it special*. Basingstoke: Palgrave Macmillan.
Searle, John R. 1969. *Speech acts: An essay in the philosophy of language*. Cambridge: Cambridge University Press.
Searle, John R. 1979. *Expression and meaning: Studies in the theory of speech act*. Cambridge: Cambridge University Press.
Searle, John R. 1983. *Intentionality: An essay in philosophy of mind*. Cambridge: Cambridge University Press.
Searle, John R. 1992. *The rediscovery of the mind*. Cambridge, MA: The MIT Press.
Shibatani, Masayoshi & Theodora Bynon (eds.). 1995. *Approaches to language typology*. Oxford: Oxford University Press.
Simone, Raffaele. 2015. *Come la democrazia fallisce*. Milano: Garzanti.
Smith, Neil & Deirdre Wilson. 1980. *Modern linguistics: The results of Chomsky's revolution*. Bloomington: Indiana University Press.
Sokal, Alan & Jean Bricmont. 1999. *Fashionable nonsense: Postmodern intellectuals' abuse of science*. New York: Picador.
Sperber, Dan. 1996. *Explaining culture*. Oxford: Basil Blackwell.
Sperber, Dan & Deirdre Wilson. 1985–1986. Loose talk. *Proceedings of the Aristotelian Society* 86. 153–171.
Sperber, Dan & Gloria Origgi. 2000. Evolution, communication, and the proper function of language. In Peter Carruthers & Andrew Chamberlain (eds.), *Evolution and the human mind: Language, modularity and social cognition*, 140–169. Cambridge: Cambridge University Press.
Sperber, Dan & Deirdre Wilson. 1995 [1986]. *Relevance: Communication and cognition*, 2nd edn. Oxford: Basil Blackwell.
Sperber, Dan, Fabrice Clément, Christophe Heintz, Olivier Mascaro, Hugo Mercier, Gloria Origgi & Deirdre Wilson. 2010. Epistemic vigilance. *Mind & Language* 25 (4). 359–393.
Stalnaker, Ronald C. 1977. Pragmatic presuppositions. In Andy Rogers, Bob Wall & John P. Murphy (eds.), *Proceedings of the Texas conference on performatives, presuppositions and implicatures*, 135–147. Arlington: Center for Applied Linguistics. Reprinted in Stalnaker 1999.
Stalnaker, Ronald C. 1999. *Context and content: Essays on intentionality in speech and thought*. Oxford: Oxford University Press.
Stanley, Jason. 2018. *How fascism works: The politics of us and them*. New York: Random House.

Stukker, Ninke, Ted Sanders & Arie Verhagen. 2009. Categories of subjectivity in Dutch causal connectives: A usage-based analysis. In Ted Sanders & Eve Sweetser (eds.), *Causal categories in discourse and cognition*, 119–171. Berlin: Mouton de Gruyter.

Sweetser, Eve. 1990. *From etymology to pragmatics: Metaphorical and cultural aspects of semantic structure*. Cambridge: Cambridge University Press.

Terkourafi, Marina, Benjamin Weissman & Joseph Roy. 2020. Different scalar terms affected by face differently. *International Review of Pragmatics* 12. 1–43.

Todorov, Tzvetan. 1966. Les catégories du récit littéraire. *Communications* 8. 125–151.

Tomasello, Michael. 2003. *Constructing a language: A usage-based theory of language acquisition*. Cambridge, MA: Harvard University Press.

Tomasello, Michael. 2008. *Origins of human communication*. Cambridge, MA: The MIT Press.

Traugott, Elisabeth Closs & Richard B. Dasher. 2002. *Regularity in semantic change*. Cambridge: Cambridge University Press.

van der Auwera, Johan. 2009. The Jespersen cycles. In Elly van Gelderen (ed.), *Cyclical change*, 35–71. Amsterdam: John Benjamins.

van der Henst, Jean-Baptiste, Laure Carles & Dan Sperber. 2002. Truthfulness and relevance in telling the time. *Mind & Language* 17 (5). 457–466.

van der Henst, Jean-Baptiste, Hugo Mercier, Hiroshi Yama, Yayoi Kawasaki & Kuniko Adachi. 2006. Dealing with contradiction in a communicative context: A cross-cultural study. *Intercultural Pragmatics* 3 (4). 487–502.

van Dijk, Teun A. 1977. *Text and context: Explorations in the semantics and pragmatics of discourse*. London: Longman.

Walter, Henriette. 1994. *L'Aventure des langues en Occident*. Paris: Robert Laffont.

Weinreich, Uriel, William Labov & Marvin I. Herzog. 1968. Empirical foundations for a theory of language change. In Winfred P. Lehmann & Yakov Malkiel (eds.), *Directions for historical linguistics*, 97–195. Austin: University of Texas Press.

Weinrich, Harald. 1973. *Le temps: Le récit et le commentaire*. Paris: Seuil.

Wichmann, Anne, Nicole Dehé & Dagmar Barth-Weingarten (eds.). 2009. *Where prosody meets pragmatics*. Bingley: Emerald.

Wilson, Deirdre. 2003. Relevance and lexical pragmatics. *Italian Journal of Linguistics* 15 (2). 273–291.

Wilson, Deirdre & Dan Sperber. 1981. On Grice's theory of conversation. In Paul Werth, *Conversation and discourse*, 155–178. London: Croom Helm.

Wilson, Deirdre & Dan Sperber. 2004. Relevance Theory. In Laurence R. Horn & Gregory Ward (eds.), *The handbook of pragmatics*, 607–632. Oxford: Basil Blackwell.

Wilson, Deirdre & Dan Sperber. 2012. *Meaning and relevance*. Cambridge: Cambridge University Press.

Zufferey, Sandrine. 2012. 'Car, parce que, puisque' revisited: Three empirical studies on French causal connectives. *Journal of Pragmatics* 44 (2). 138–153.

Zufferey, Sandrine. 2015. *Acquiring pragmatics: Social and cognitive perspectives*. London: Routledge.

Zufferey, Sandrine & Bruno Cartoni. 2012. English and French causal connectives in contrast. *Languages in Contrast* 12 (2). 232–250.

Zufferey, Sandrine, Jacques Moeschler & Anne Reboul. 2019. *Implicatures*. Cambridge: Cambridge University Press.

Name index

Amis, Martin 178
Anderson, Stephen R. 13, 30, 51,
Austin, John L. 122
Aymé, Marcel 147–148

Banfield, Ann 95, 158, 181–184
Barthes, Roland 59
Berlin, Brent 104
Bickerton, Derek 75
Bleuler, Eugen 124
Blochowiak, Joanna 207
Bonnefon, Jean-François 125
Borges, Jorge Luis 186–187
Brown, Penelope 7, 119, 122–125

Carston, Robyn 90, 203, 206
Cavalli-Sforza, Luca 15, 30
Charlie Hebdo 200–204
Chomsky, Noam 3, 5, 64, 67, 71–75, 99, 101, 111, 142
Coe, Jonathan 181
Corneille, Pierre 173
Crystal, David 13, 17, 29, 61

Dennett, Daniel 53–55, 79
Diamond, Jared 15, 18, 30, 57
Ducrot, Oswald 145, 161, 181, 193

Eco, Umberto 56, 158

Fauconnier, Gilles 167–168
Fitch, W. Tecumseh 3, 64, 73, 75, 211
Flaubert, Gustave 182
Frege, Gottlob 5
Freud, Sigmund 37, 151, 178
Fruttero, Carlo 178

Goffman, Ervin 120–121, 131
Greenberg, Joseph H. 19–20
Grice, H. Paul 21, 52, 55–56, 78–81, 83, 85, 118–119, 121, 125, 162, 170, 192, 201
Grisot, Cristina 207, 212–213

Hauser, Marc 3, 46, 51–52, 64, 73–75, 78
Horn, Laurence R. 174, 202–203, 206

Jackendoff, Ray 6, 63, 75–78, 97
Jespersen, Otto 42
Johnson, Mark 46, 105, 107–108, 165–166

Kahneman, Daniel 151
Kay, Paul 104
King, Martin Luther 152–153

Labov, William 100, 114–116, 179–180
Lakoff, George 46, 105, 107–108, 164–166
Lakoff, Robin 118
Leech, Geoffrey 119
Levinson, Stephen C. 3, 6–7, 103, 119, 122–125, 129–131, 191
Longobardi, Giuseppe 40
Lucentini, Franco 178

Martineau, France 42–43
Mercier, Hugo 90, 98, 152, 155
Mithen, Steven 51, 149–150
Moeschler, Jacques 4, 6, 84, 109, 117, 125, 127, 132–135, 140, 145–146, 151, 159, 174–175, 179, 190–194, 203, 206, 208, 213, 216
Mosegaard Hansen, Maj-Britt 42
Newmeyer, Frederick J. 3, 20, 102, 150

Obama, Barack 141, 152, 154
Ortony, Andrew 162

Pinker, Steven 2, 31–33, 39, 63–64, 75–76, 97, 102–103, 125
Pollock, Jean-Yves 31, 67
Potts, Christopher 209
Pullum, Geoffrey K. 3, 102

Reboul, Anne 3–6, 46, 49, 51–53, 64–65, 76, 83–85, 95, 125, 132–134, 140, 146, 155, 157, 182, 185, 190–191

Reddy, Michael 46, 107–108
Rizzi, Luigi 70

Sapir, Edward 101
Saussure, Ferdinand de 35, 99–100
Schegloff, Emanuel 128–129
Schlenker, Philippe 183, 189
Sciascia, Leonardo 178–179
Searle, John R. 98, 122, 125, 132–133, 157, 162–163
Sperber, Dan 4–6, 47–48, 56–57, 63, 85–88, 90, 97–98, 121, 152–153, 155–156, 162, 164, 171–173, 179

Stalnaker, Ronald C. 193, 209
Stendahl 135

van der Auwera, Johan 42

van der Henst, Jean-Baptiste 79, 90, 103, 155
Walter, Henriette 17, 34
Wilson, Deirdre 4, 6–7, 47–48, 56–57, 63, 85–88, 106, 121, 153, 156, 158, 162, 164, 171–173, 179

Zufferey, Sandrine 4, 6, 33, 84, 125, 144–145, 191

Subject index

accessibility 193, 209
adaptation 74
agent 77
ambiguity 6, 20
anaphoric pronoun 133
antonym 174
aposemantism 52
approximation 164

Batesian mimicry 52
biolinguistics 64, 97
broadening 107

category 165
causal chain 185
Chinese 3, 16
code 4, 6, 46
– linguistic 47
cognitive environment 133, 172–173
– mutual 48, 154
coherence 136, 140–142, 144, 146, 149
cohesion 136
– marker of 136, 138–142
common ground 37, 49
– conversational 48, 193–194
communication 46
– evolution of 5
– human-machine 213
– implicit 89
– ostensive-inferential 63
competence 66
– linguistic 127
– discourse 127
compositionality 61
concept 35, 65, 99, 104, 197
– ad hoc 106
connective 65, 127–128, 144–146, 203
– pragmatic 139
connector 168–169
context 1, 58, 85–86, 105–107, 133, 194
– communication 103
– discourse 183
– social 100, 114
– of thought 183

– of utterance 183
– threatening 125
contextual
– assumption 58, 60, 88, 156
– dependency 105
contradiction 174
contrariety 174
contrary predicate 174
conversation analysis 128
cooperation 78, 116, 118, 121, 131
cooperative principle 79, 85, 122, 130
creole 75
cue 52

denotation 108
derivation 71
dialect 115
diglossia 14, 31, 113
discourse 134
– analysis 128
– connective 139
– context 183
– pragmatics 146–149
– relation 142–146
– free indirect 181–184

echolocation 51
effect
– MaxContrary 174
– non-propositional 149–151, 153–154, 156, 171, 173, 187
– poetic 150, 154, 171–173
– positive cognitive 86, 88, 156
– propositional 149, 154, 173
ellipsis 136
emotion 123, 149–150, 152, 210
English 16–19, 22–28, 34–37, 61, 70, 103, 115, 144–145, 184, 213
entailment 193, 209
ethnomethods 128
exaptation 64
explanation 143, 180
explicature 192–193, 209
expression 183

face 119, 120
- negative 122
- positive 122
- face-work 120
factive 52–53, 55, 194
faculty of language 72
- in the broad sense 73
- in the narrow sense 3, 64, 73
figure of speech 81, 161–162
focus 77
forclusive 43, 112
French 4, 14–28, 34–43, 109–113
FTA (face-threatening act) 122–125

garden-path sentence 38
German 14, 17–19, 22–24, 28, 31, 35–37, 211–212
grammatical
- category 77
- function 77
grammaticalisation 41

Homo
- neanderthalis 51
- sapiens 15, 75, 150
homologous 74
Hopi 2
HOT (higher-order thought) 53

identification principle 167–168
idioms 61
illocutionary act 122
implicature 137, 154, 190
- conversational 81, 193, 209
- conventional 193, 209
- weak 171
indexicals 6, 183
inference 4, 58, 63, 88, 209
inflexion 77
information 21, 46–49, 52, 54, 58, 77, 150
- background 57, 159
- foreground 159
- relevant 86
Inslekampx 32
intention
- communicative 47, 63
- global communicative 147

- global informative 147
- informative 47, 63, 79
intentional system 54
interchange
- remedial 120
- supportive 120
interface
- conceptual-intentional 73–74, 99, 210
- sensorimotor 73–74, 99, 210
- semantics-pragmatics 208, 212
intonation 46
irony 160

Japanese 19, 35, 46
jargon 37

language 60
- acquisition 14, 32–33, 54, 67
- evolution 5, 75–76, 78, 83
- external 67
- internal 67
- of thought 65
- origin of 210–211
- standard 14
- vernacular 14
langue 66, 99–100
lexicon 60–61
linguistic
- determinism 101
- relativism 101
litotes 174

machine translation 211–213
maxims of conversation 78, 81, 119, 122
- manner 21–22, 80, 170
- quality 80–81, 85, 162
- quantity 21, 80, 85, 125, 201
- relation 80, 83, 174
meaning
- autonomy of 105
- communicated 192
- natural 52, 55
- non-natural 55–56
- non-truth-conditional 90
- speaker 58, 66, 82
merge 70
metaphor 160

– conduit 107
– constructivist approach 164
– decipherment 190
– non-constructivist approach 162–164
metonymy 40, 160
model
– code 56, 62
– idealised cognitive 166
– inferential 62
– of necessary and sufficient conditions 165
morphology 33, 77, 136, 206
– French 24, 35
move 70
myside bias 155

narration 143, 180
narrative 157, 176, 178
narrowing 107
negation
– descriptive 202
– French 41–43
– metalinguistic 194, 202

ostension 4, 47

parole 66, 100
performance 6, 67–68, 72, 115, 127, 150
phoneme 112
phonology 3, 60, 62
pidgin 75
Pirahã 3
politeness 116–126
polysemy 6, 60
poverty of stimulus 34
pragmatics 1, 4, 6, 66, 122, 131, 190, 206, 208–209, 211, 216
– acquisition of 33
preference organization 130
premise 58
presupposition 49, 84, 190, 193, 209
procedure
– of comprehension 156
– of production 156
proposition 65, 103, 162, 164, 201
prosody 207
protolanguage 51, 75–77

prototype 165
– theory 165

quantifier 125

recursion 3, 5, 64, 73–74
reductionism 99, 132
relevance 87
– conditional 129
– cognitive principle of 86
– communicative principle of 86
– presumption of optimal 86
representation
– propositional 150
– non-propositional 150
Romanian 3
Romansh 30
semantics 3, 33, 60, 62, 77–78, 166, 208–209
– cognitive 168

sign (Hauser) 51
sign (Saussure) 99
signal 35, 53
signifiant 99
signifié 99
skaz 182
strength 193
style 173, 184
subcontrariety 174
subject of consciousness (self) 182
superpragmatics 7, 190, 200
Swahili 13
syntax 3, 6, 33, 60, 62, 77–78, 206
– French 22, 24
– narrow 73–74, 99, 210
– protosyntax 77

target 168
temporal order 176, 179–180, 184, 187
thematic role 77
theory
– of argumentation 155
– of mental spaces 168
– of mind 79
trigger 168
Turing test 190

universal grammar 3
utterance 87–88, 133, 156, 193
- context of 183
- comprehension of 7, 82, 85–87, 122, 131, 146–147; 156–157, 187, 193
- meaning 78, 192

variationist sociolinguistics 101

Yupno 14

zeugma 161

www.ingramcontent.com/pod-product-compliance
Lightning Source LLC
Chambersburg PA
CBHW071737150426
43191CB00010B/1615